TRAINS OF ALABAMA

*Short Lines, Railyards, Engines,
Heritage Units, Railfan Photos, & More*

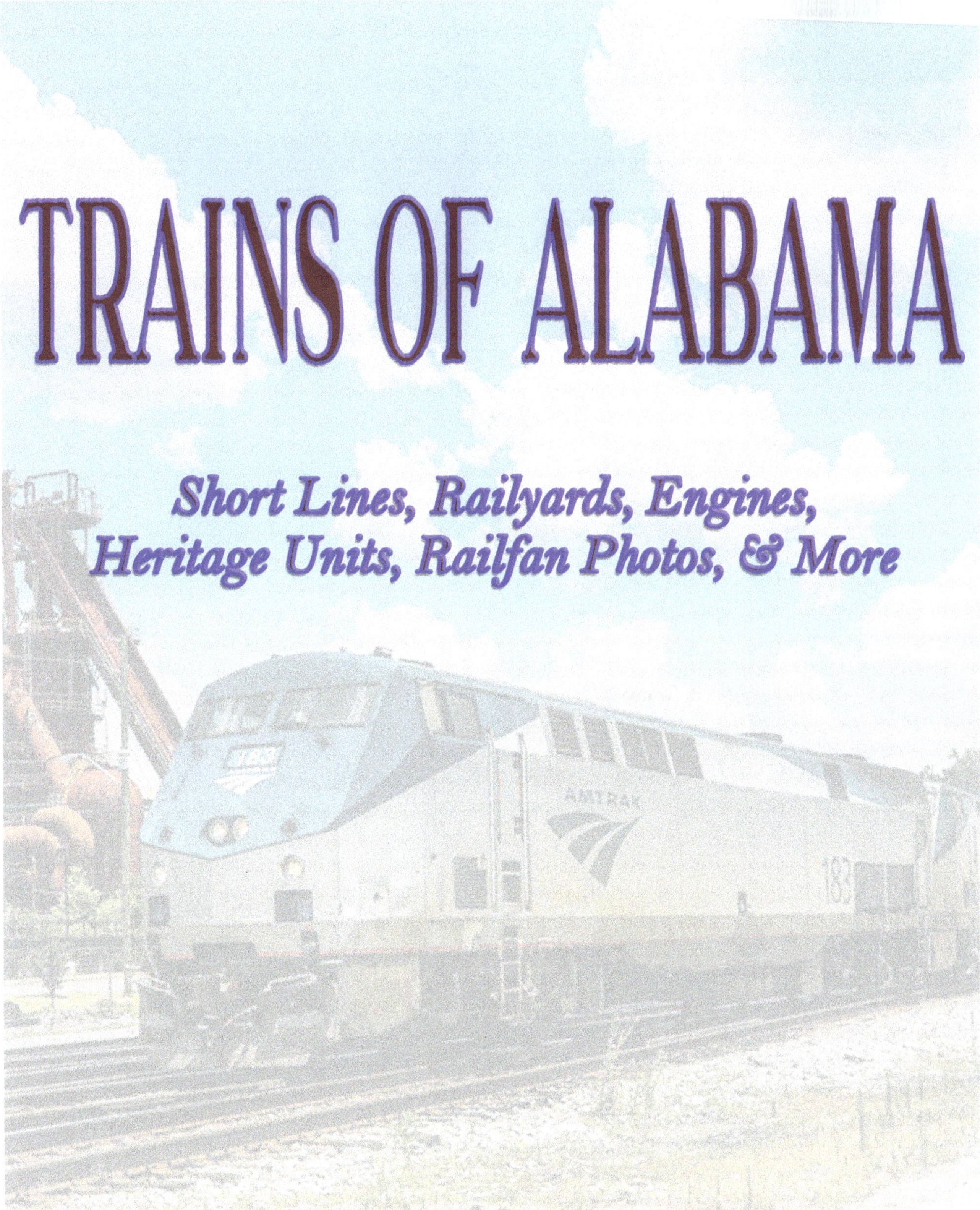

TRAINS OF ALABAMA
Short Lines, Railyards, Engines, Heritage Units, Railfan Photos, & More

Introduction by Angie Birmingham

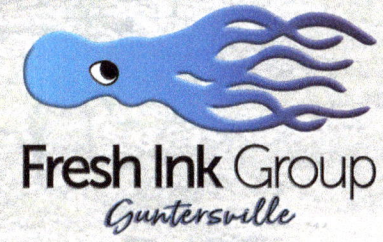

Fresh Ink Group
Guntersville

Trains of Alabama
Short Lines, Railyards, Engines, Heritage Units, Railfan Photos, & More

Copyright © 2024
by Brayden Dexter Greene
All rights reserved

Fresh Ink Group
An Imprint of:
The Fresh Ink Group, LLC
1021 Blount Avenue #931
Guntersville, AL 35976
Email: info@FreshInkGroup.com
FreshInkGroup.com

Edition 1.0 2024

Cover design by Stephen Geez / FIG
Book design by Amit Dey / FIG
Associate publisher Beem Weeks / FIG

Except as permitted under the U.S. Copyright Act of 1976 and except for brief quotations in critical reviews or articles, no portion of this book's content may be stored in any medium, transmitted in any form, used in whole or part, or sourced for derivative works such as videos, television, and motion pictures, without prior written permission from the publisher.

Cataloging-in-Publication Recommendations:
PHO011010 PHOTOGRAPHY / Individual Photographers / Artists' Books
TRA004020 TRANSPORTATION / Railroads / Pictorial
PHO015000 PHOTOGRAPHY / Photojournalism

Library of Congress Control Number: 2024917315

ISBN-13: 978-1-964998-11-4 Softcover
ISBN-13: 978-1-964998-21-1 Hardcover
ISBN-13: 978-1-964998-13-8 Ebooks

DEDICATION

*To my parents,
Logan and Amanda,
for supporting me through everything*

TABLE OF CONTENTS

Introduction by Angie Birmingham 1

Norfolk Southern 3

CSX and BNSF 63

Shortline: Huntsville and Madison County Railroad Authority (HMCR). . . 89

Shortline: Alabama and Tennessee River Railroad (ATN). 101

Amtrak 119

About Brayden Dexter Greene 131

INTRODUCTION

*By World Wildlife
Photographer Angie Birmingham*

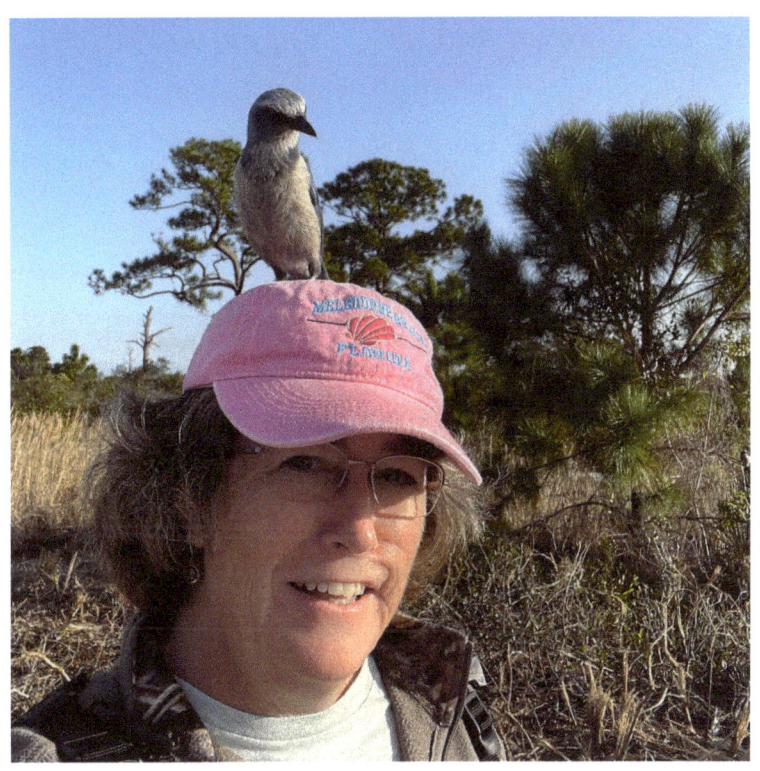

In a world brimming with images, photography stands out as a powerful medium of expression, creativity, and storytelling. For young minds, it offers more than just the ability to capture moments; it provides a unique lens through which they can explore their passions, tell their stories, and connect with the world around them.

Brayden Dexter Greene, a 14-year-old from the suburbs of Birmingham, Alabama, has this spirit of exploration and creativity. From an early age, Brayden developed a keen interest in studying and photographing birds, reptiles, abandoned buildings, and trains. His fascination with trains reflects a deep appreciation for their timeless charm and the sense of adventure they embody. This passion has driven him to embark on a personal summer project before starting high school—photographing and writing this book.

Photography encourages young people like Brayden to observe the world more closely, to notice the details often overlooked in the hustle of daily life. Through his camera's viewfinder, Brayden captures the intricate beauty of locomotives, the vibrant colors of rail cars, and the ever-changing landscapes through which trains travel. This heightened sense of awareness fosters mindfulness and a deeper connection to his surroundings.

In addition to his work with trains, Brayden has expanded his photographic journey to include abandoned homes and other buildings in rural America, laying the groundwork for his next book. His ability to find beauty in forgotten places and bring their stories to life through his lens is a testament to his growing talent and dedication.

Photography is more than just a hobby for Brayden; it is a continuous learning journey. He is constantly experimenting with his equipment and styles, eager to refine his skills and share his images with others. His journey serves as an inspiration for other young photographers, demonstrating that age is no barrier to pursuing one's passions and achieving artistic growth.

This book is a testament to Brayden's creativity, passion, and vision. It showcases his journey, challenges, and triumphs, highlighting the profound impact that photography can have on personal and artistic development. As you turn through these pages, you will witness the world through the eyes of a young photographer fascinated by the romance and adventure of rail travel and the hidden stories of rural Alabama—full of curiosity, imagination, and boundless potential.

May this book inspire young minds to pick up their cameras, explore their surroundings, and unleash their creativity. For in every photograph lies a story waiting to be told, a moment captured forever, and a glimpse into the extraordinary perspectives of our future generation.

NORFOLK SOUTHERN

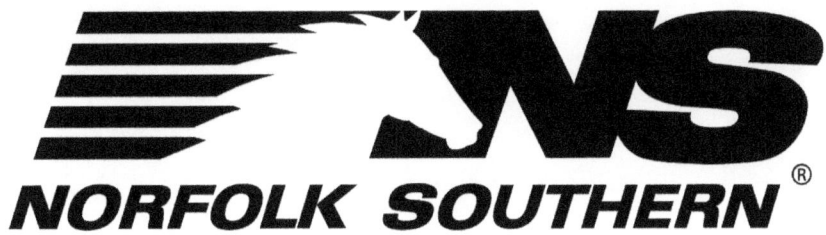

The Norfolk Southern Railroad is the most prevalent railroad company in Alabama. Two of its mainlines come together just east of Birmingham in Irondale, Alabama, at Norris Yard. The railroad serves many customers in Alabama, and is the easiest to find for railfans, with observation platforms built at the south end of the yard in Irondale and many grade crossings controlled by them in major Alabama cities.

Norris Yard is Norfolk Southern's main yard in Alabama. It's where two main lines come together to head westward to New Orleans, Meridian, and other destinations. Built by the Southern Railroad, the yard opened in 1951. Traffic is nearly constant, and there is almost always a train being taken apart. The locals hardly ever get to cross the tracks! The yard also has a large diesel shop which used to service the steam engines run on excursions by the railroad. The yard's actual operations rely on three teams of smaller EMD locomotives and "slugs," which are powered units without cabs. Each team consists of two locomotives and a slug. Railfans can watch from an observation platform built across from the Irondale Café—make sure to grab some fried green tomatoes, as this place was the inspiration for Fannie Flagg's novel!—or from a platform with an old Southern Caboose on it. I personally would recommend the caboose side because trains commonly stop on the first track and block your view. The caboose platform also offers you a view of the ATN's track down the street.

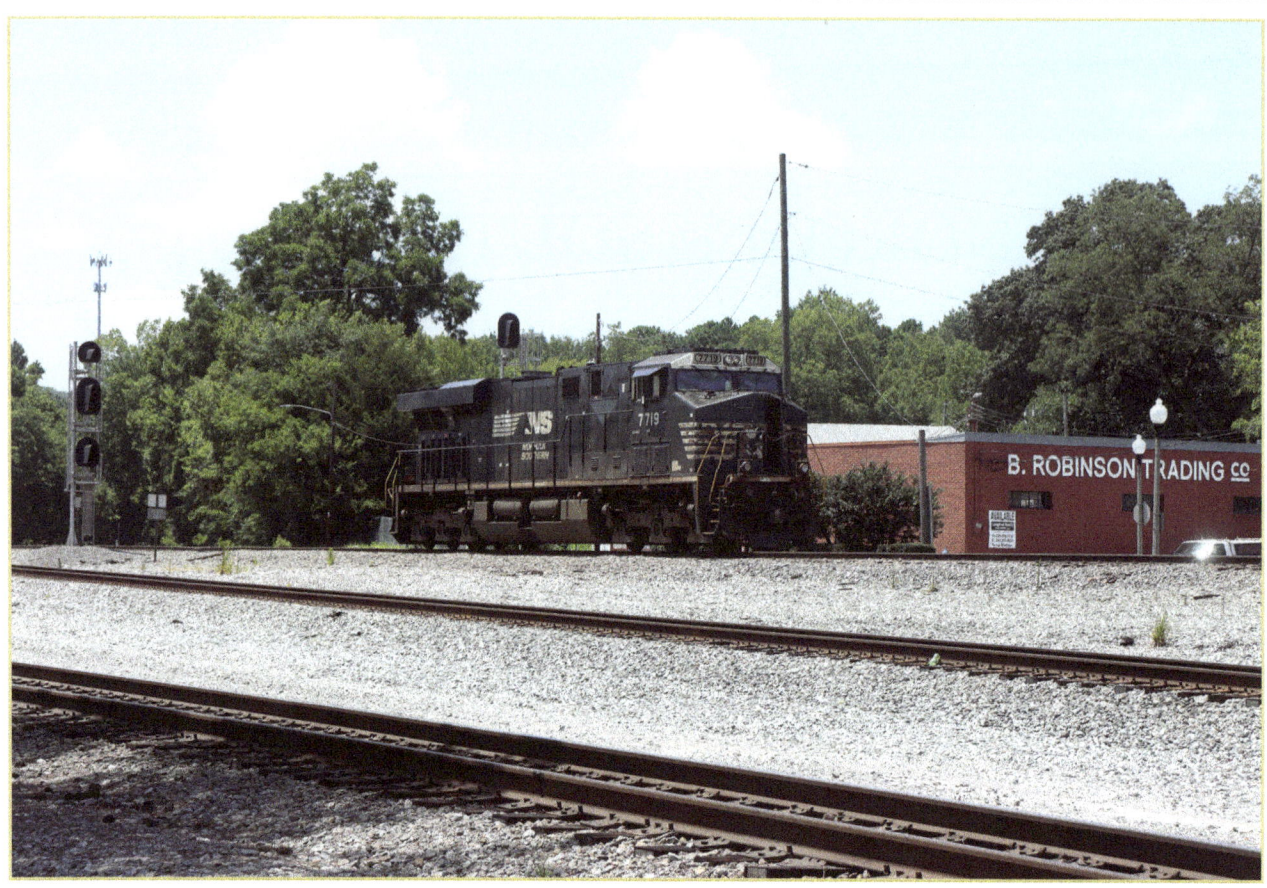

A very rusty ES44DC stands alone at the southern end of Norris Yard in Irondale.

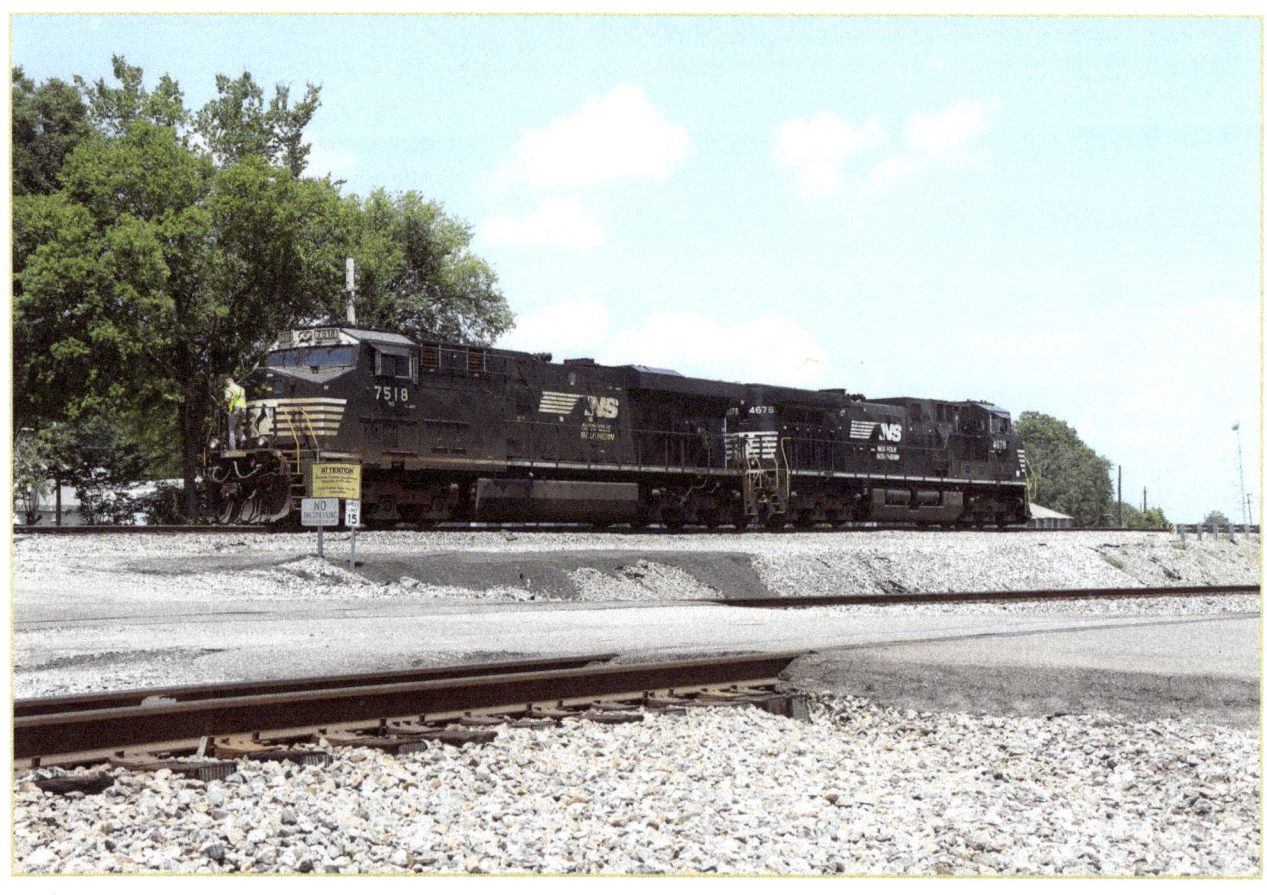

A pair of Norfolk Southern locomotives waits to lash up to a train in Irondale.

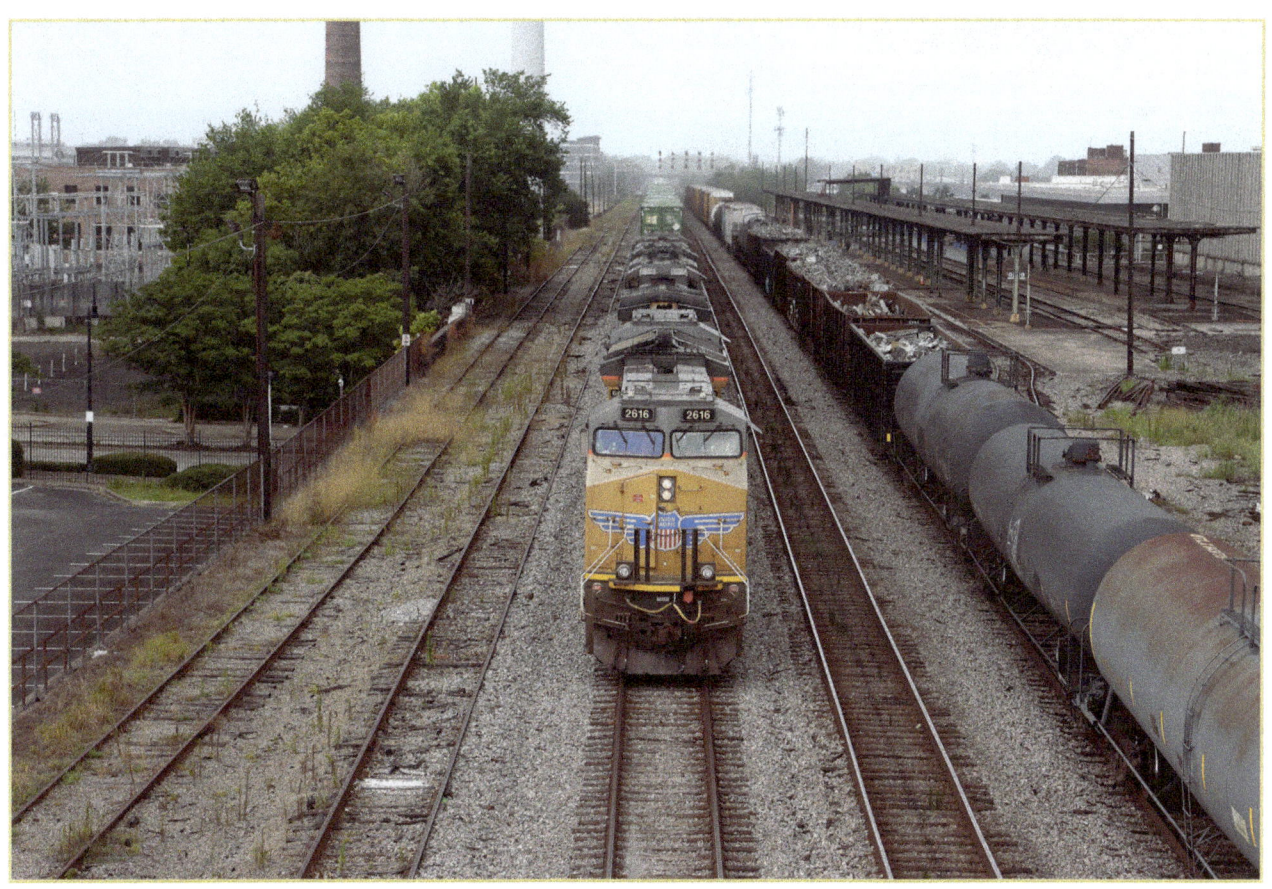

A Union Pacific run-through train passes through Birmingham, most likely on its way to Atlanta.

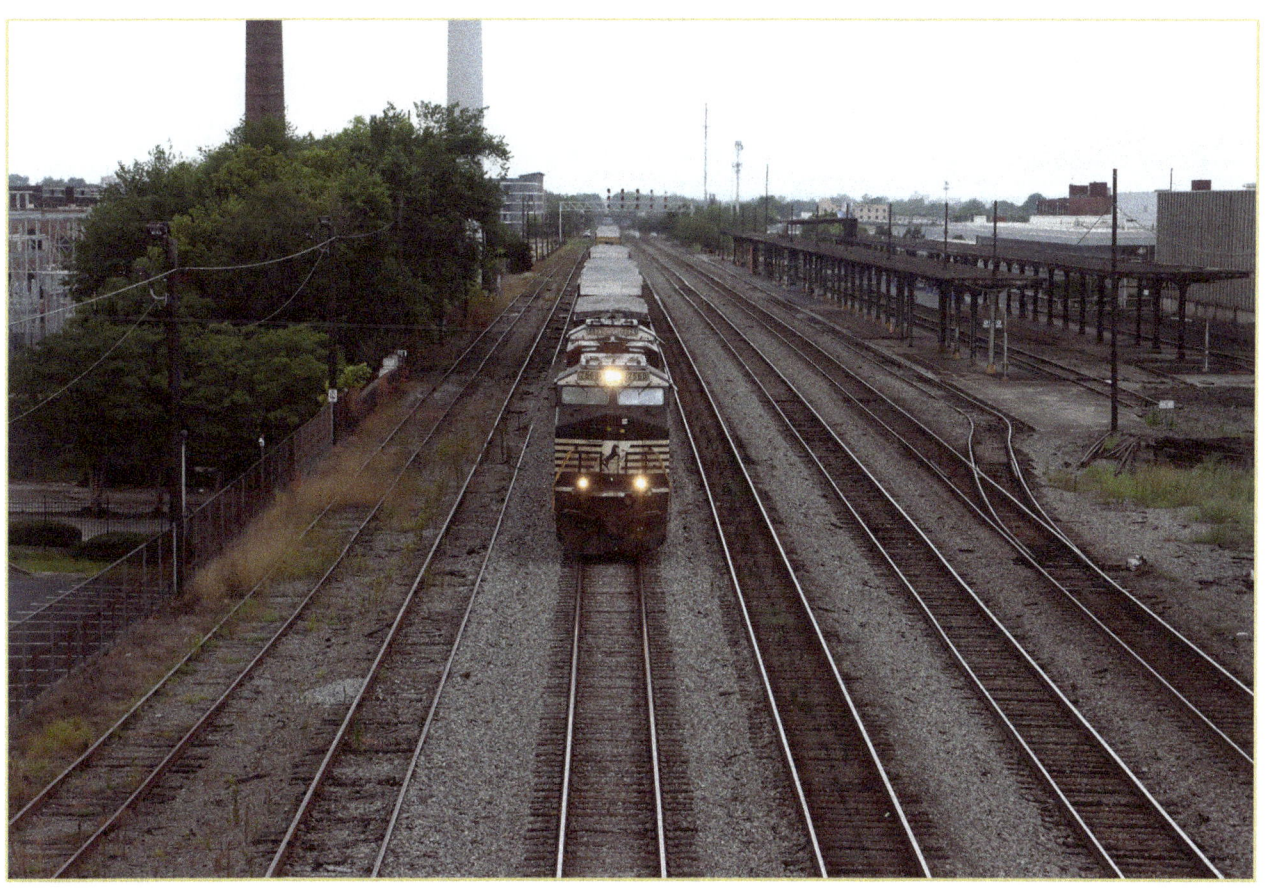

A Norfolk Southern mixed-freight train on its way to Irondale.

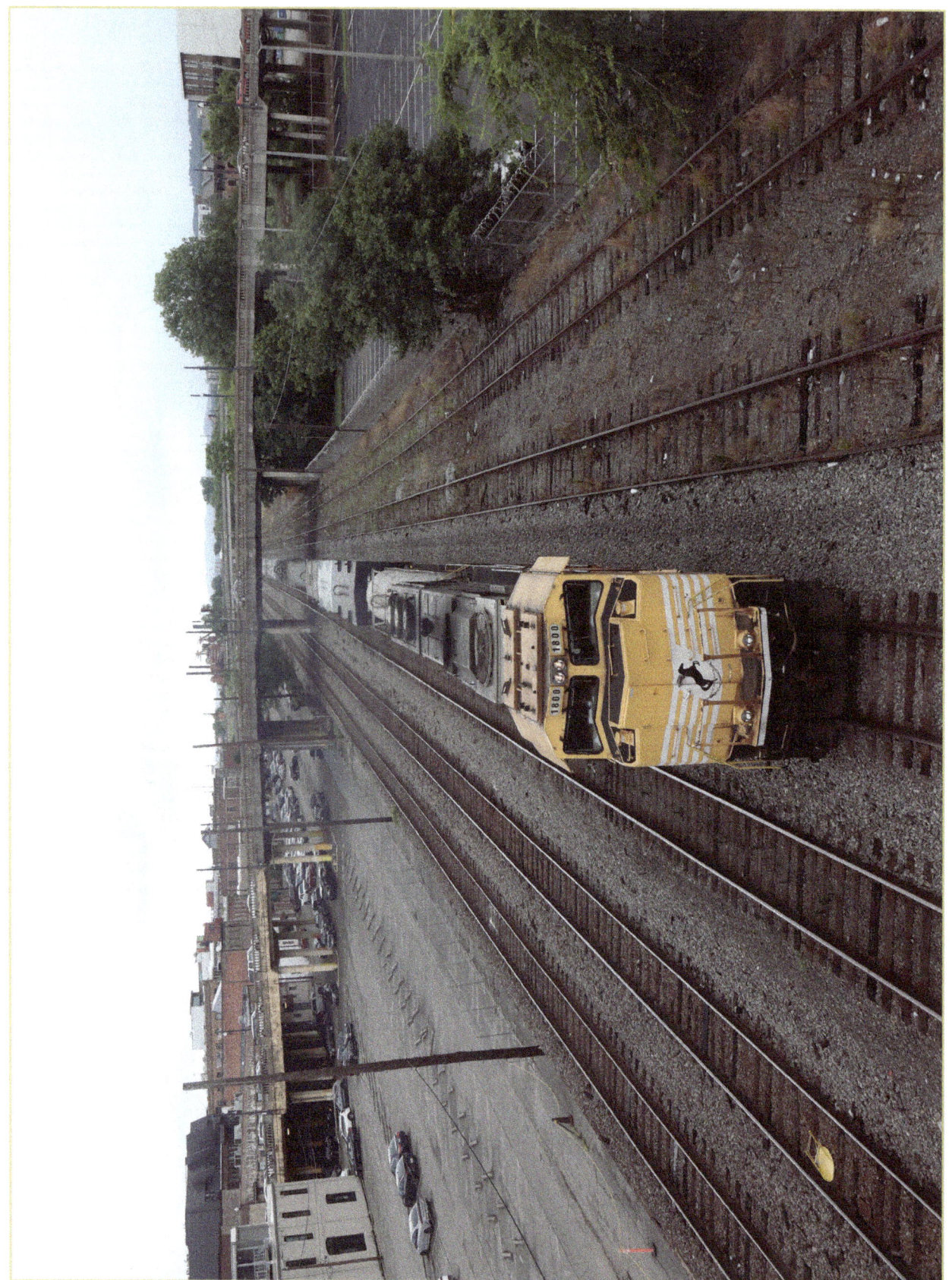

Norfolk Southern 1800, a special DC-to-AC locomotive at the rear of a mixed-freight train.

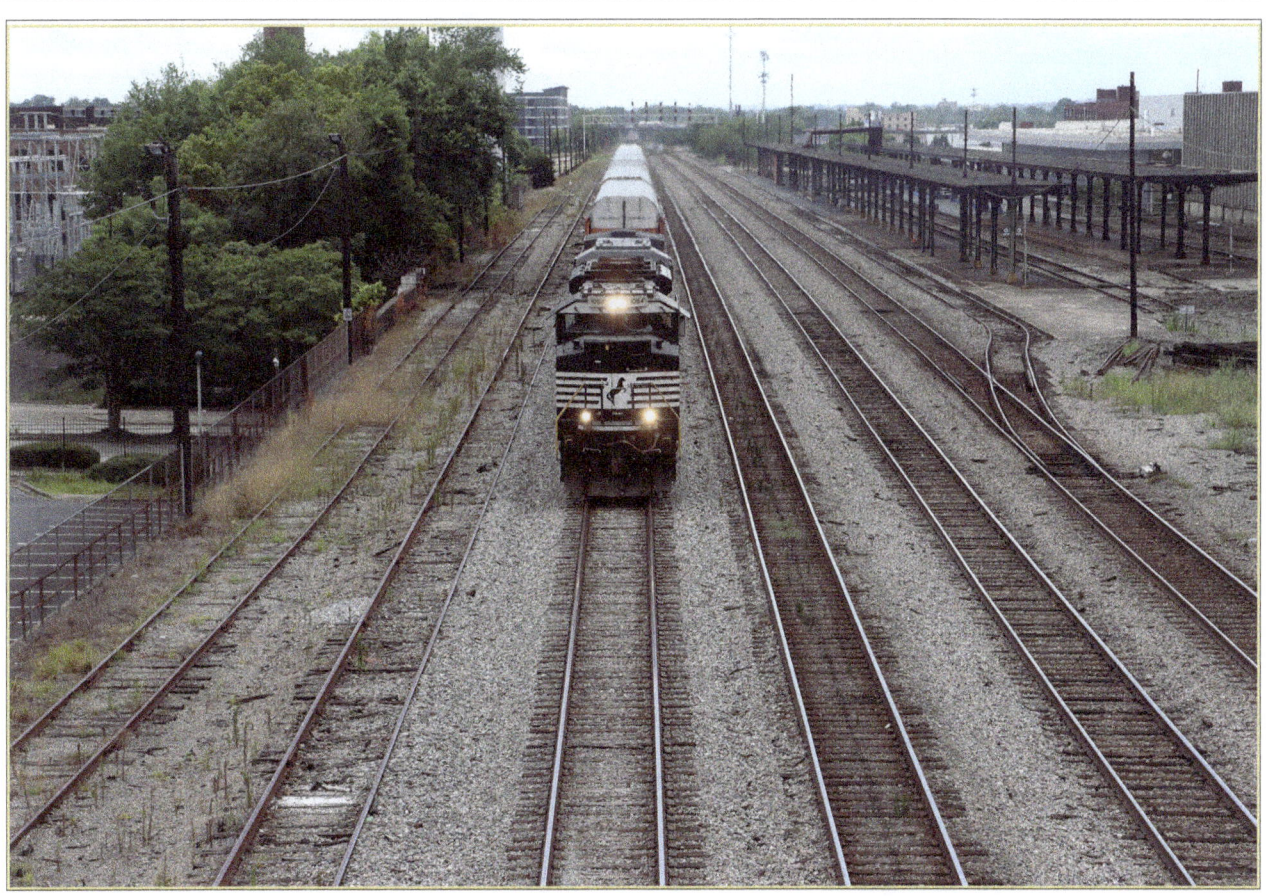
A Norfolk Southern SD70ACe leads autoracks toward Irondale.

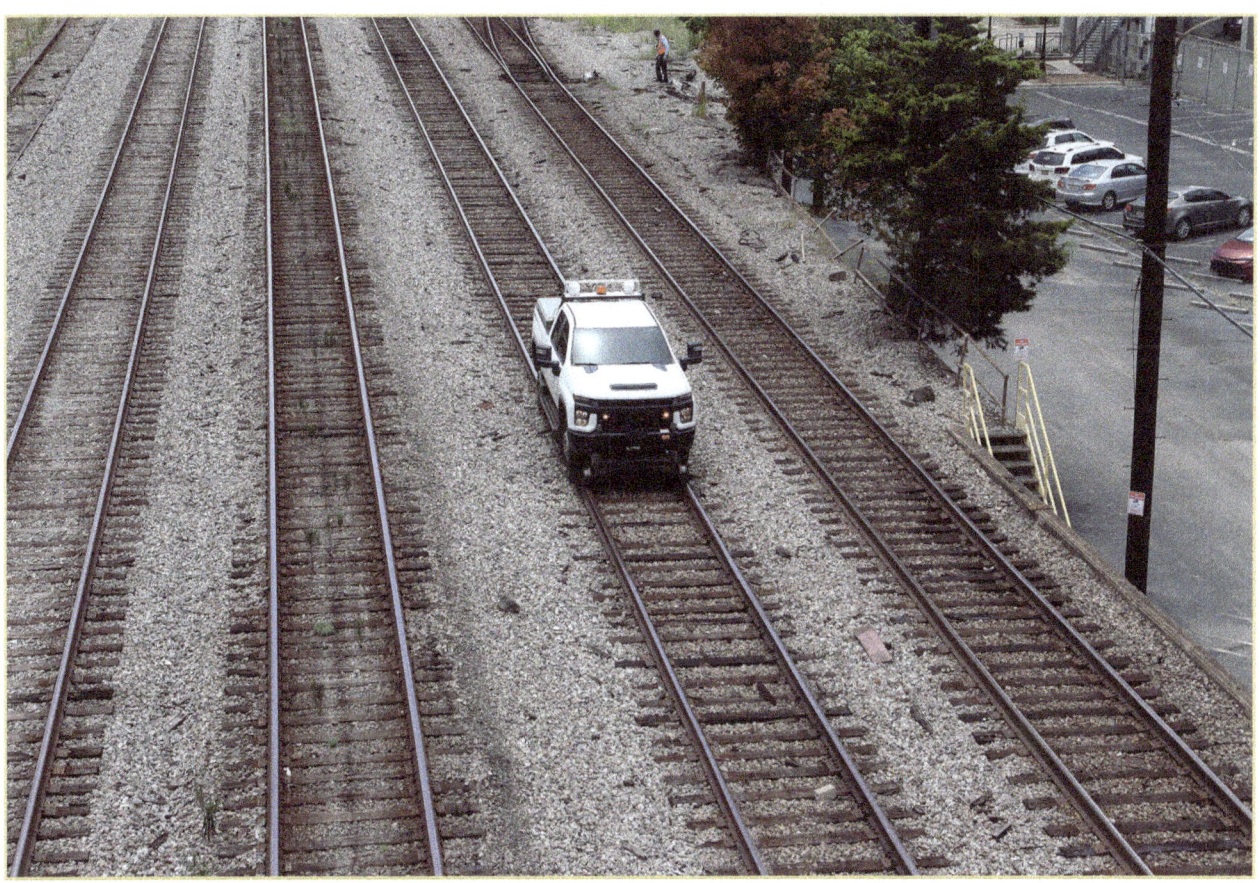
A CSX truck inspects the track while an Amtrak conductor prepares the switch for the arriving Crescent.

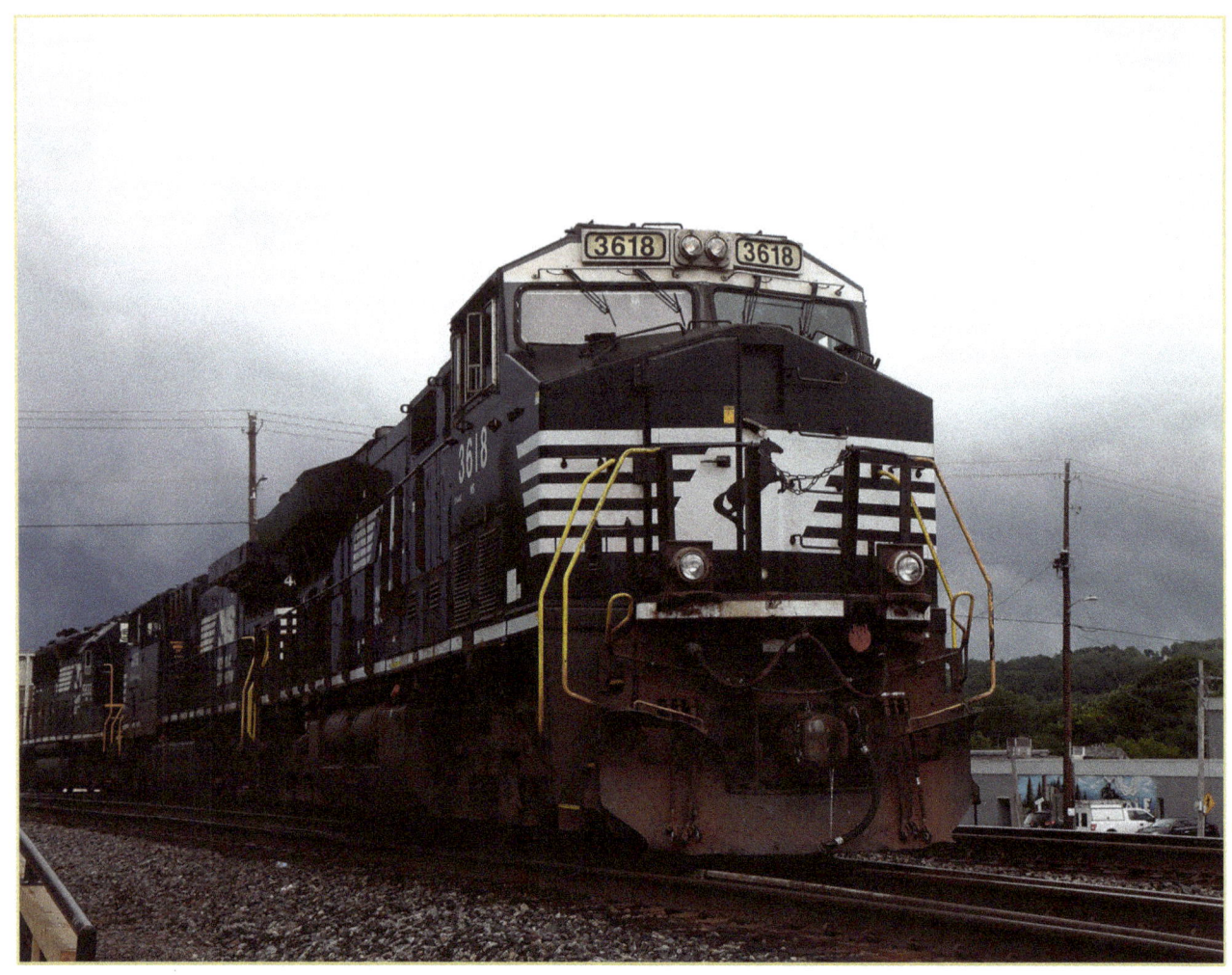

Norfolk Southern 3618 leads a train out of Irondale.

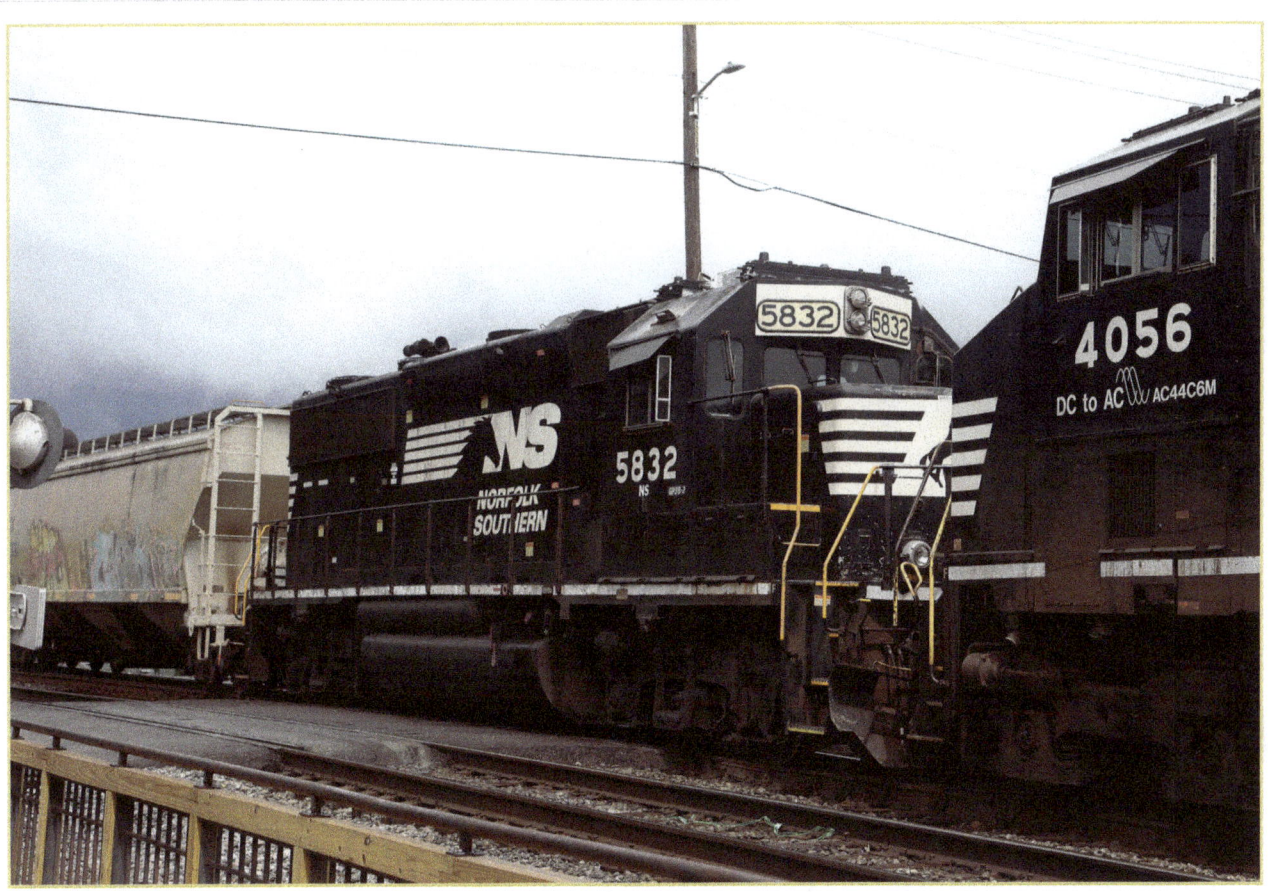
Norfolk Southern 5832, a GP38-2, is trailing on a mixed-freight heading toward Birmingham.

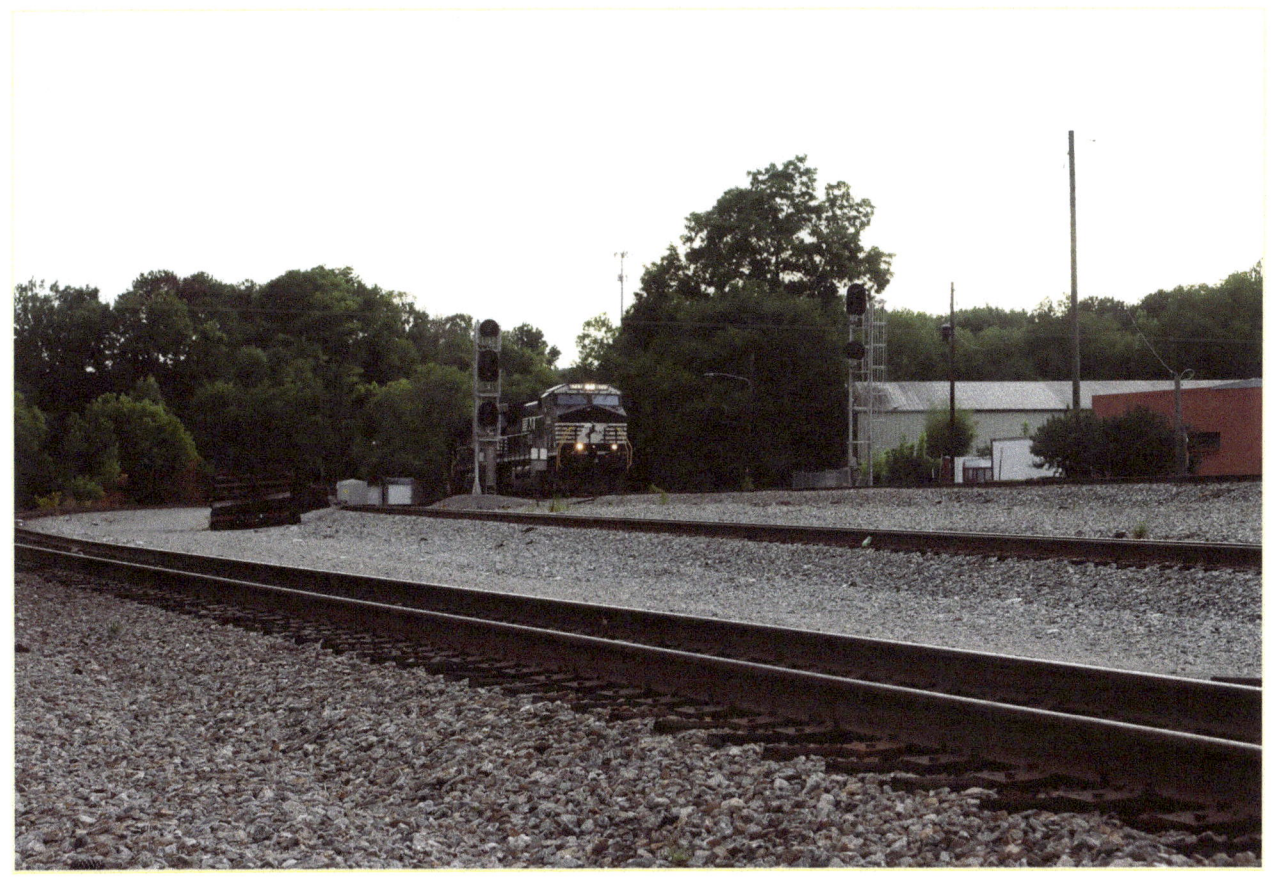
A freight train passes the signal towers on its way into Irondale.

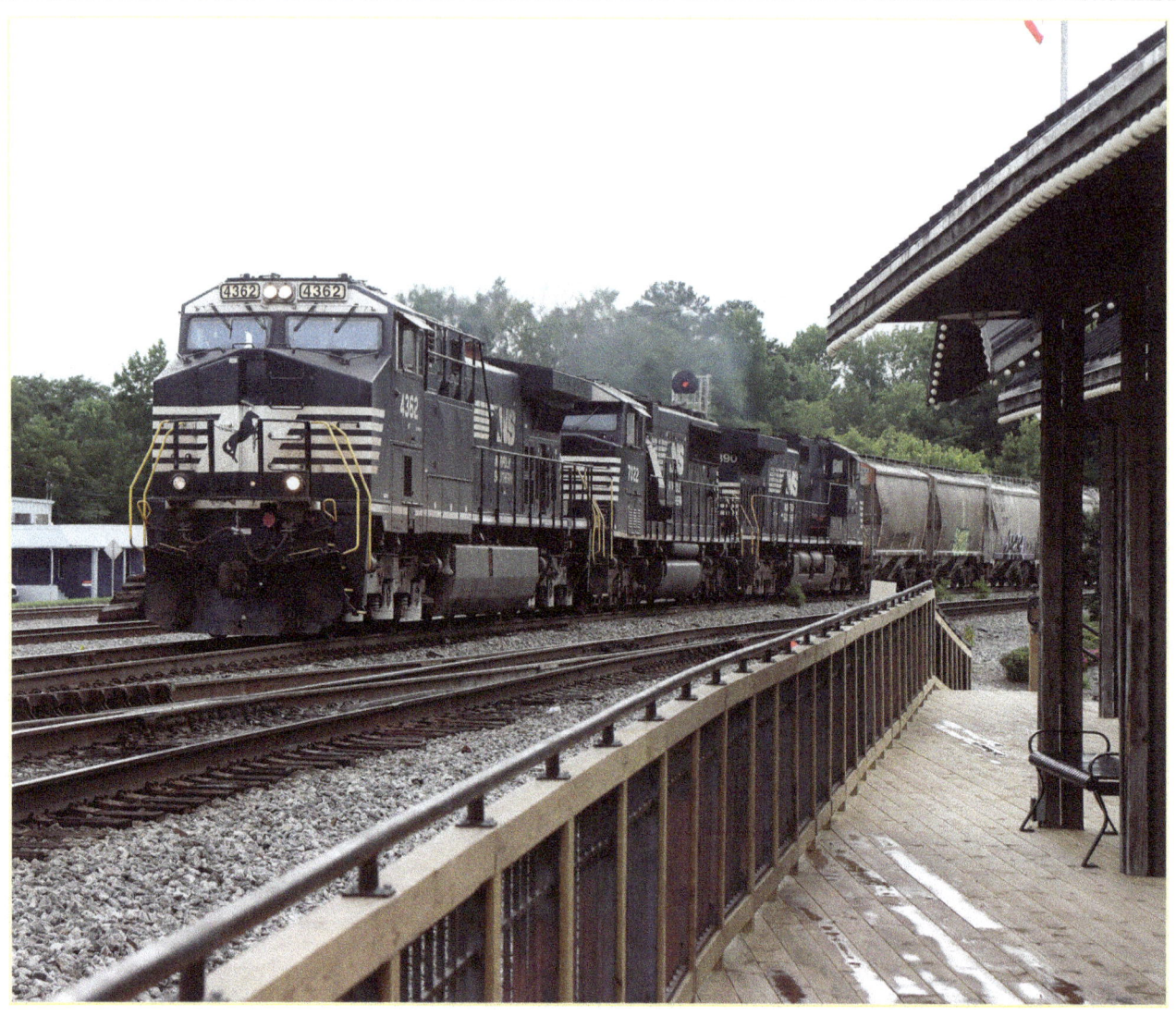
A mixed-freight passes by the train-watching platform in Irondale on a rainy day.

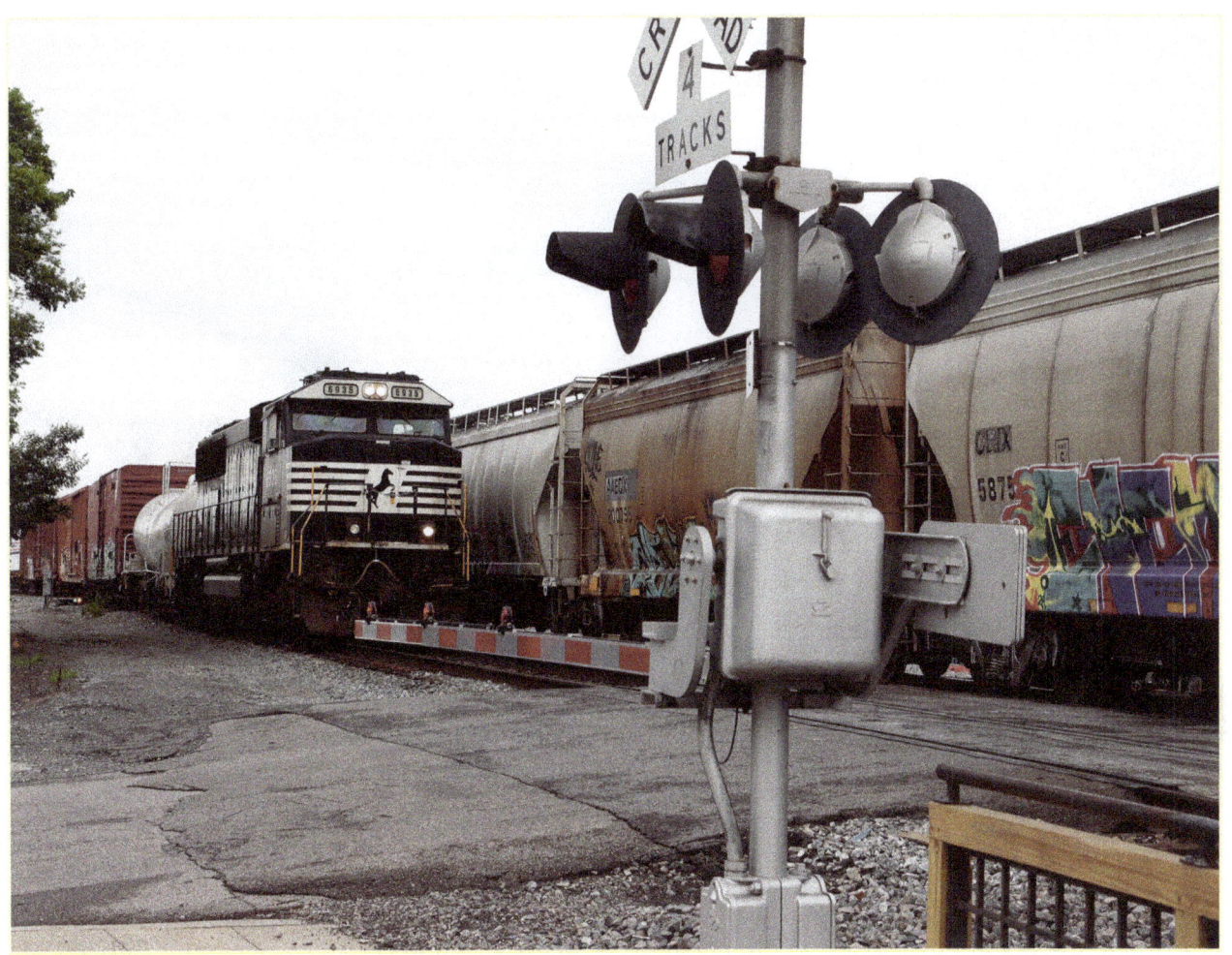
An SD60 leaves Norris Yard while some very colorful covered hoppers are entering.

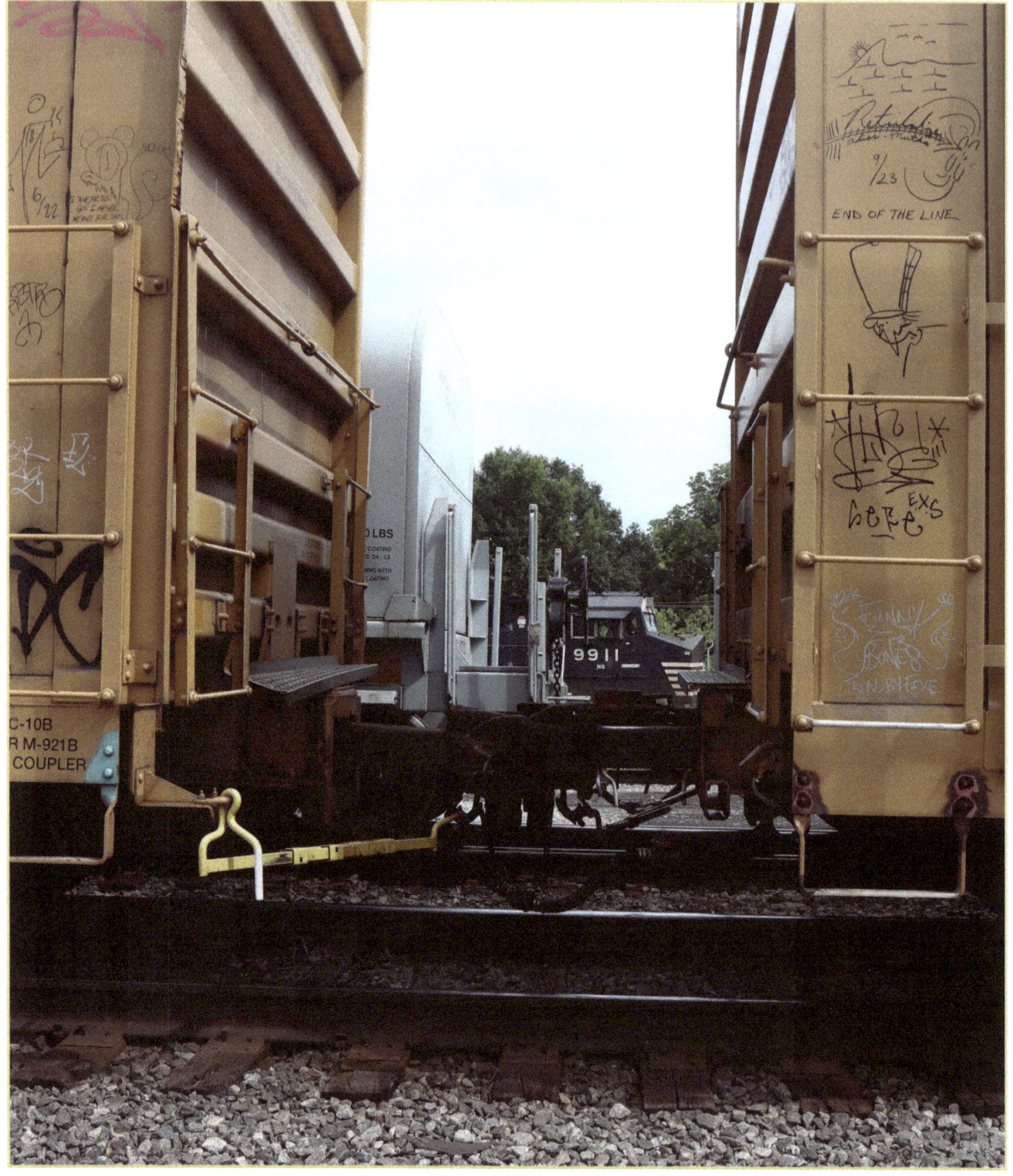

Three trains are leaving, entering, and passing through Norris Yard at the same time.

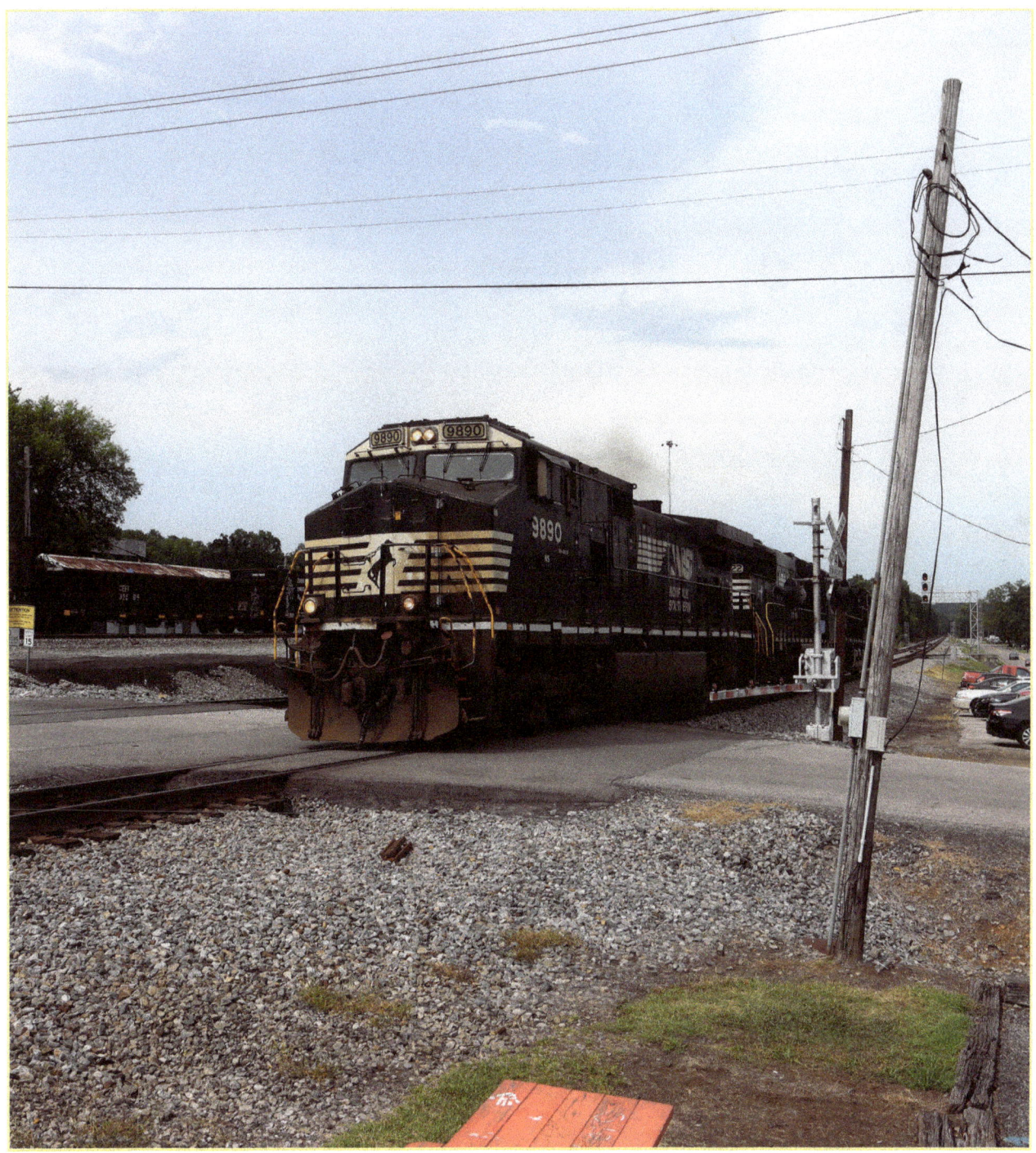
Three locomotives head toward the entrance to Norris Yard for their next assignment.

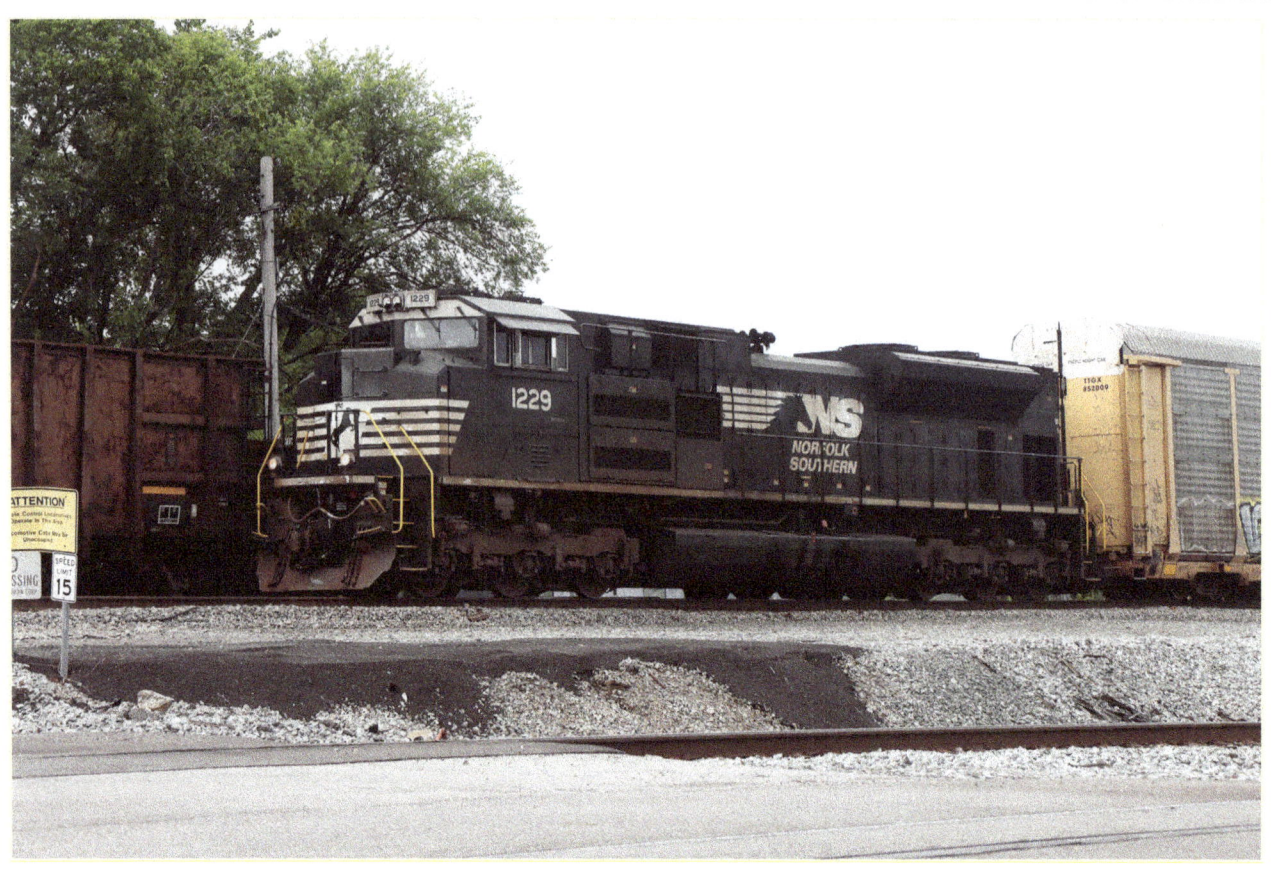

A single SD70ACe leads a freight out of Norris Yard.

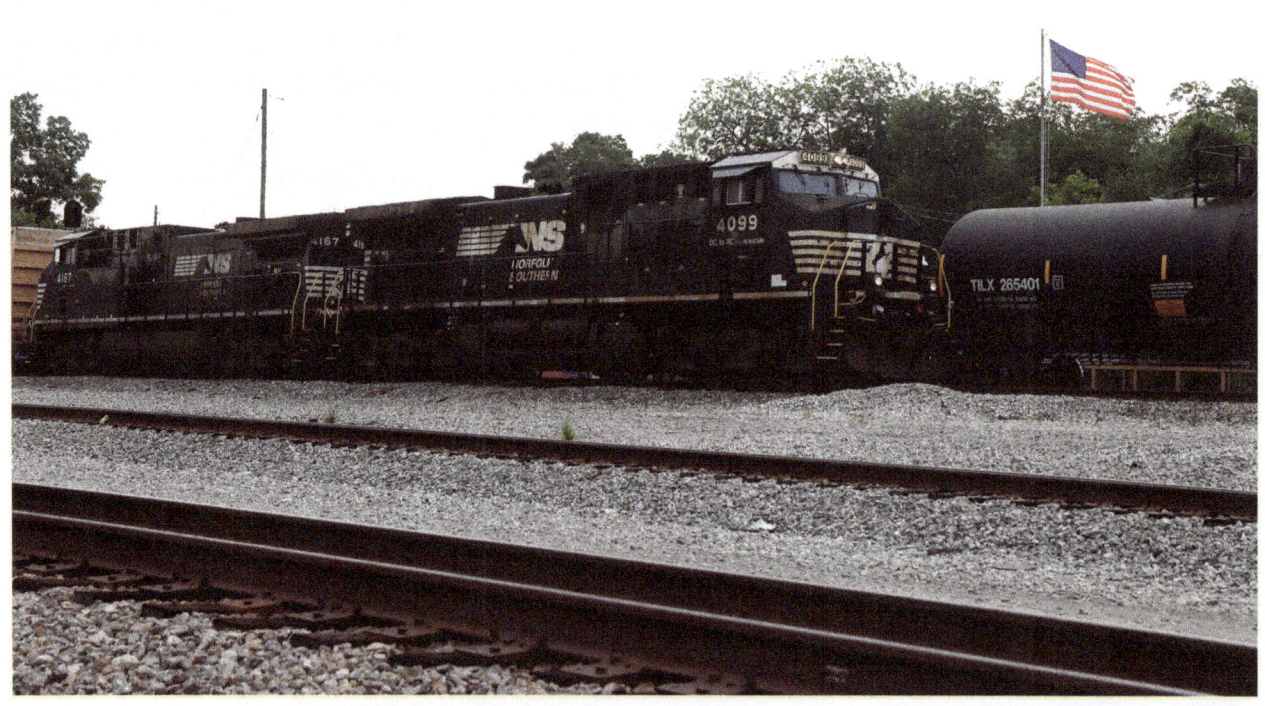

Two AC44 locomotives lead a freight into Irondale.

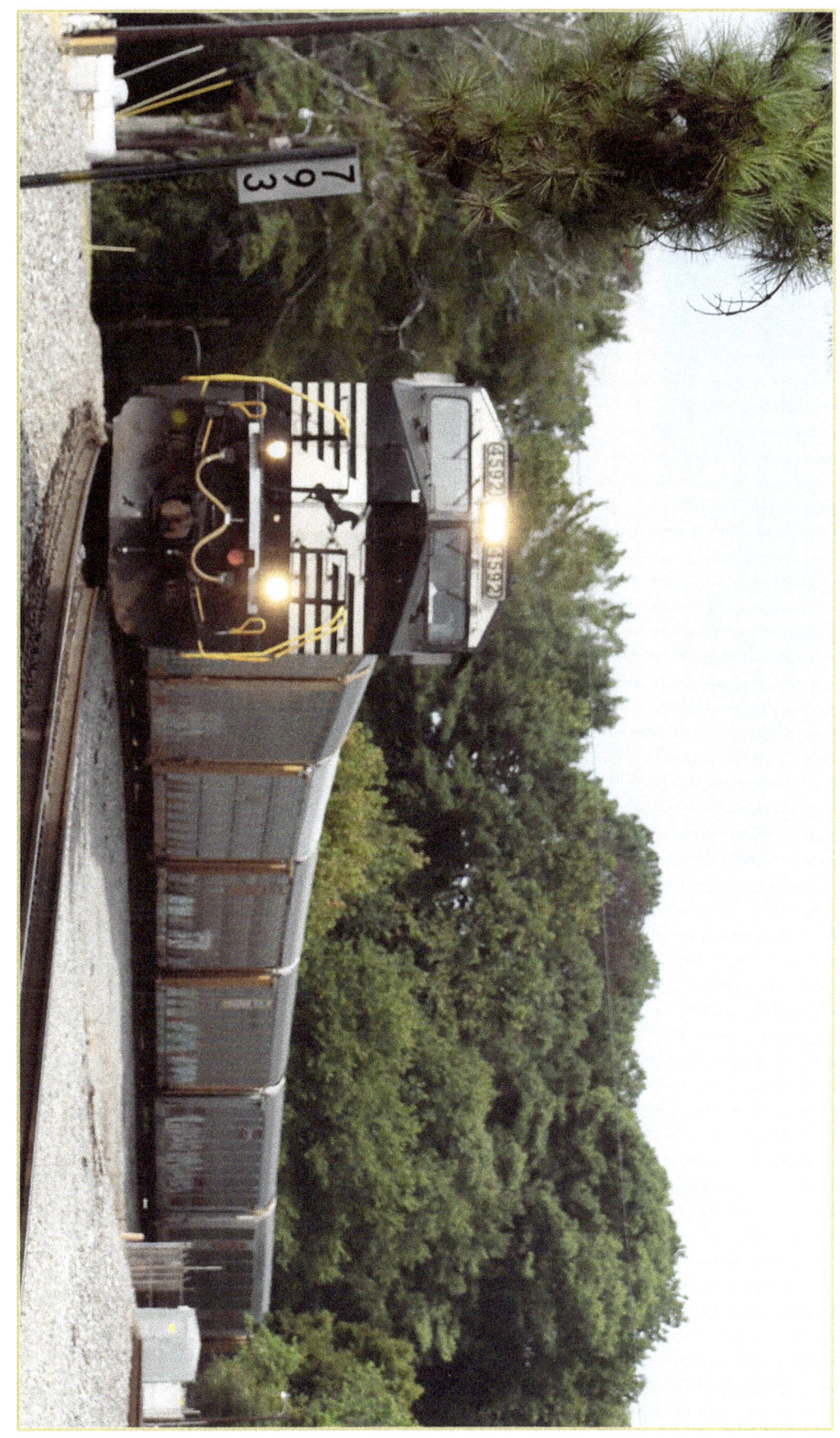

A single AC44 leads autoracks through Irondale.

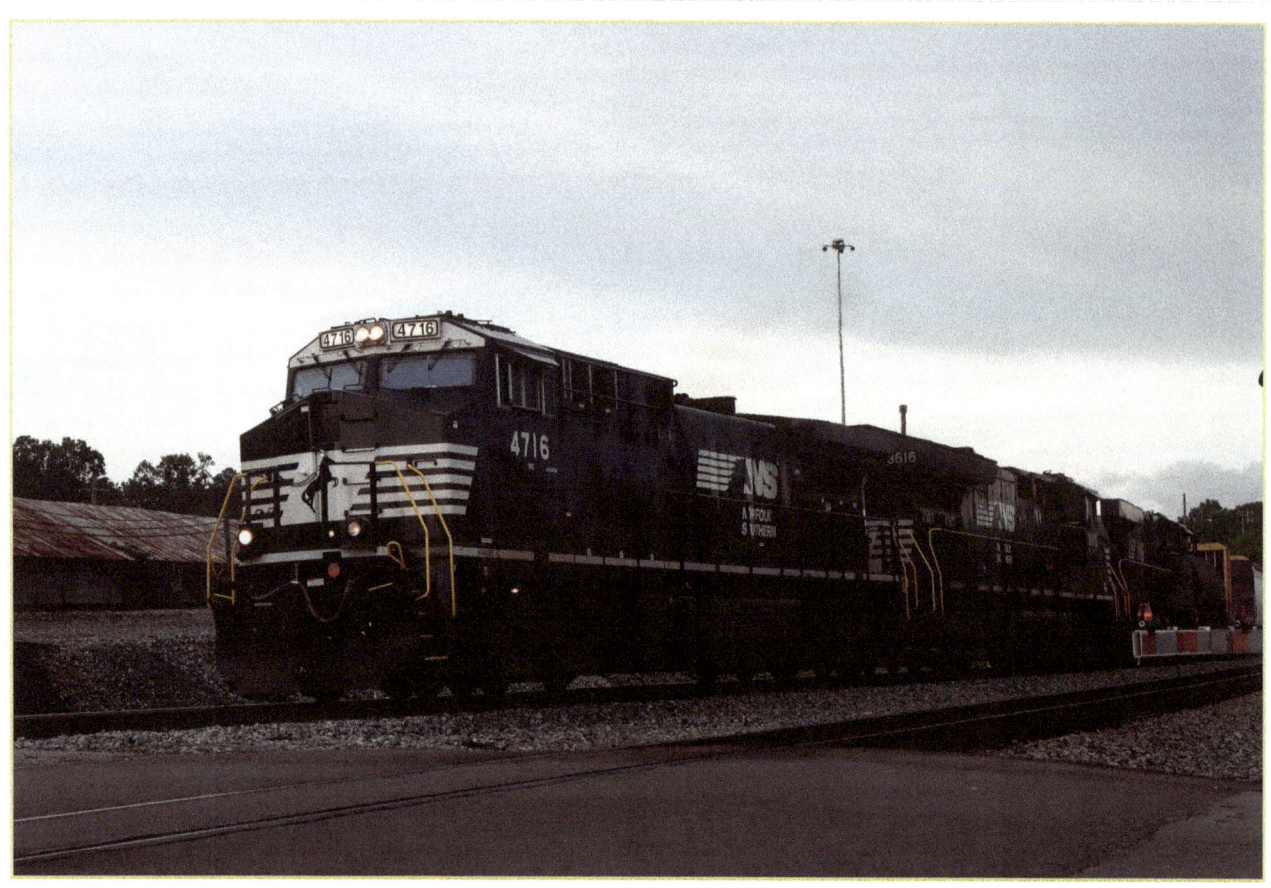

A freight train enters Irondale from the East End District mainline, which comes from Atlanta.

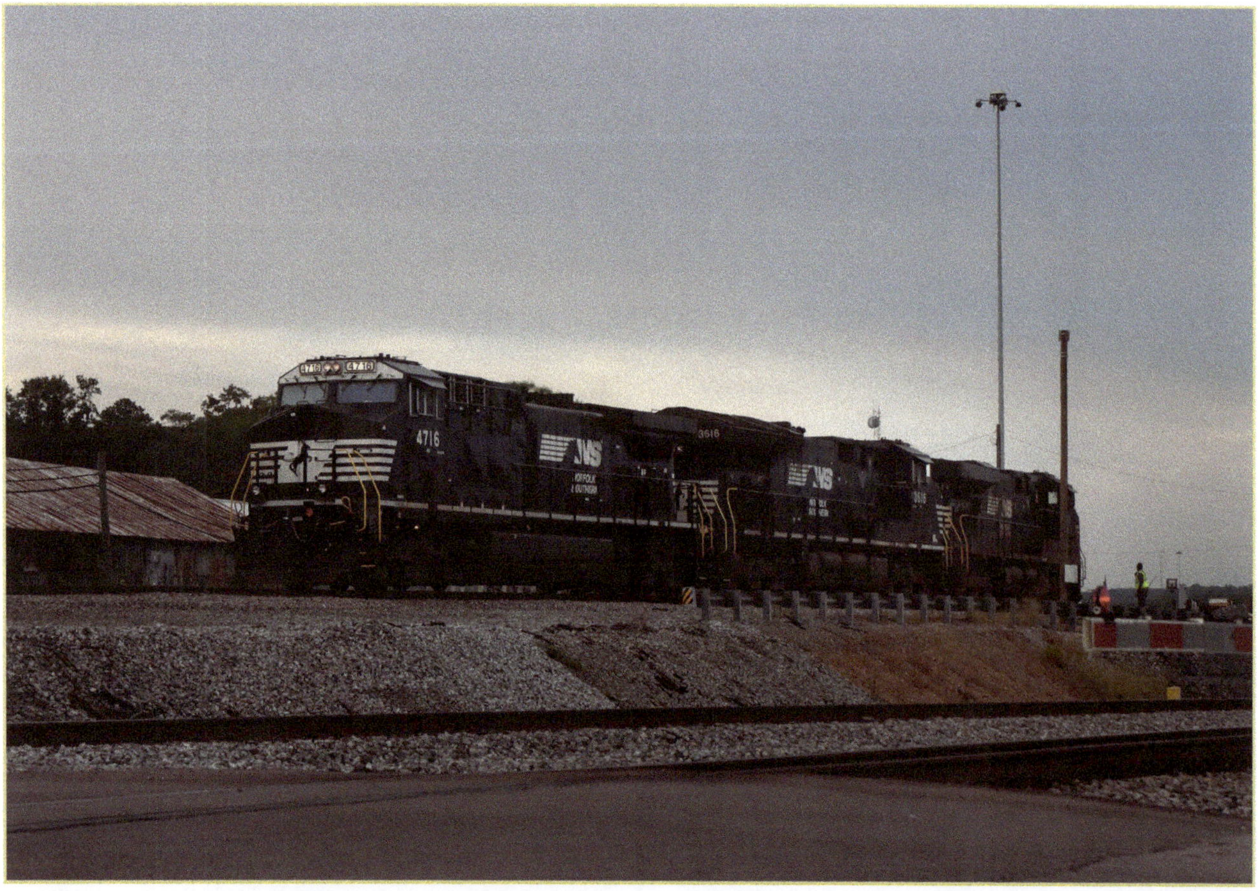

After dropping off its train, these locomotives await their next assignment.

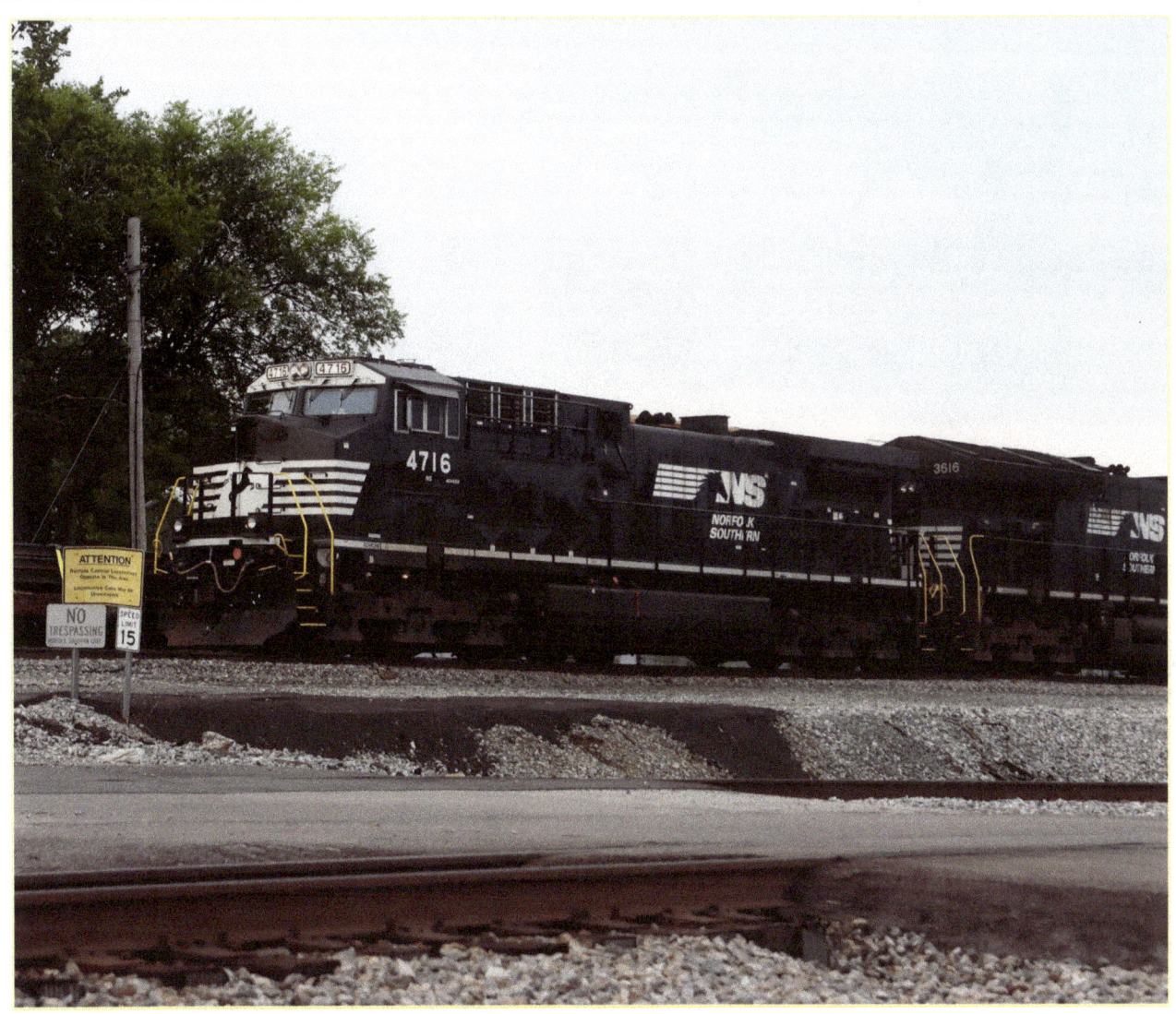

The mixed-freight backs into Norris Yard to be classified.

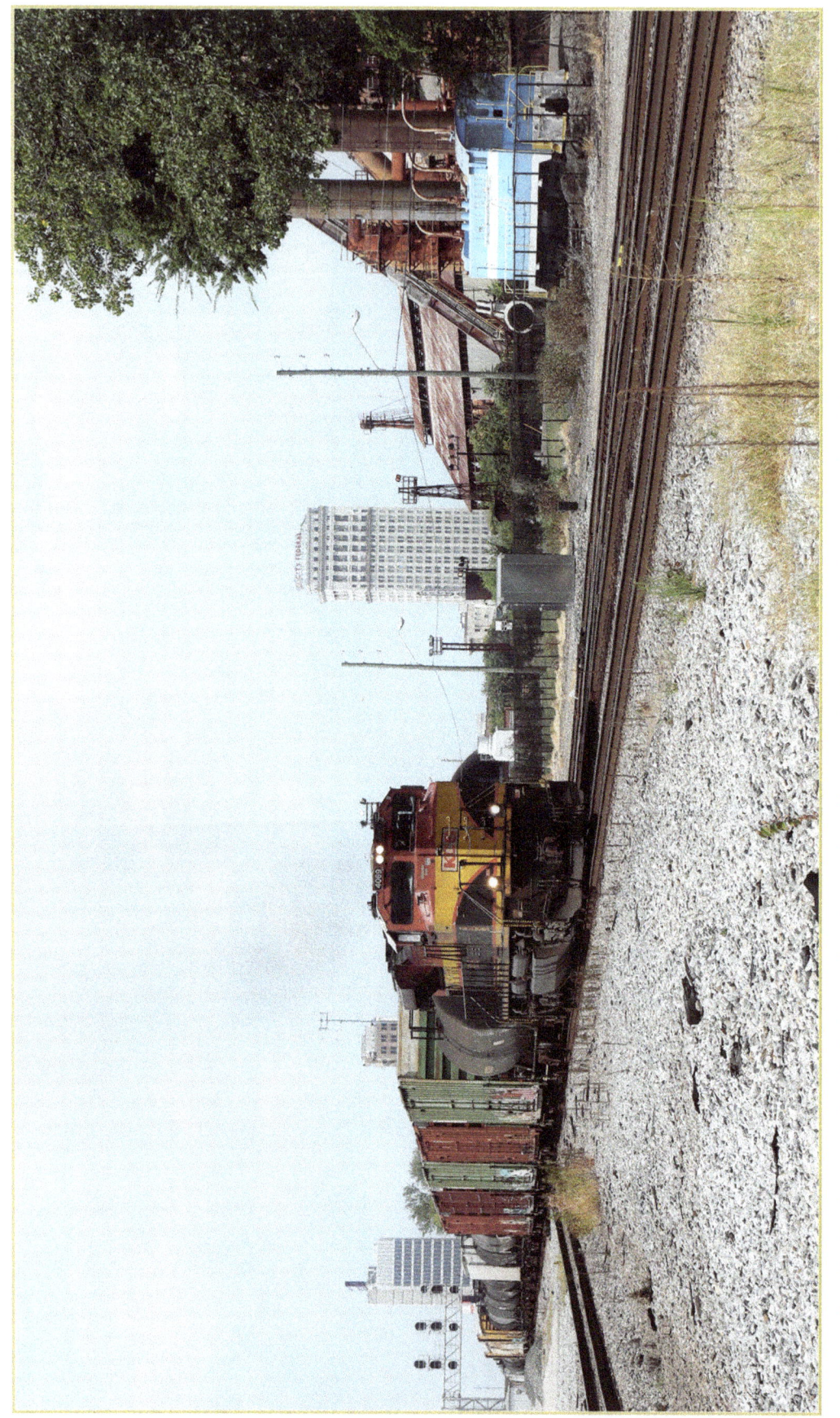

A Canadian Pacific Kansas City SD70ACe still in its original Kansas City Southern paint leads a Norfolk Southern train through Birmingham.

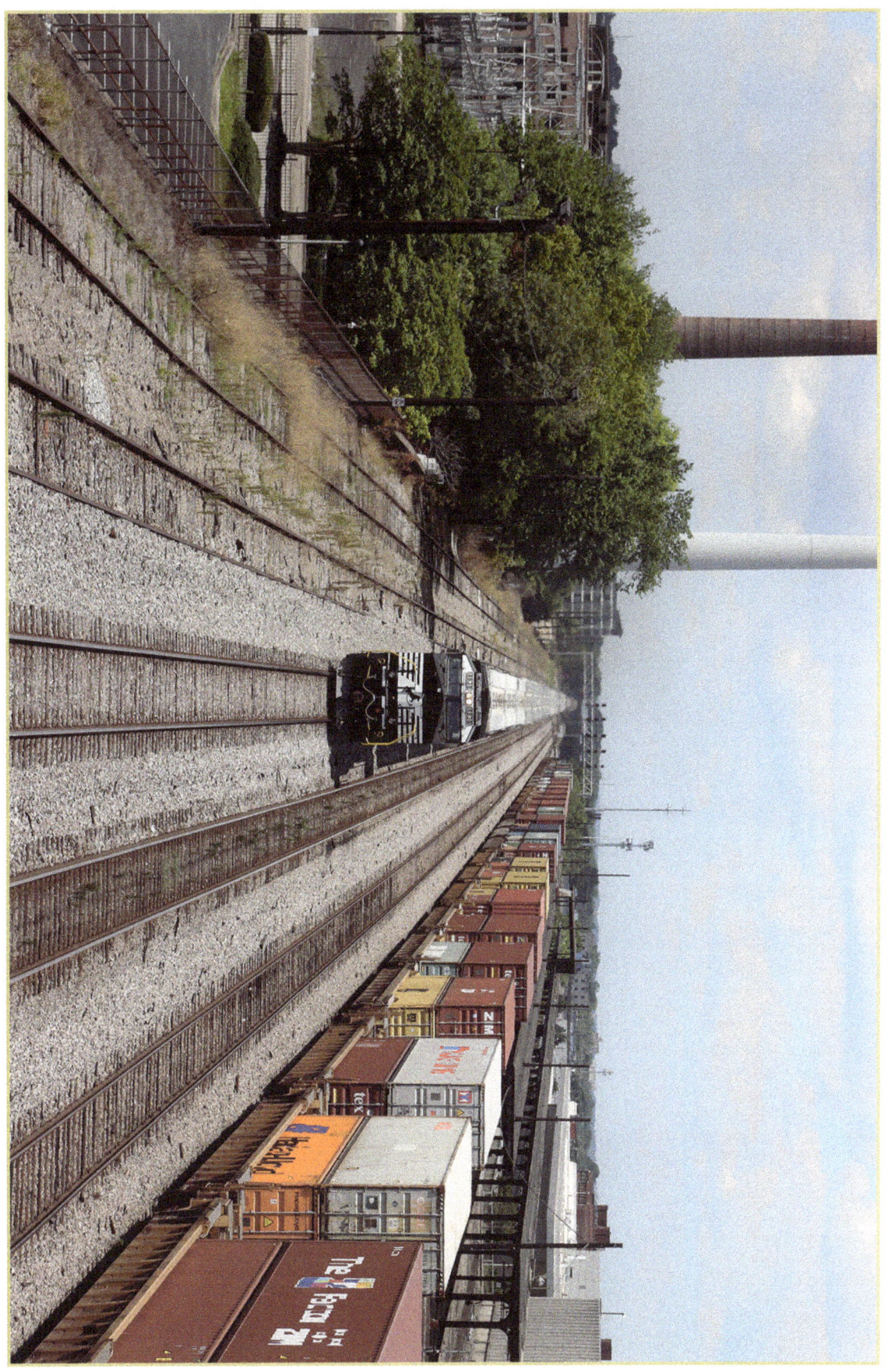

A Norfolk Southern engine leading covered hoppers comes through Birmingham while a CSX container train waits for it to pass.

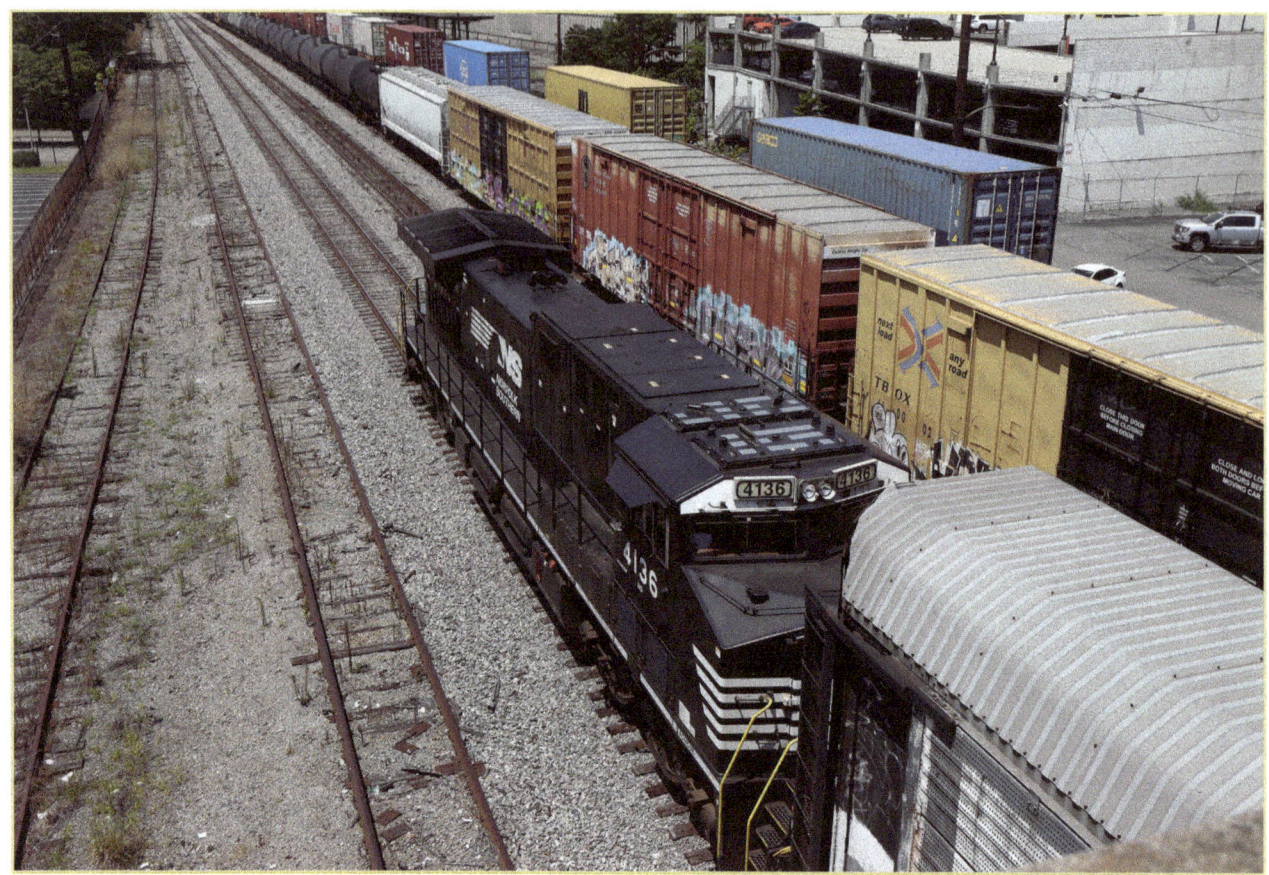
A Norfolk Southern engine pushes in the rear while passing a stopped CSX train in Birmingham.

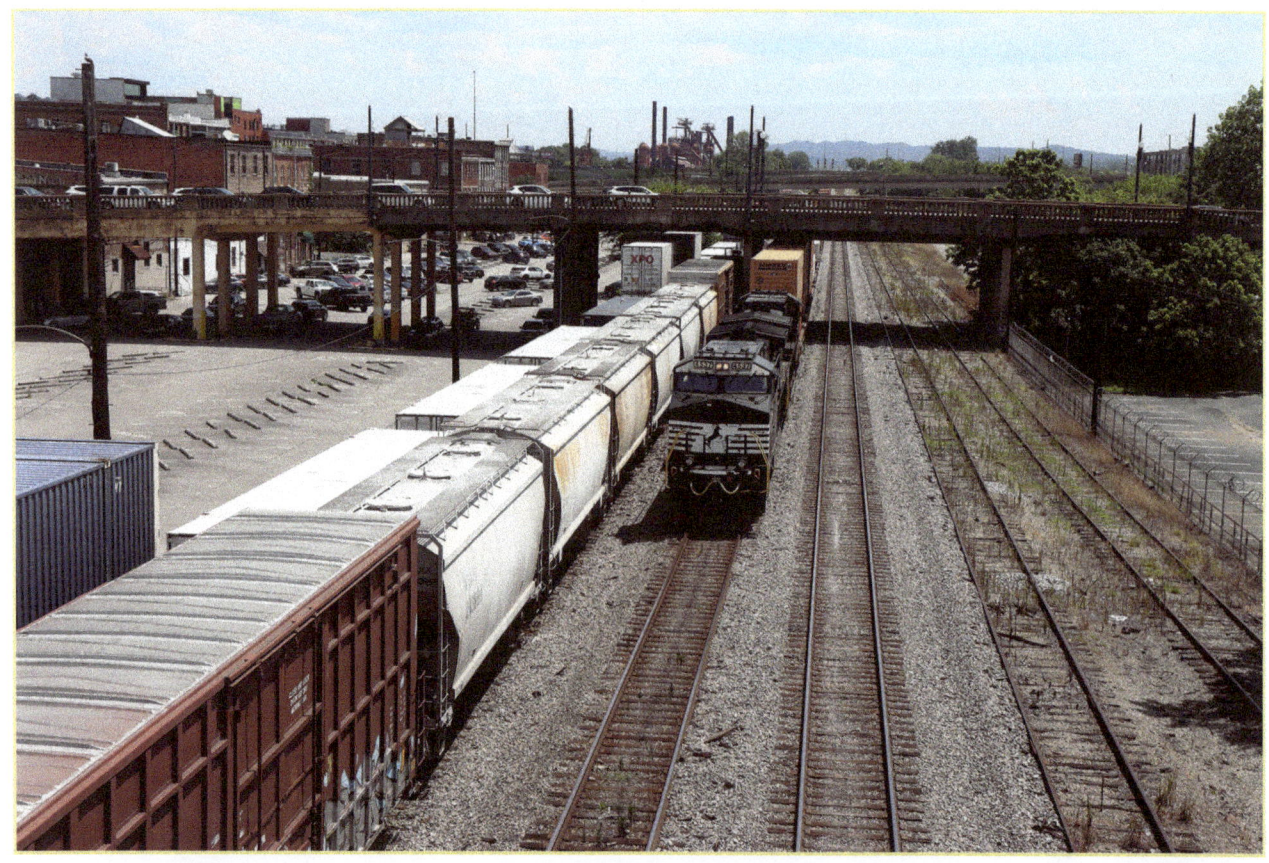
A Norfolk Southern container train stops to let the two CSX trains cross the Norfolk Southern tracks.

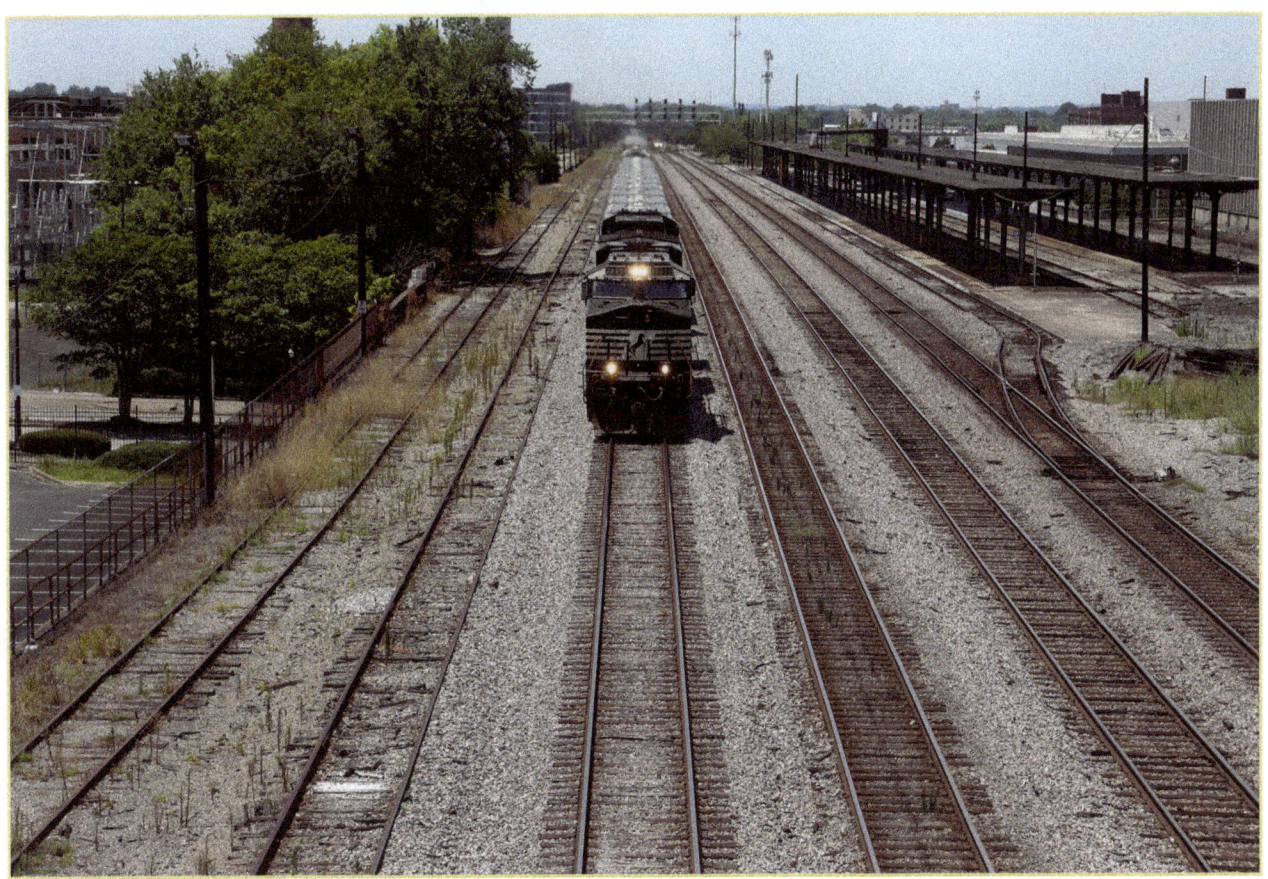
A Norfolk Southern mixed-freight passes the old L&N station, which is still used daily by Amtrak.

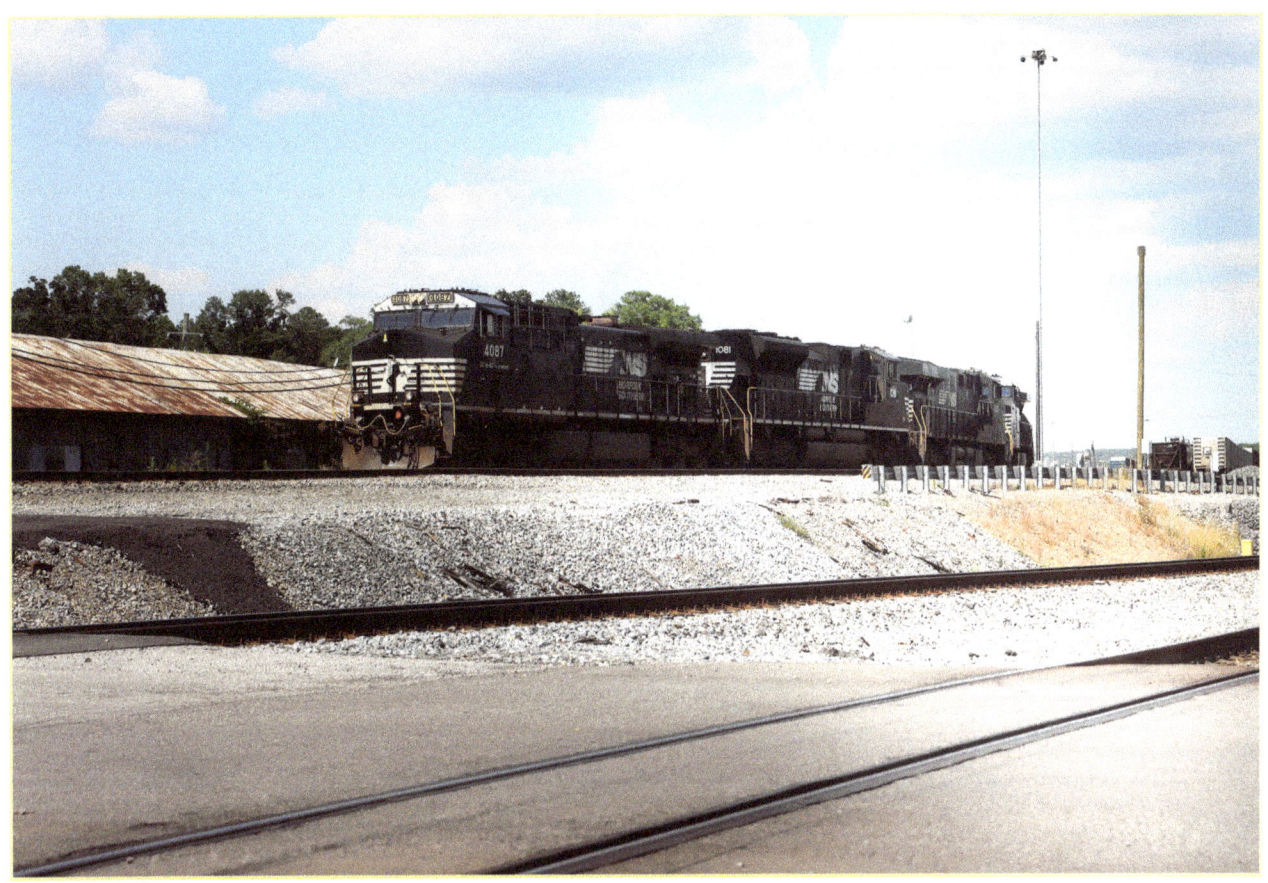
Four Norfolk Southern engines emerge from Norris Yard with a long train in tow.

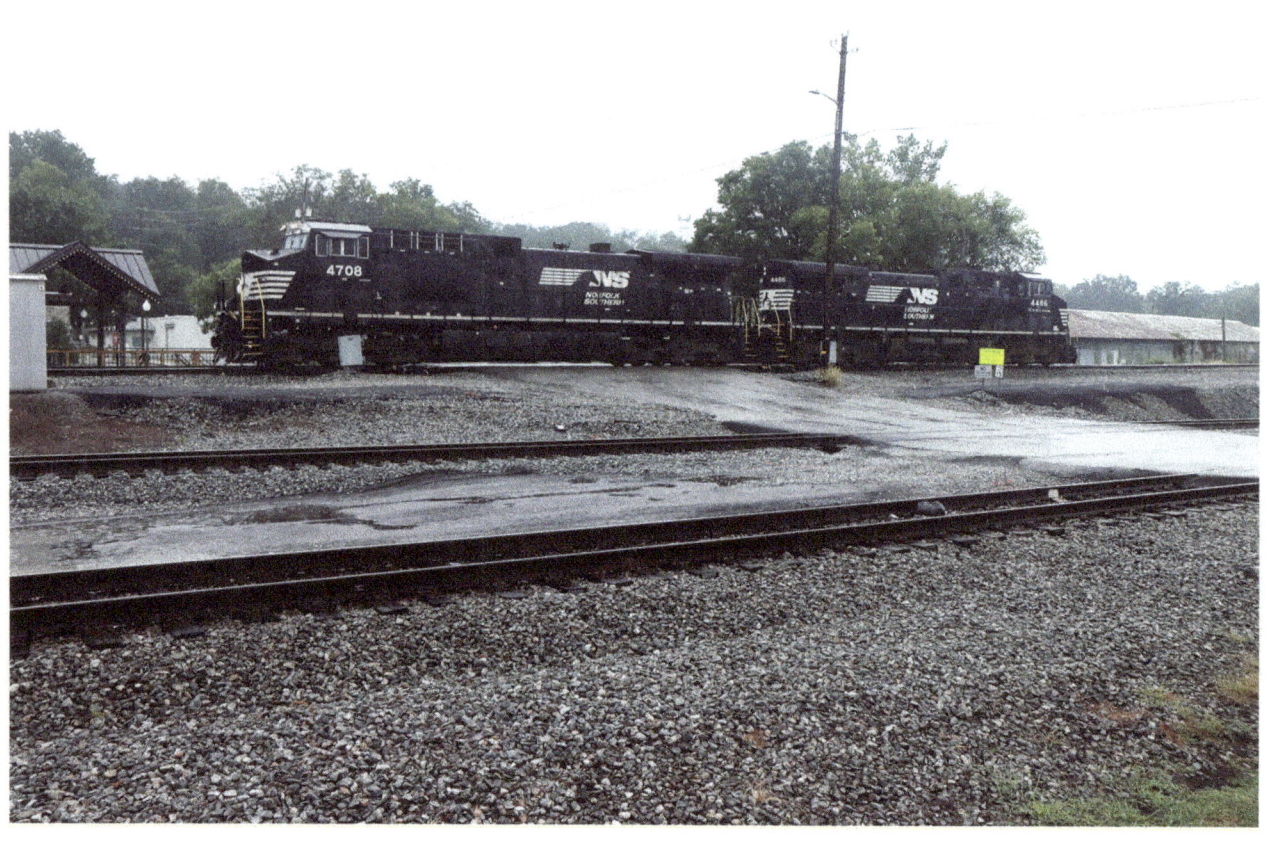
Two Norfolk Southern AC44 locomotives sit idle in the rain.

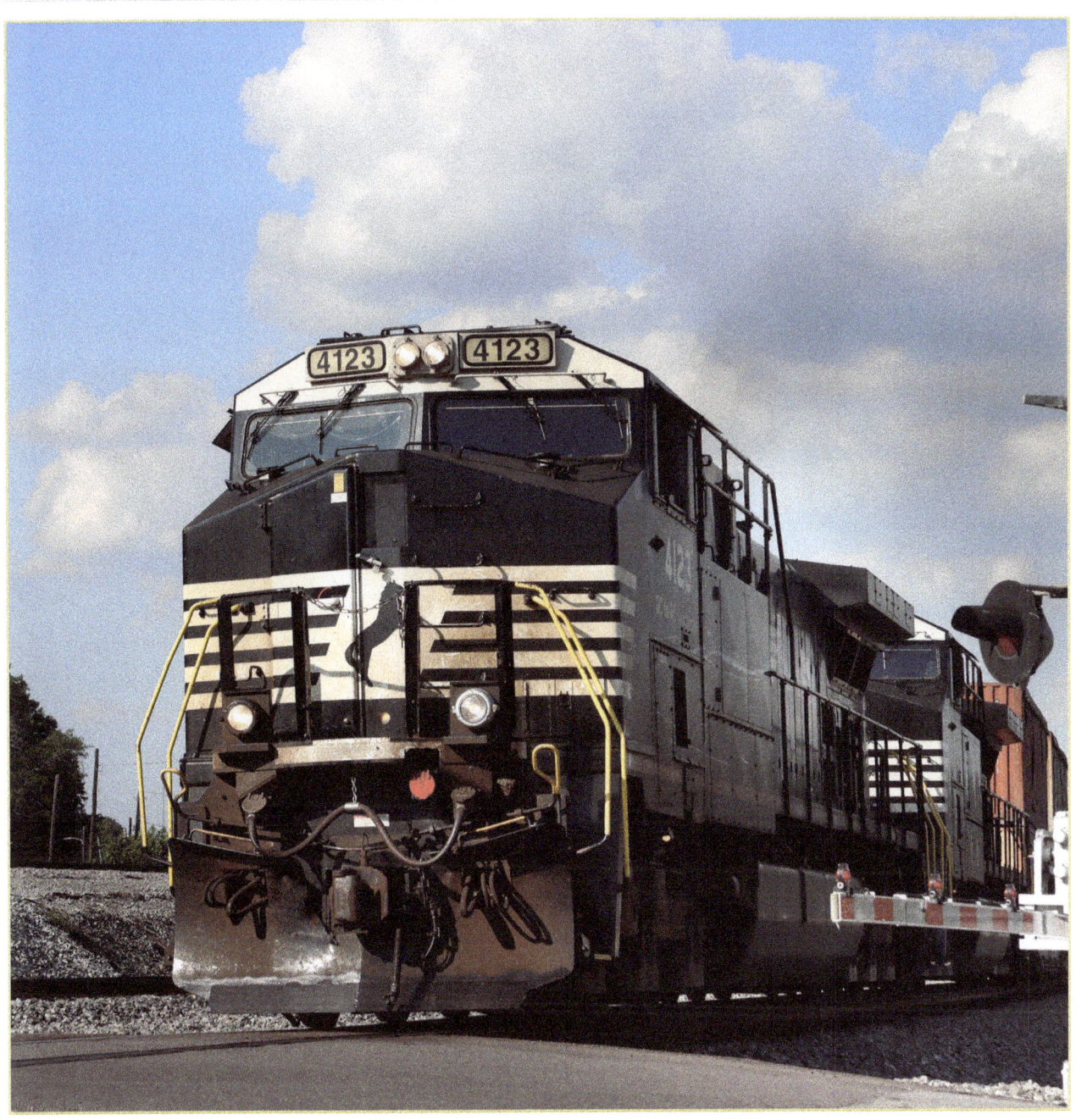
Two Norfolk Southern engines lead a container train through Irondale.

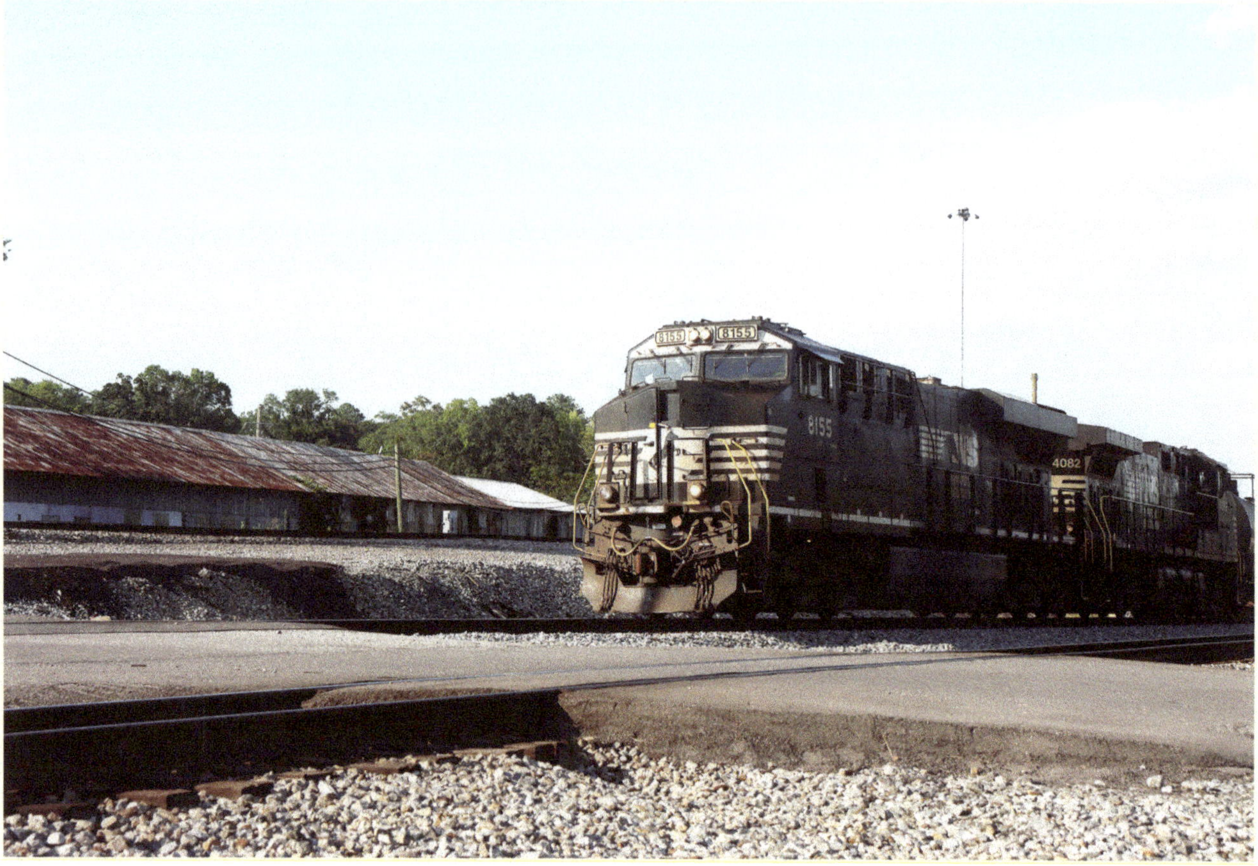

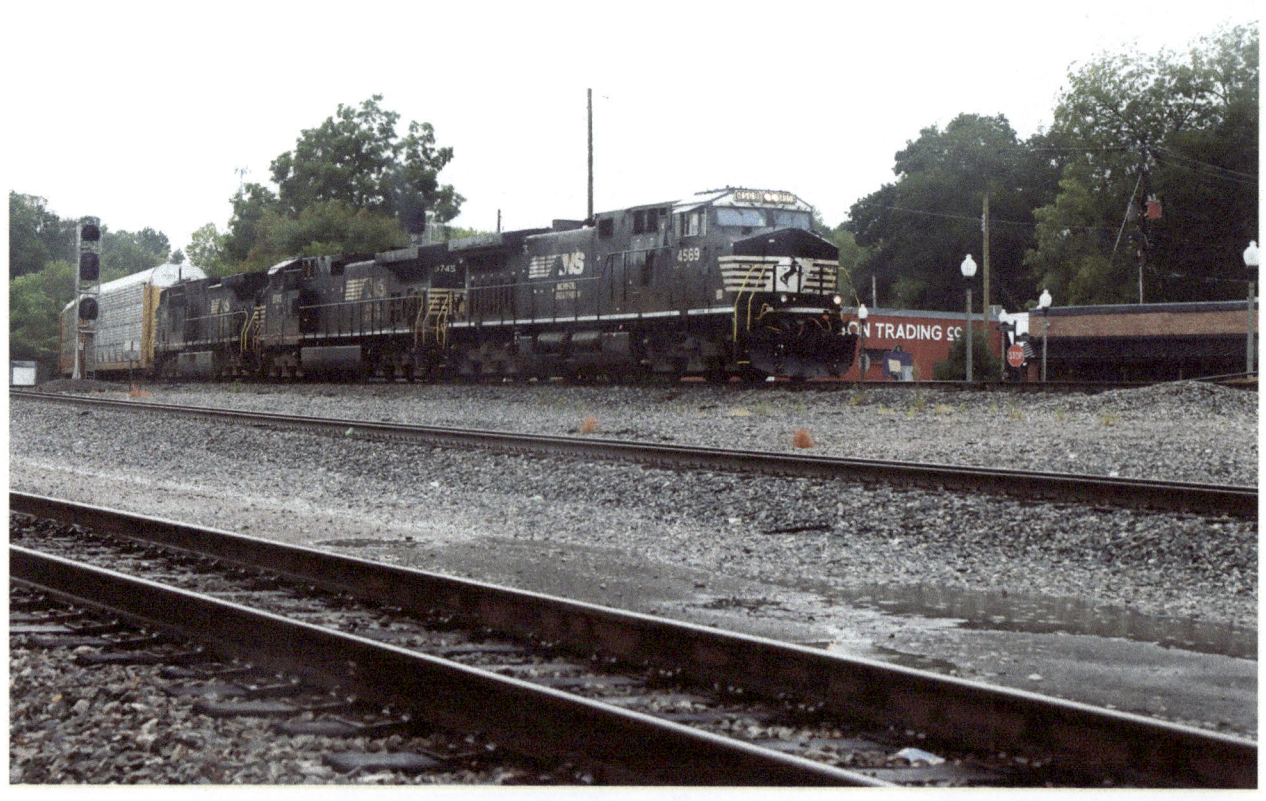

A mixed-freight passes through Irondale in the afternoon.

A train pulling autoracks that are most likely from the Mercedes plant in Tuscaloosa enters the south end of Norris Yard.

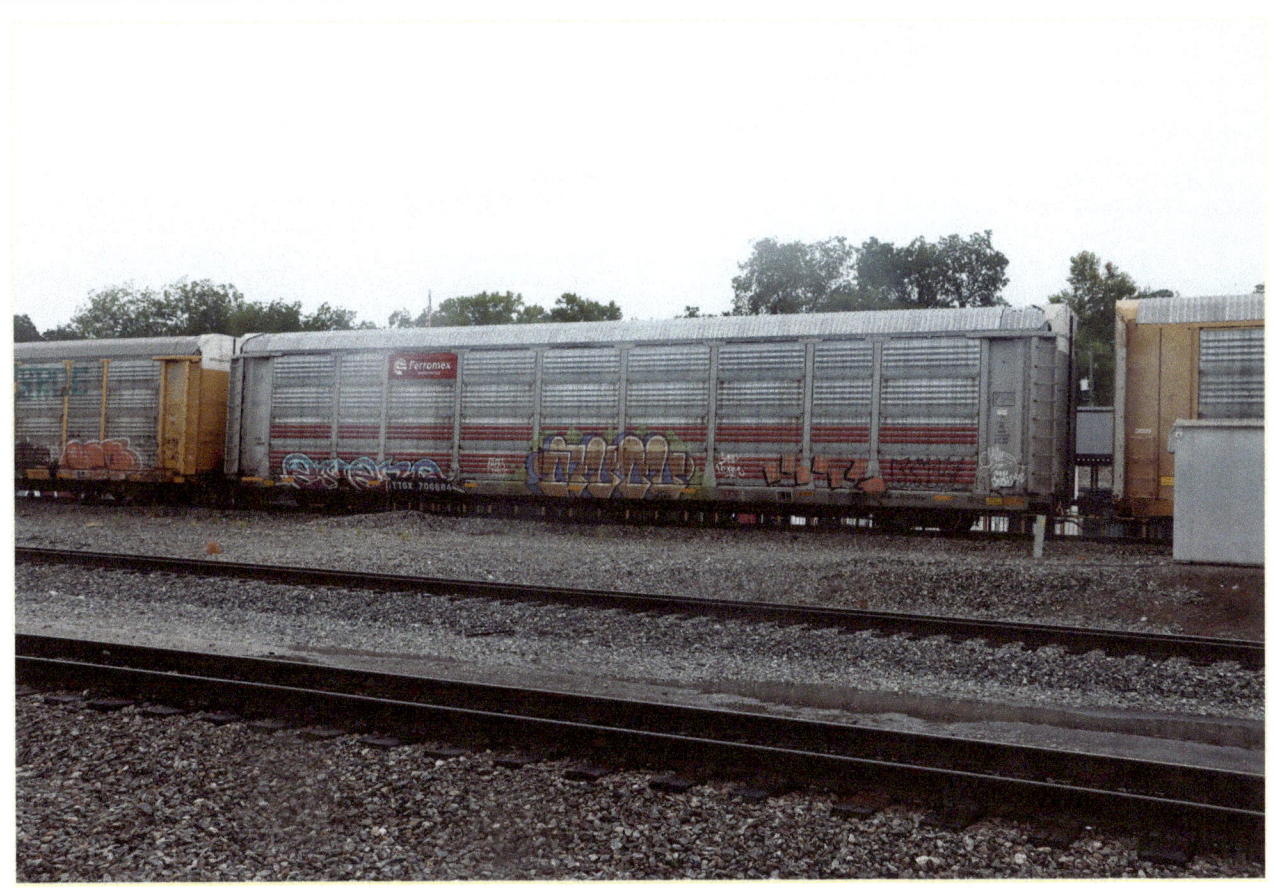
This autorack owned by Ferromex, a Mexican railroad company, traveled all the way from Mexico.

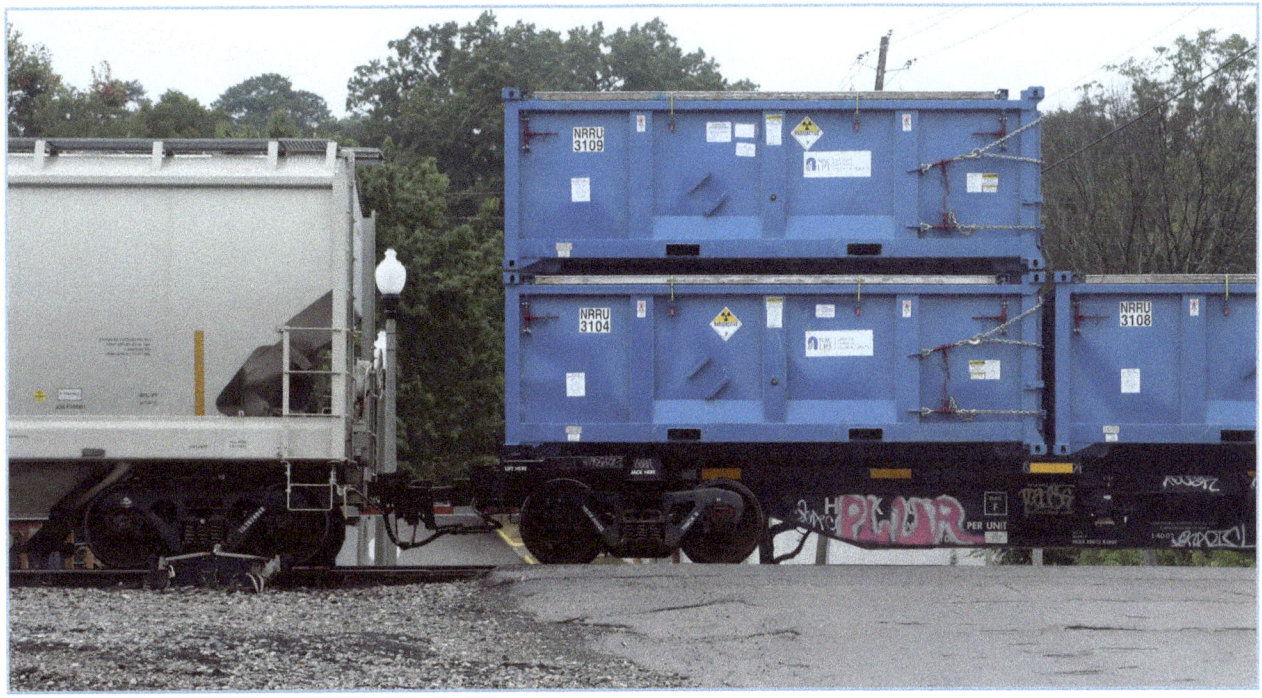
These containers are hauling radioactive material westward toward Birmingham and other destinations.

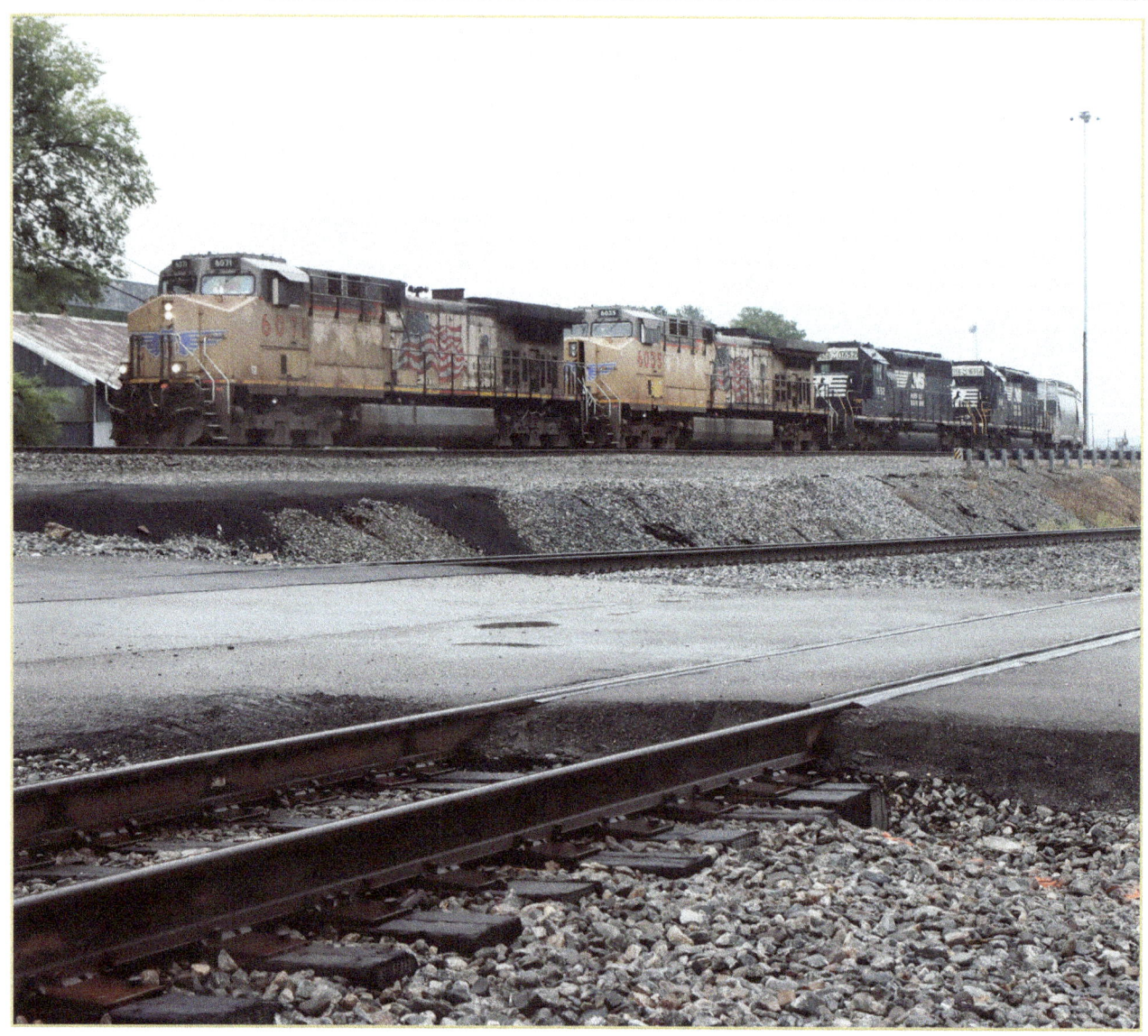
Two Union Pacific GEVOs lead two older Norfolk Southern engines out of Norris Yard.

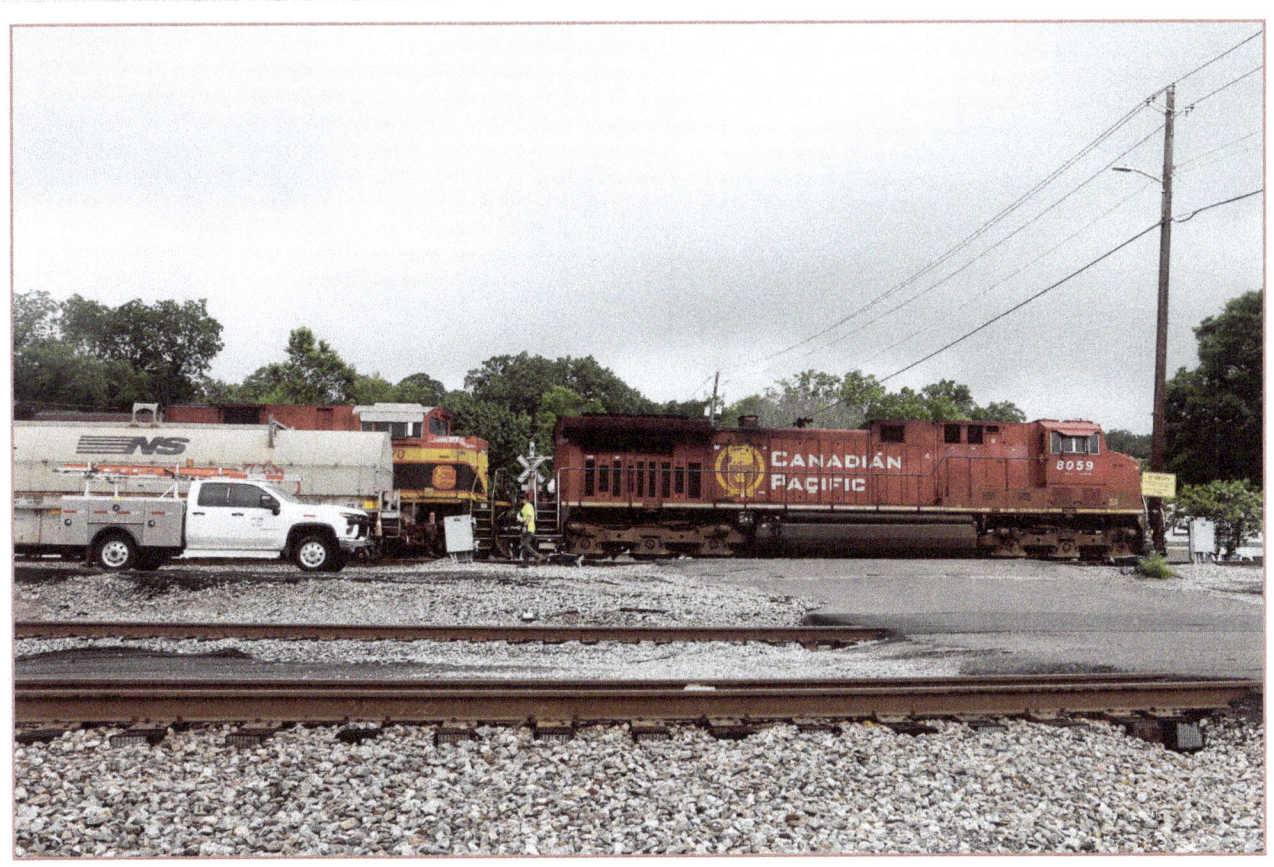

Two CPKC engines, both in original paint showing the two railroads that merged in 2024, enter Norris Yard pulling a train most likely from Meridian, Mississippi.

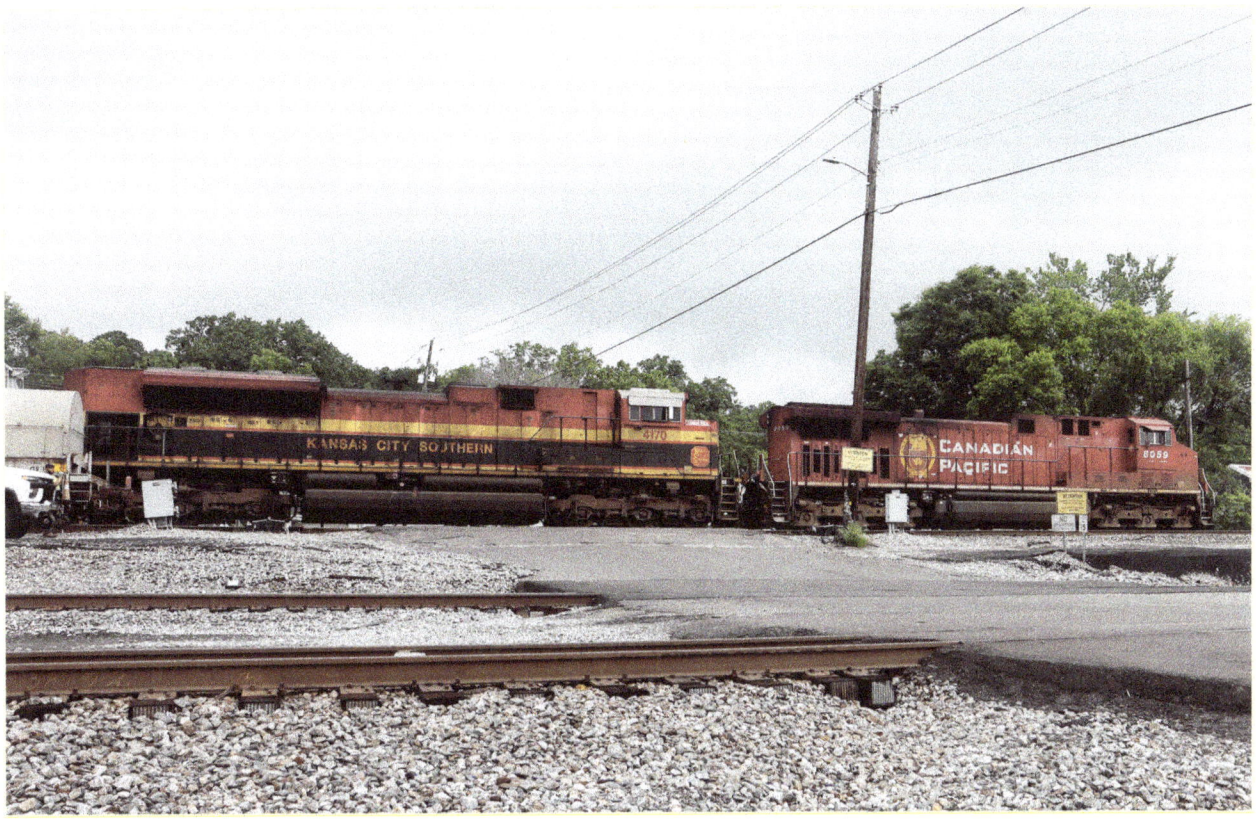

Two CPKC locomotives pull into the yard slowly while a Norfolk Southern employee works on the end of a train.

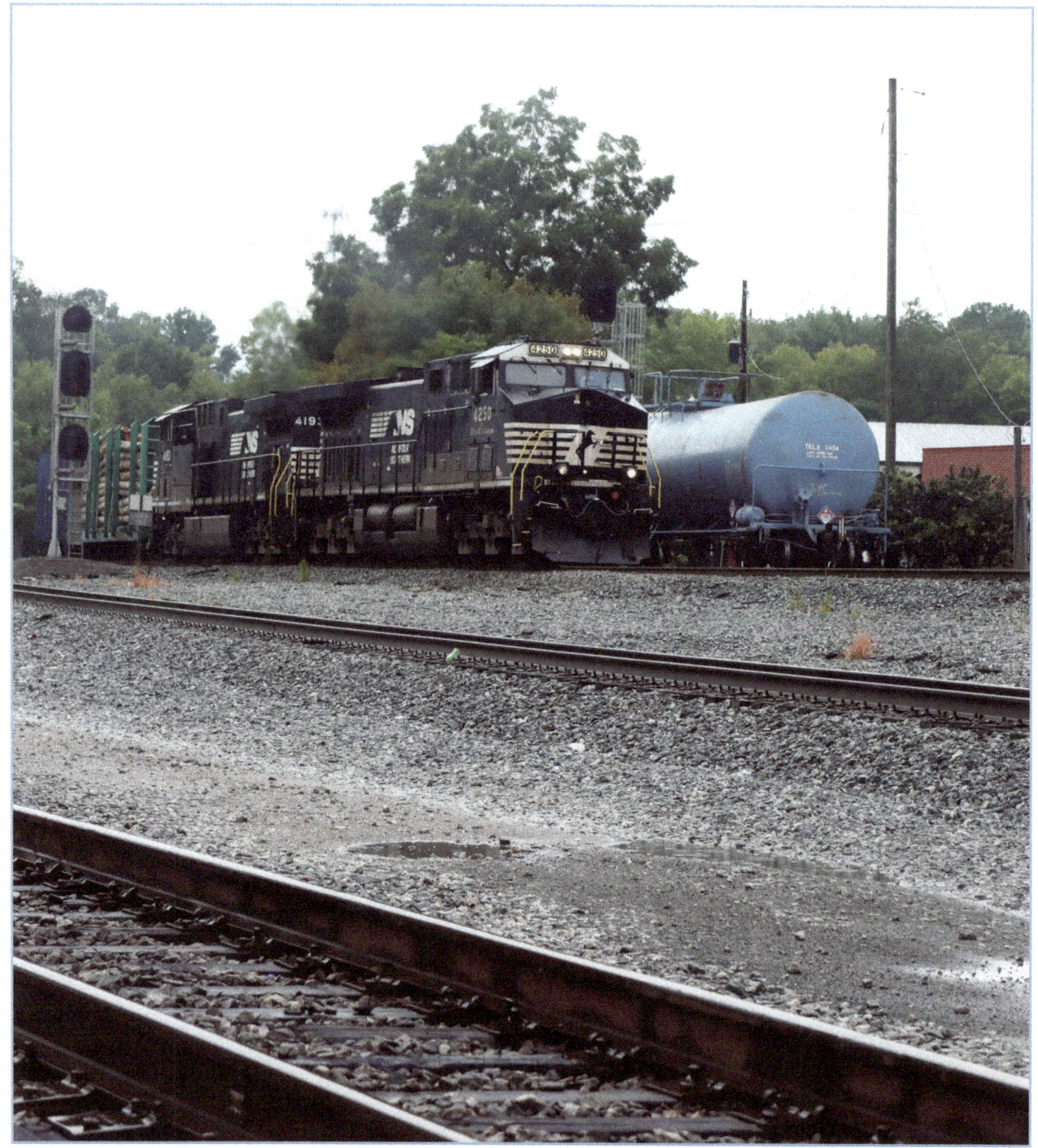
An inbound Norfolk Southern train meets an outbound at the south end of Norris Yard.

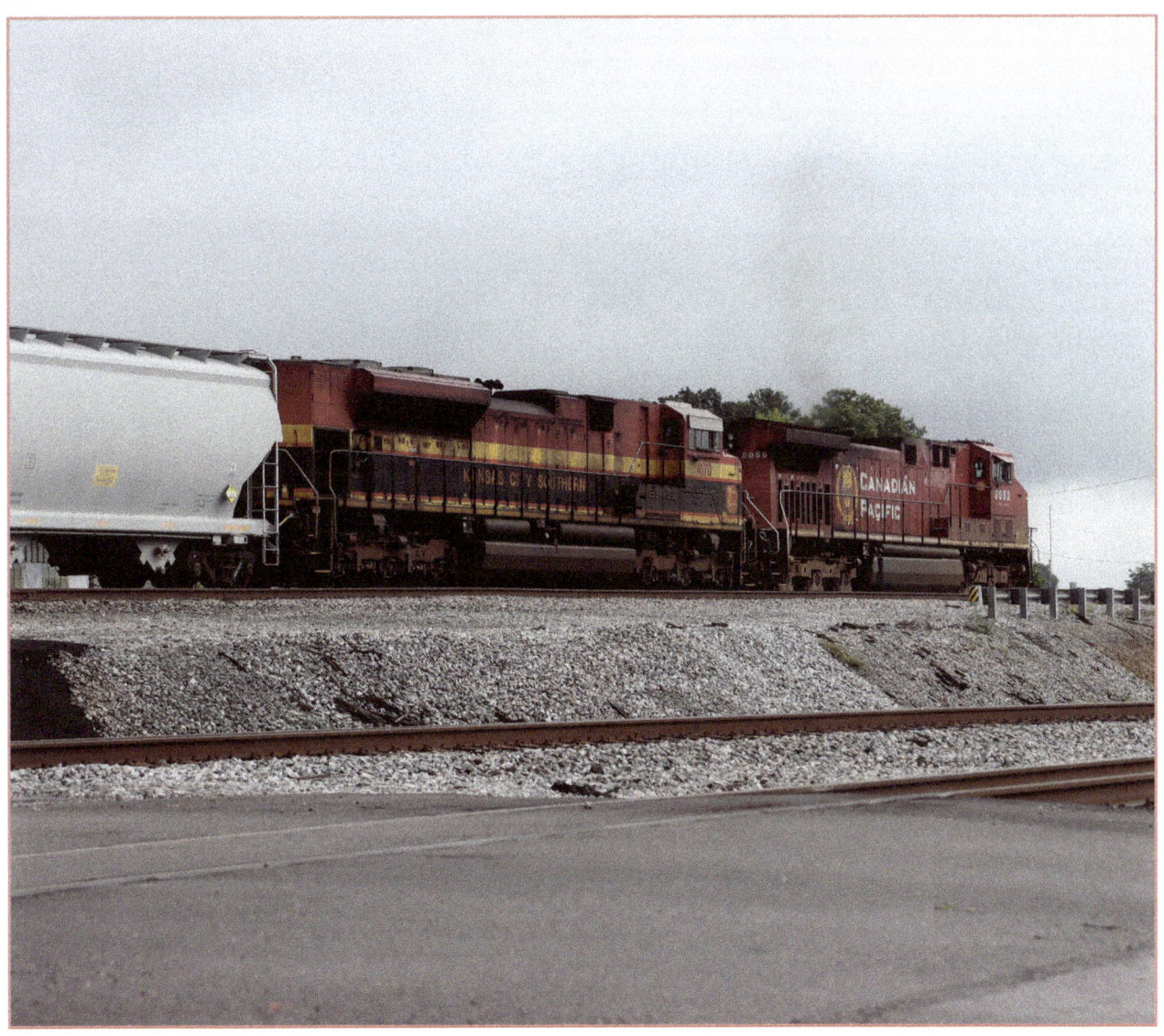

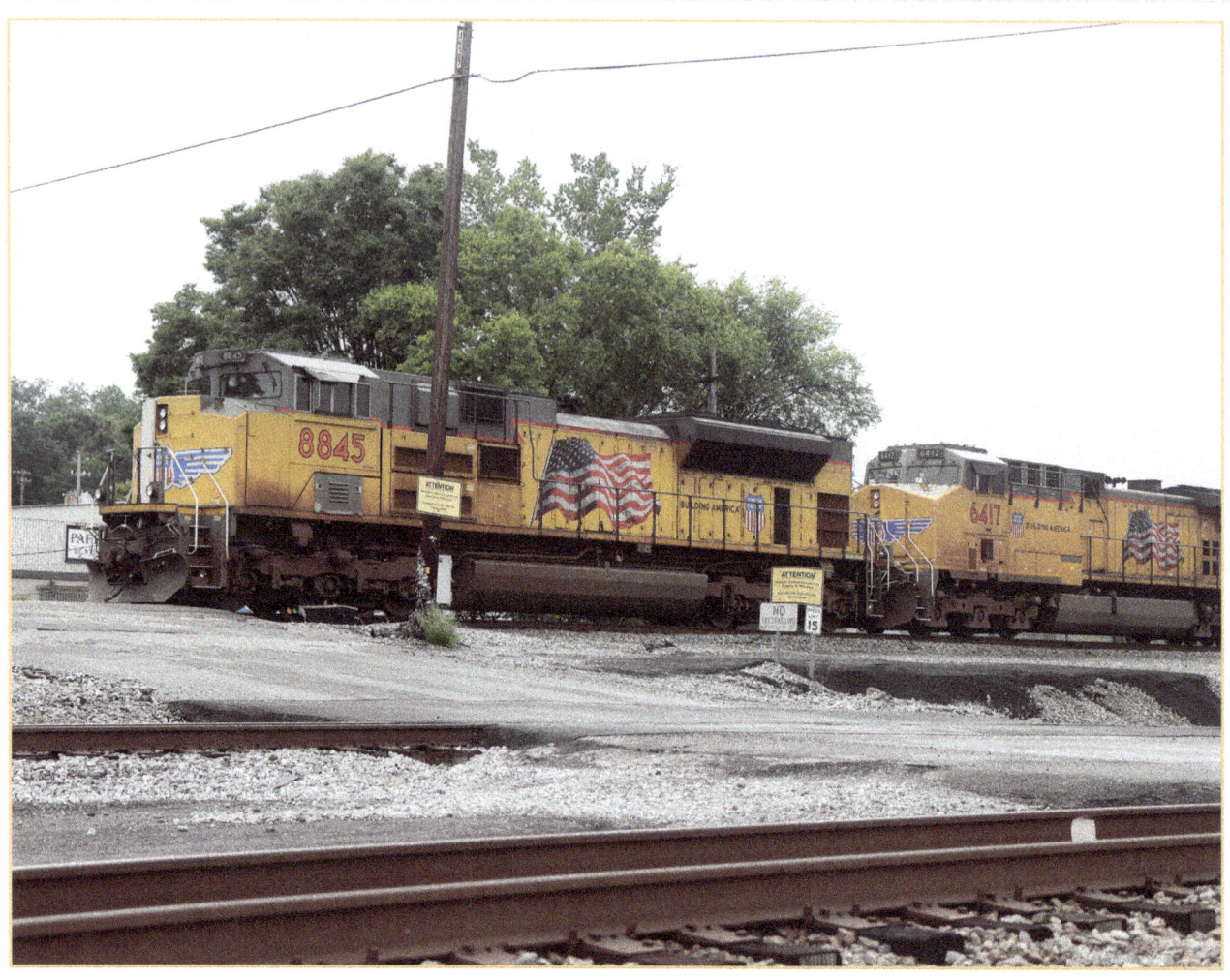

A Union Pacific SD70ACe exits the yard on a gloomy day.

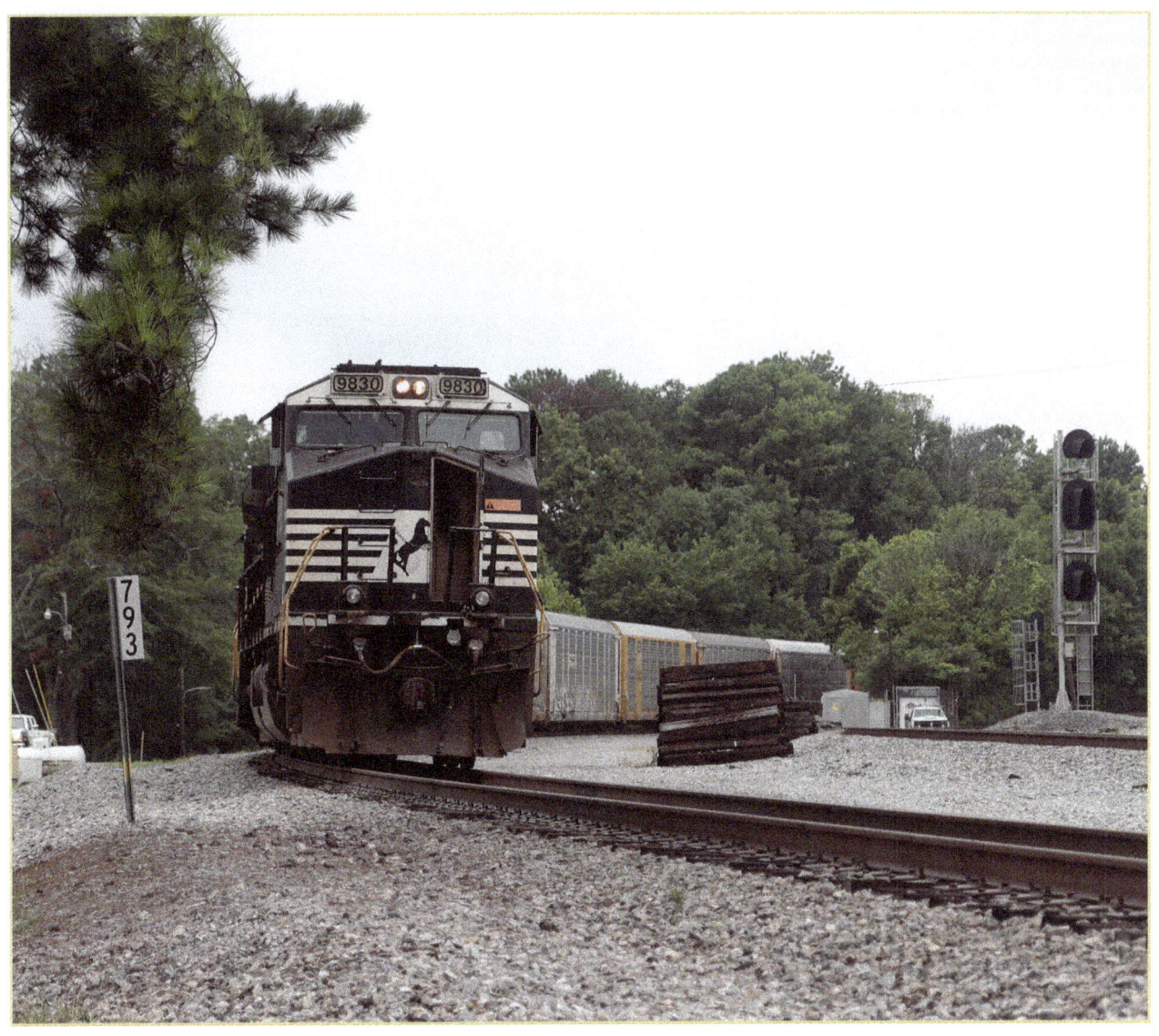
A Norfolk Southern AC44 leads autoracks toward Atlanta with the cab door wide open. This could be an accident, or the air-conditioner might not be working.

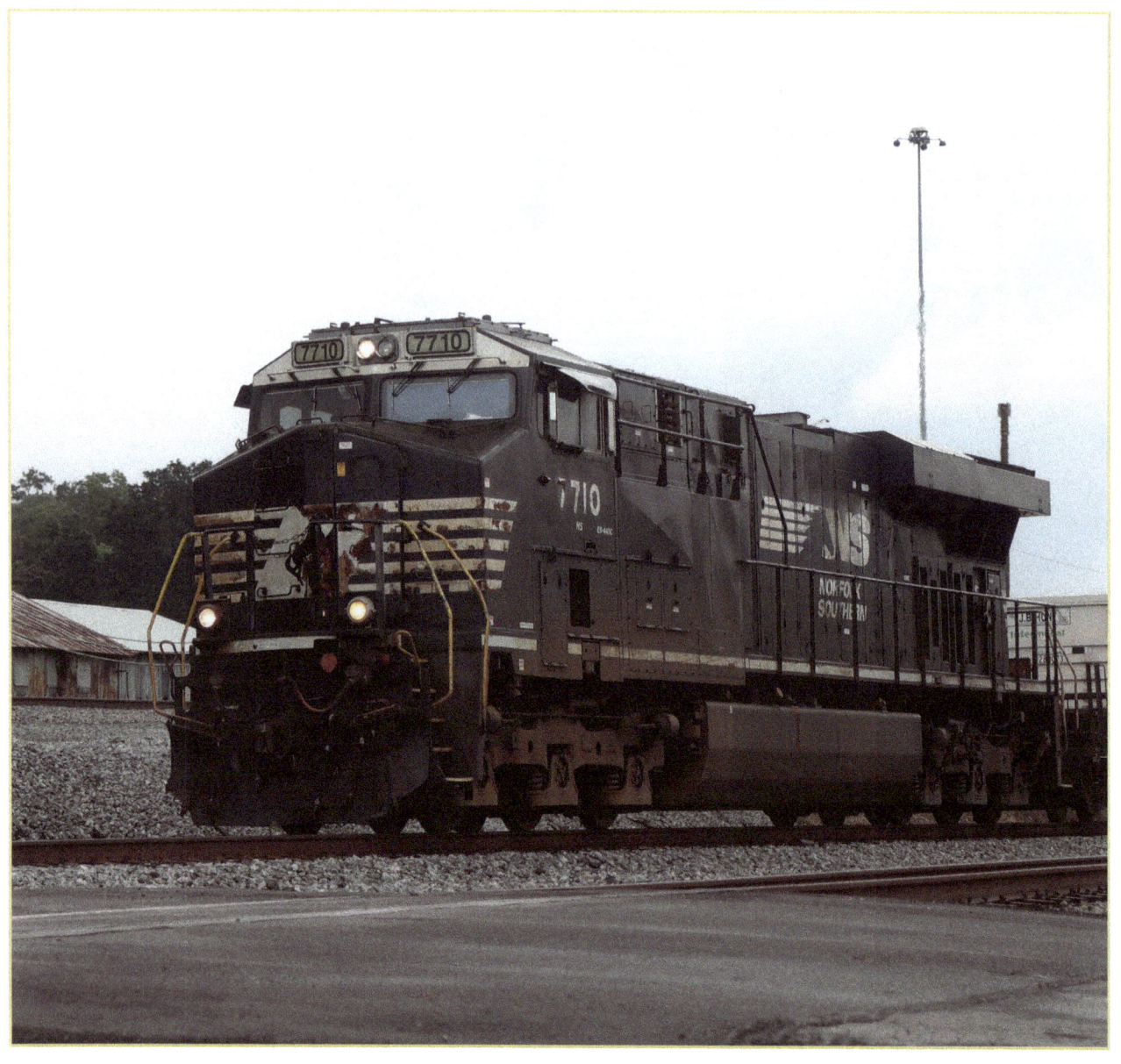
A rusty GEVO with one light out leads containers toward Birmingham.

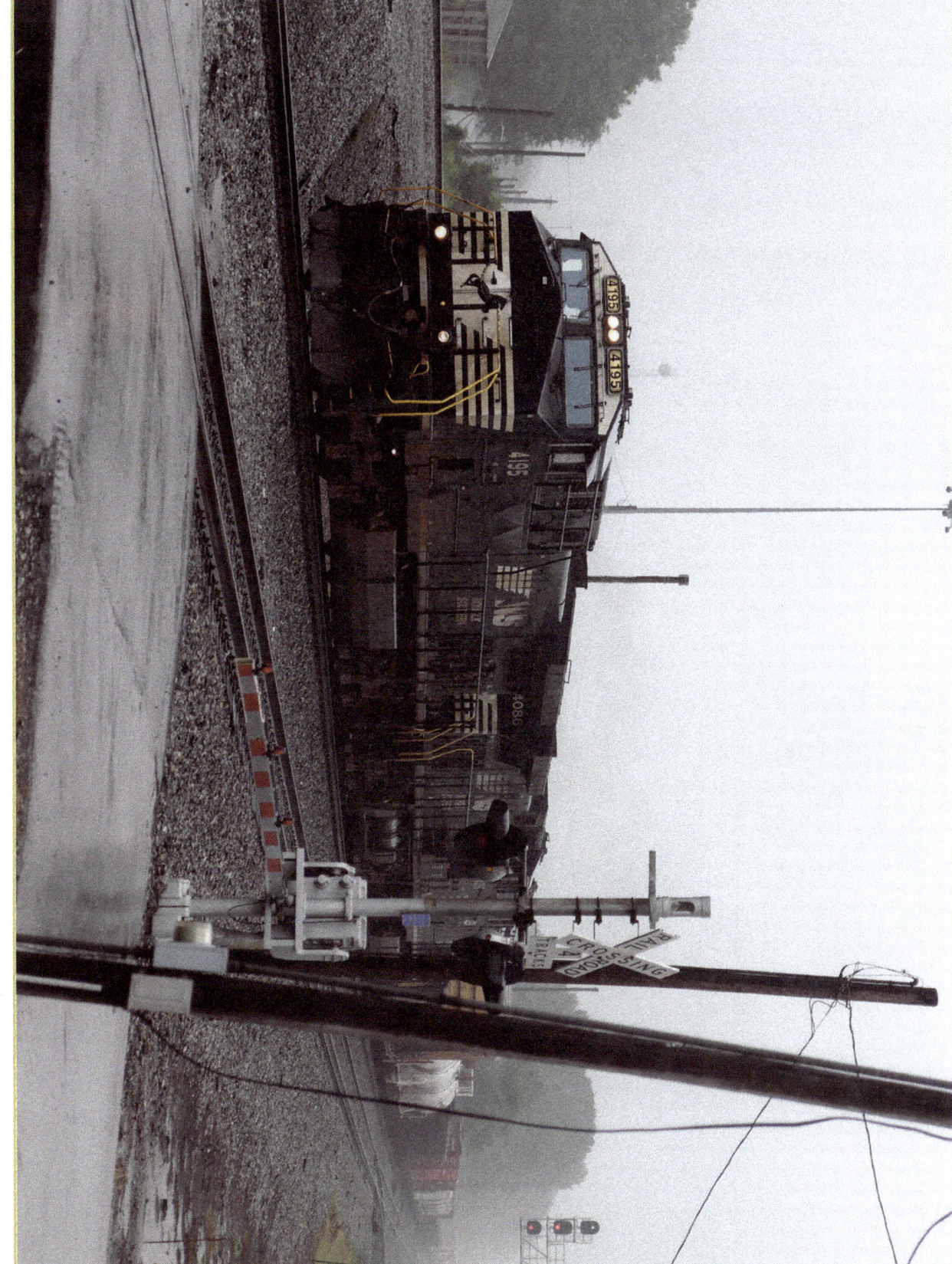

A mixed-freight races through Irondale while an eastbound train has a green signal.

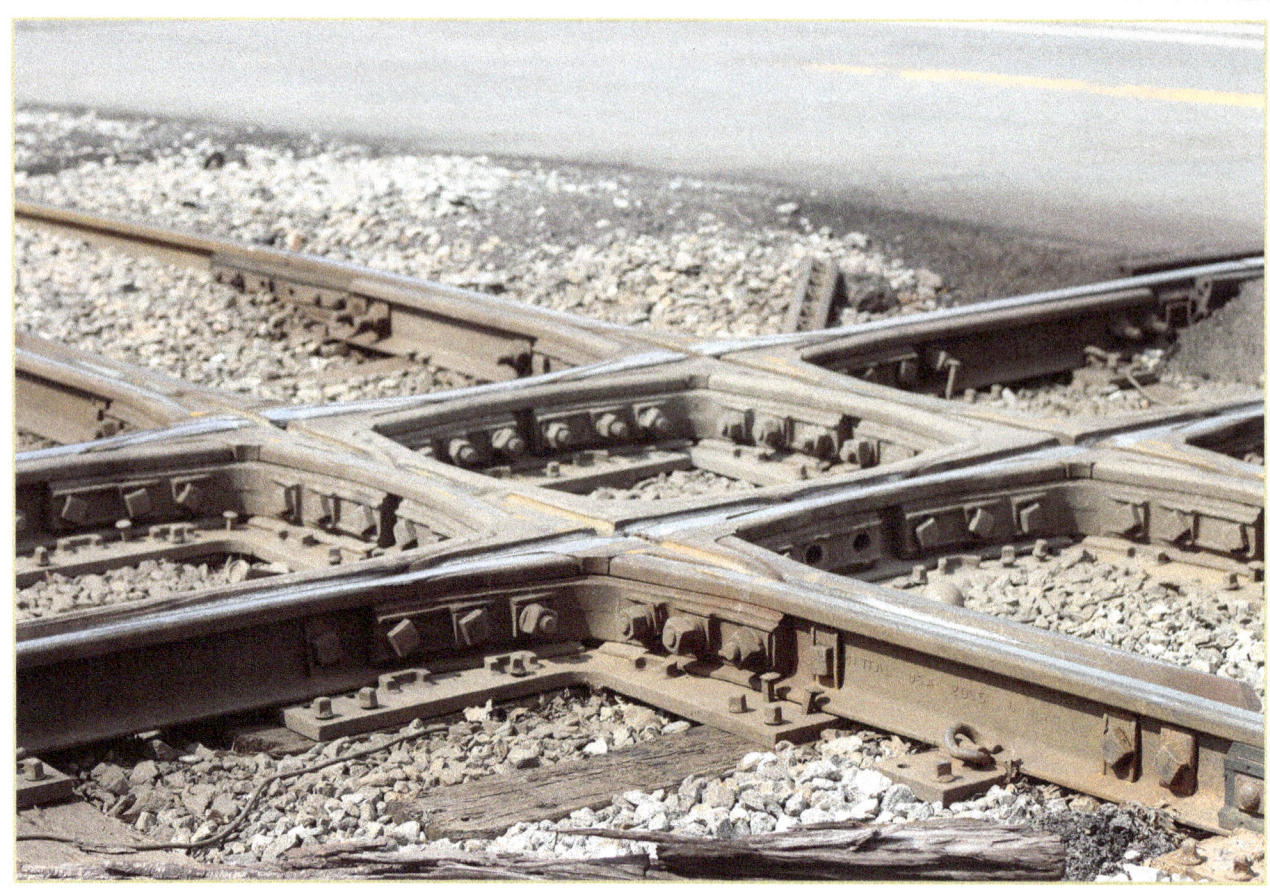

This diamond nears Sloss Furnace in Birmingham is where the Norfolk Southern crosses the Alabama and Tennessee River Railroad.

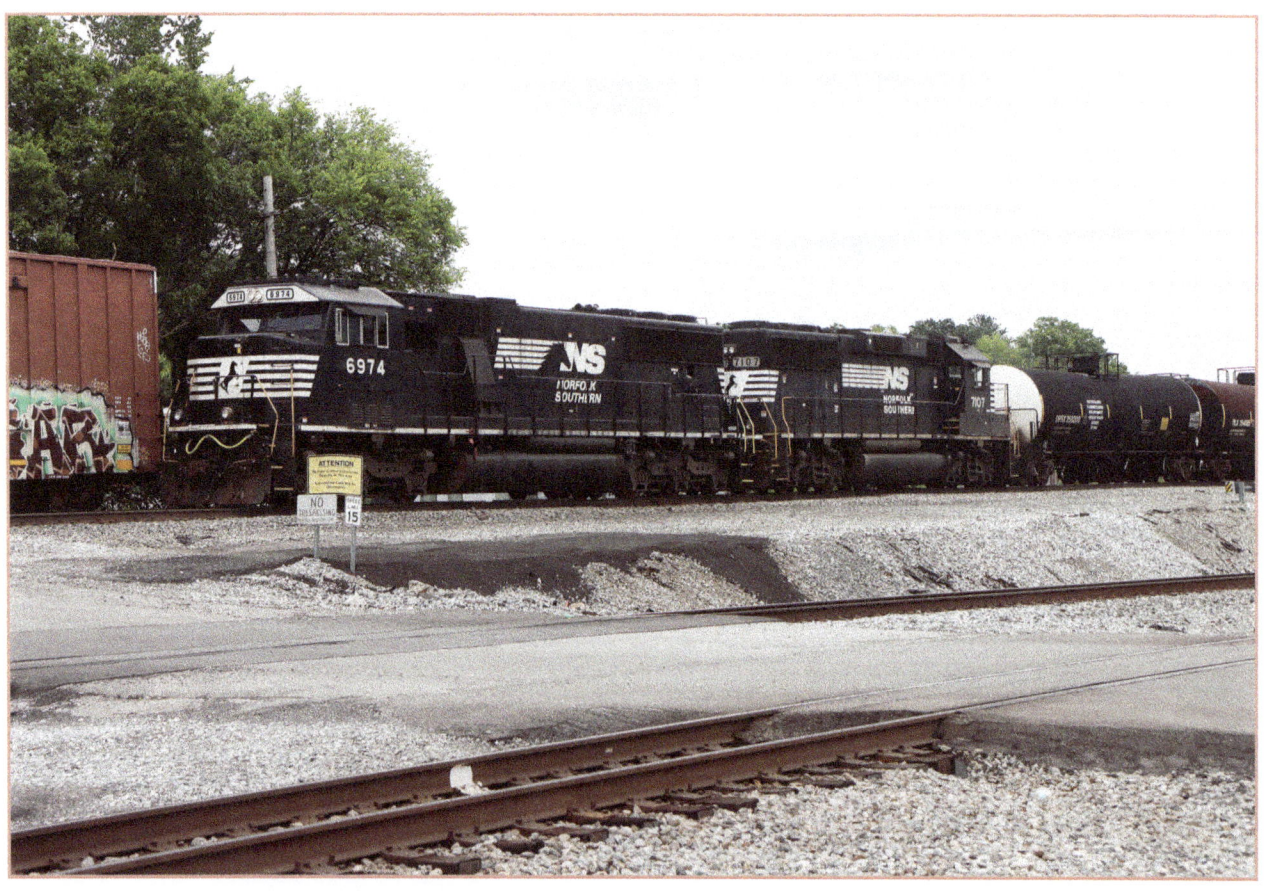

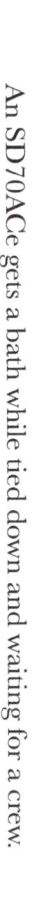

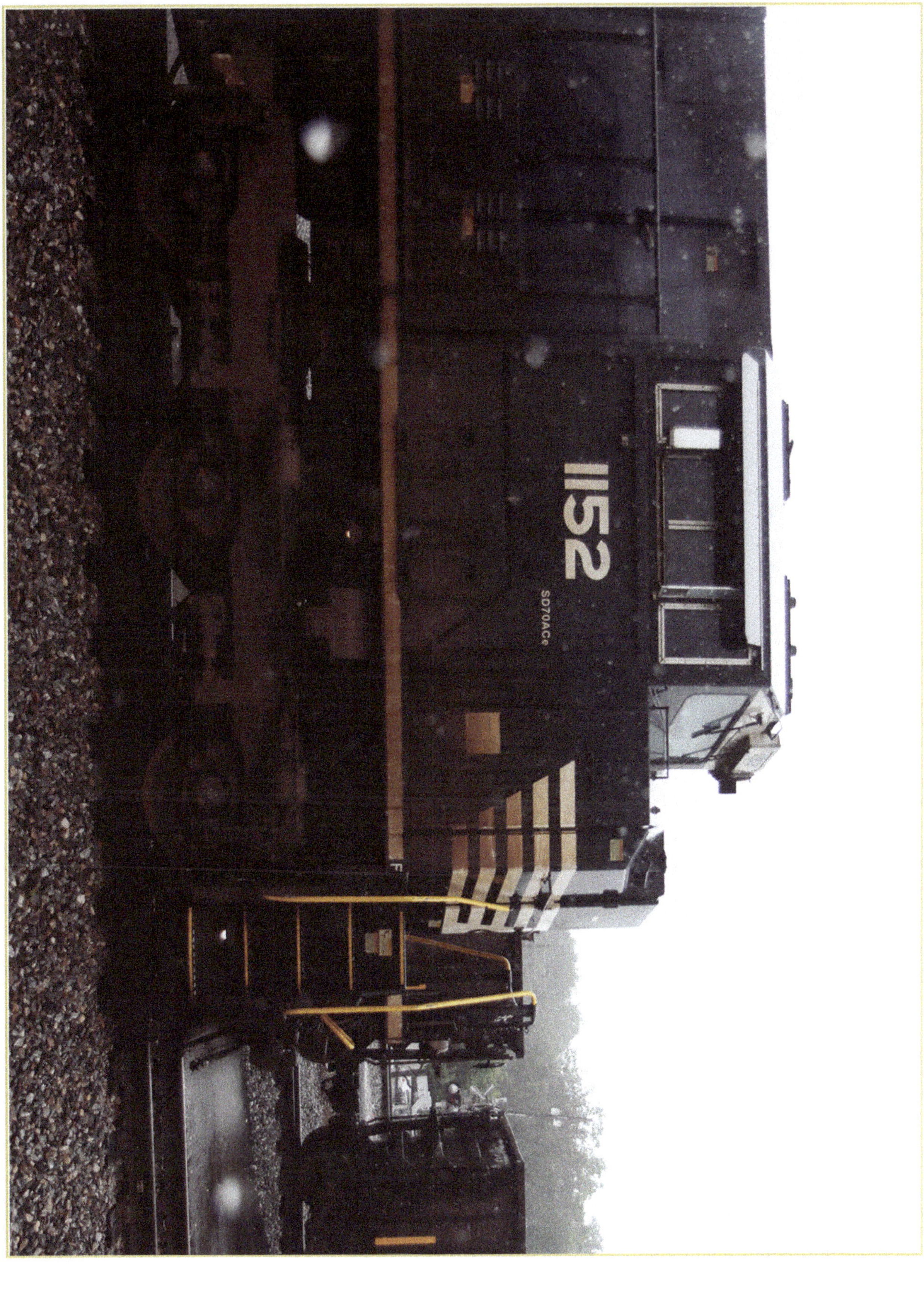

An SD70ACe gets a bath while tied down and waiting for a crew.

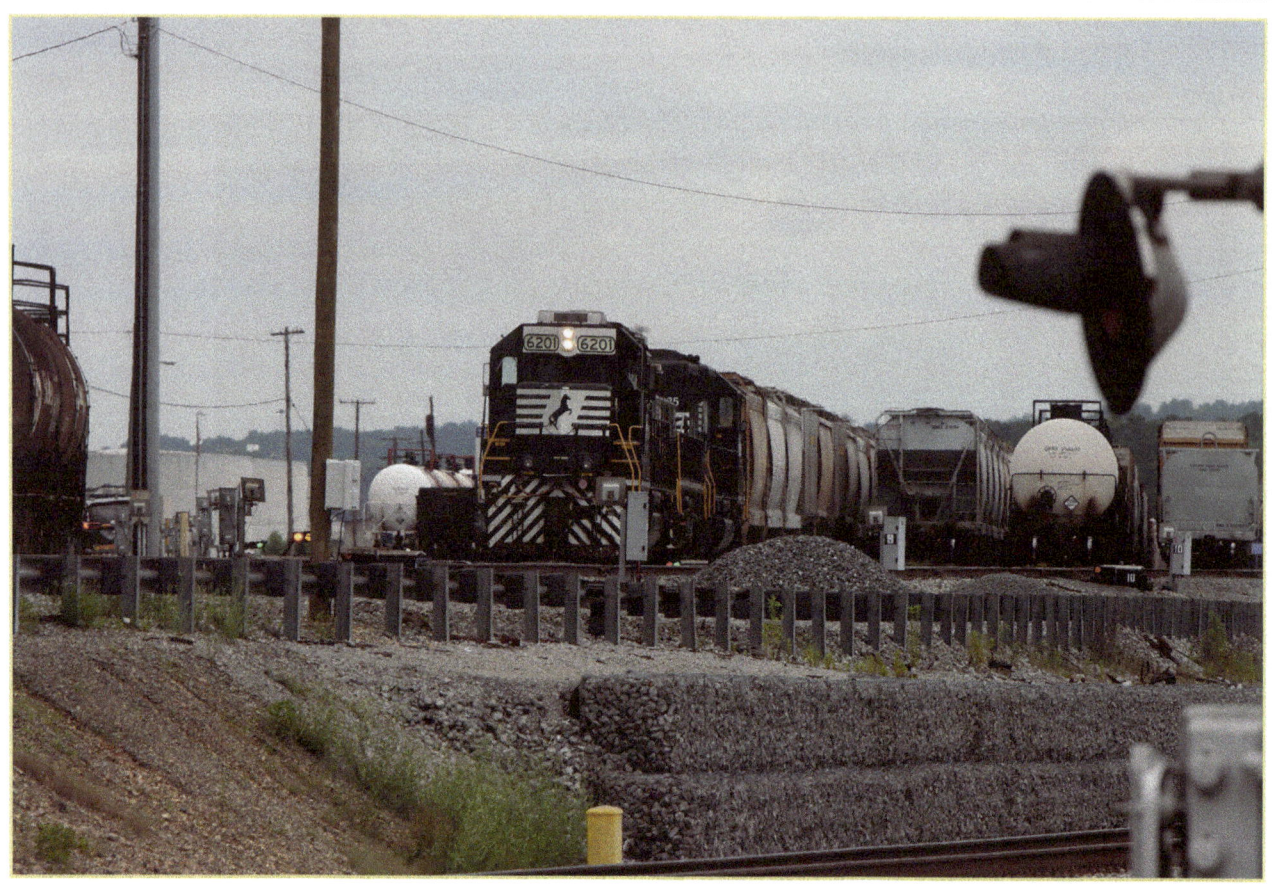

Norfolk Southern SD40-2 6201 works the yard on a cloudy day.

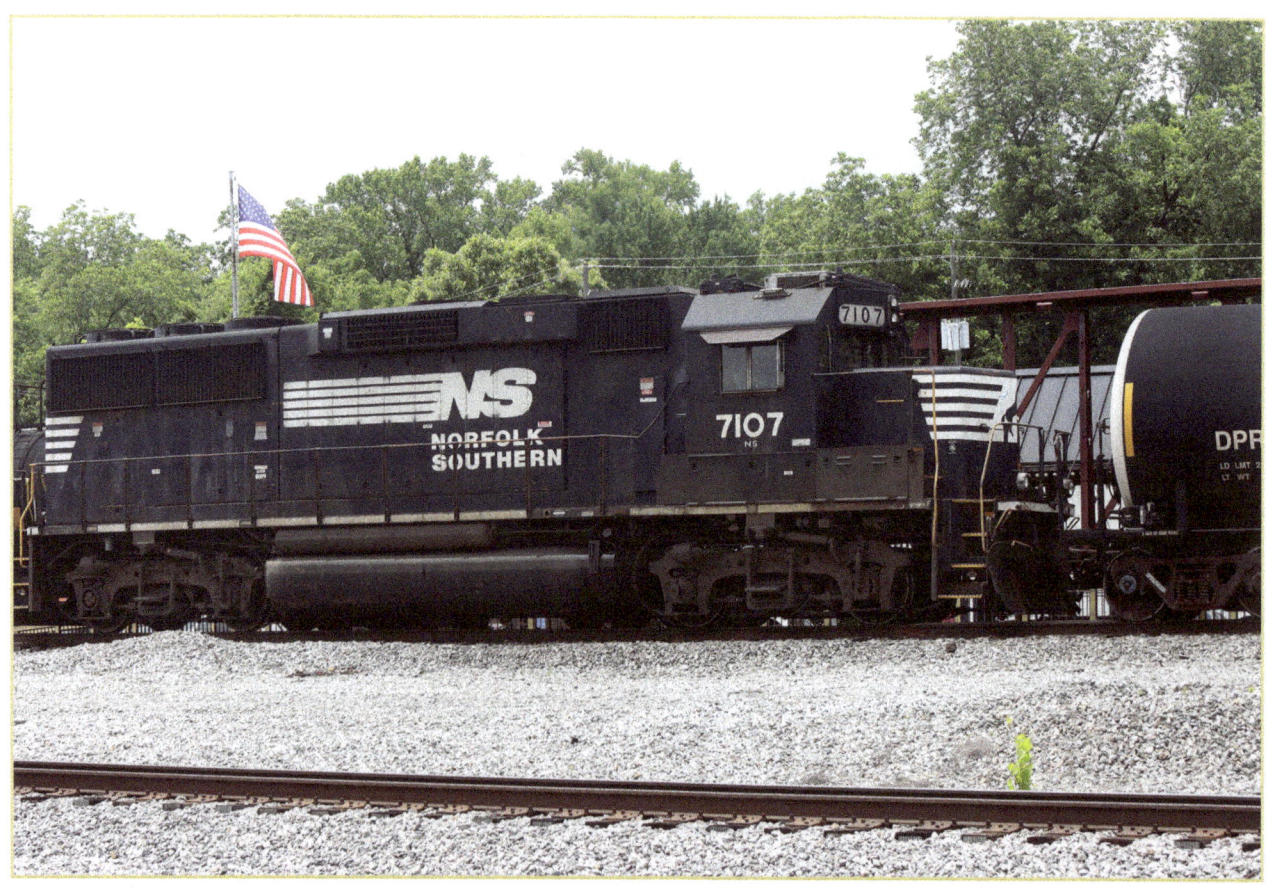

Norfolk Southern GP60 7107 trails on an outbound mixed-freight.

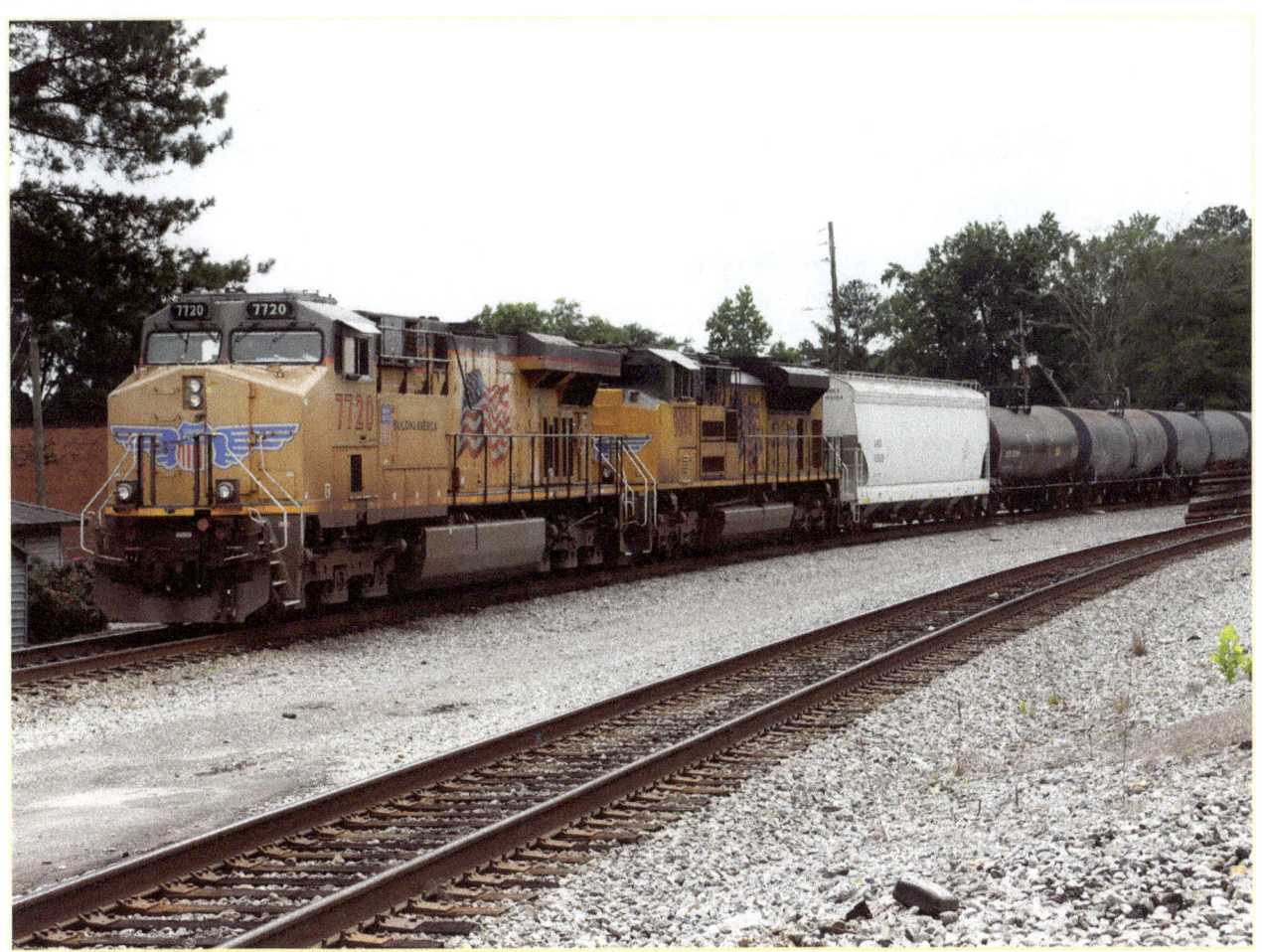
Two Union Pacific engines lead a stopped Norfolk Southern train.

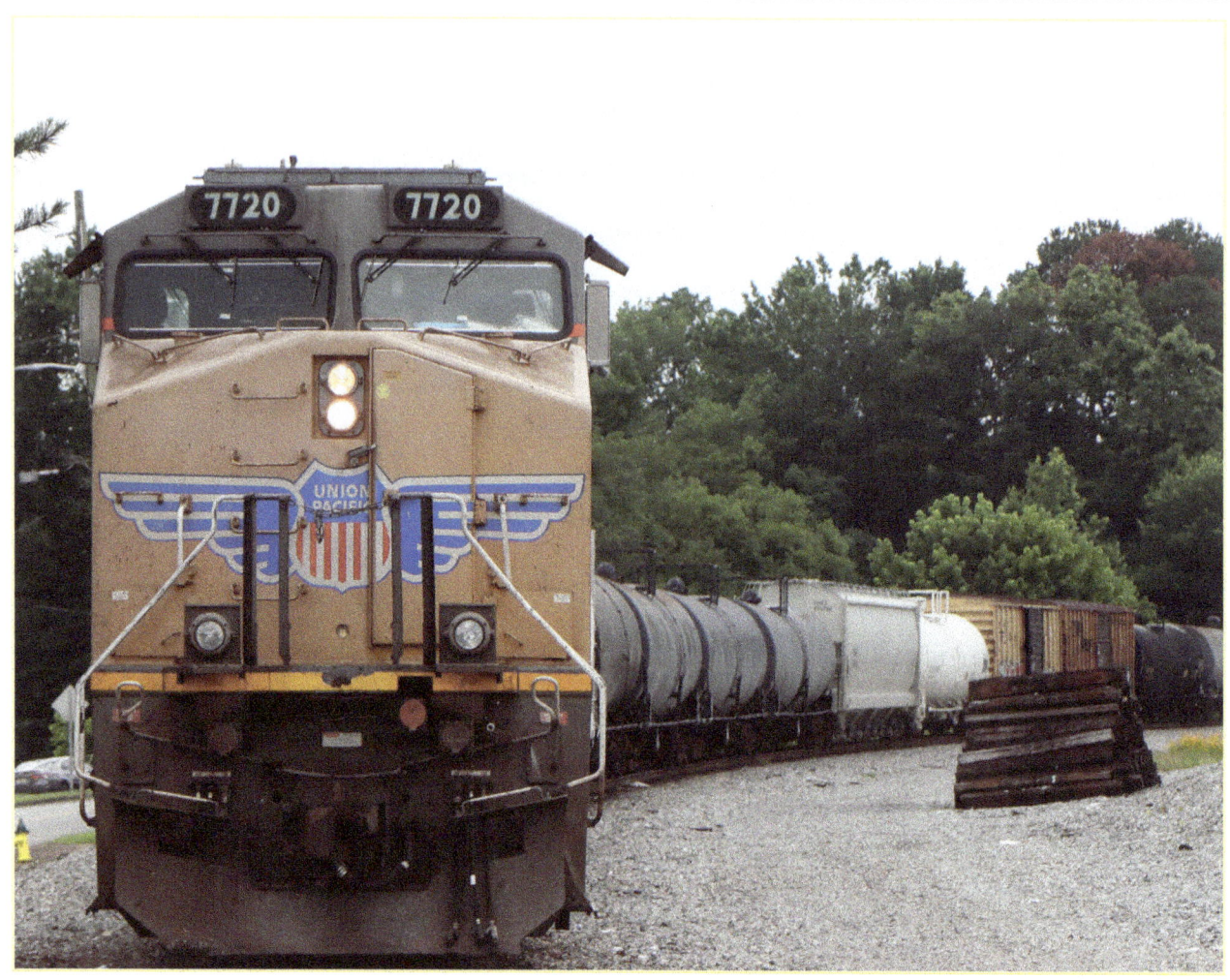
Union Pacific 7720 waits for a crew to take it toward Atlanta.

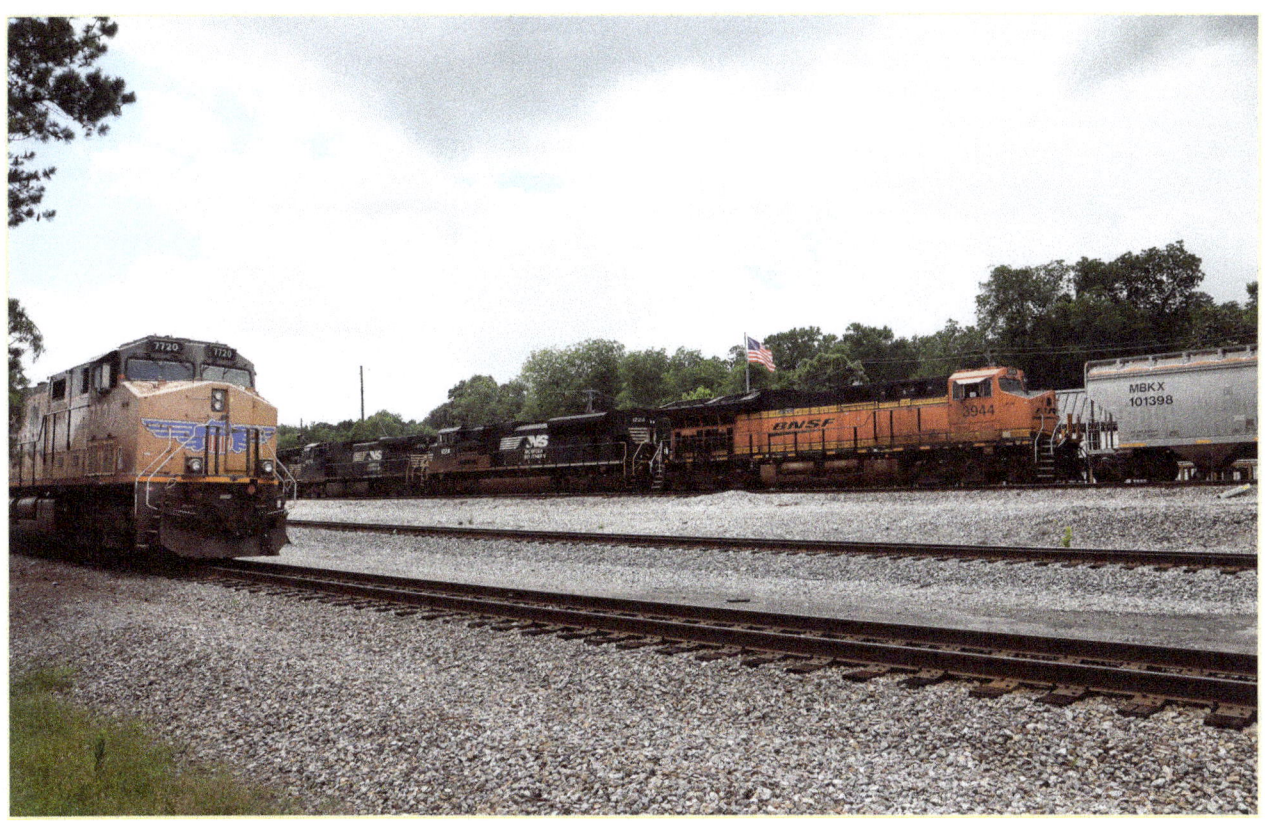

A Norfolk Southern train with a BNSF engine trailing exits Norris Yard while the Union Pacific train still waits for a crew.

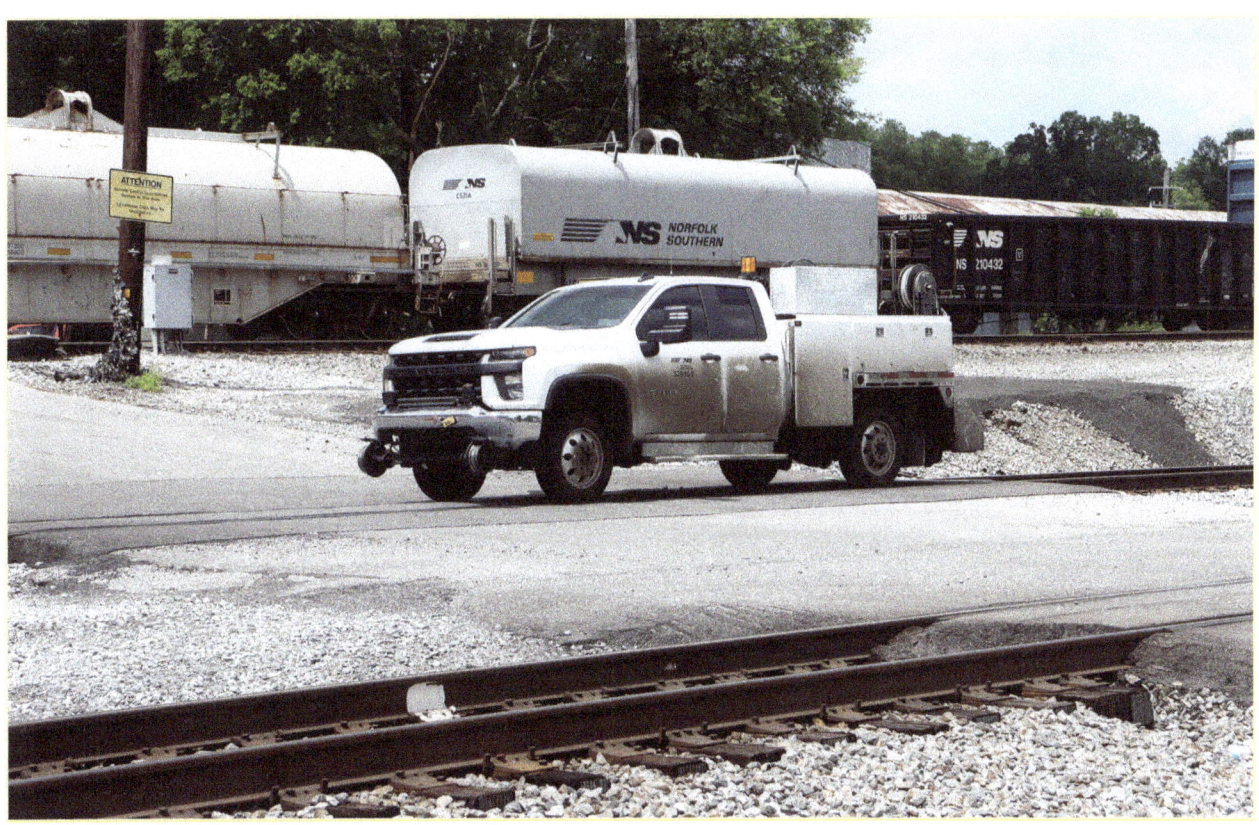

A very dirty Norfolk Southern work truck gets off the tracks in Irondale.

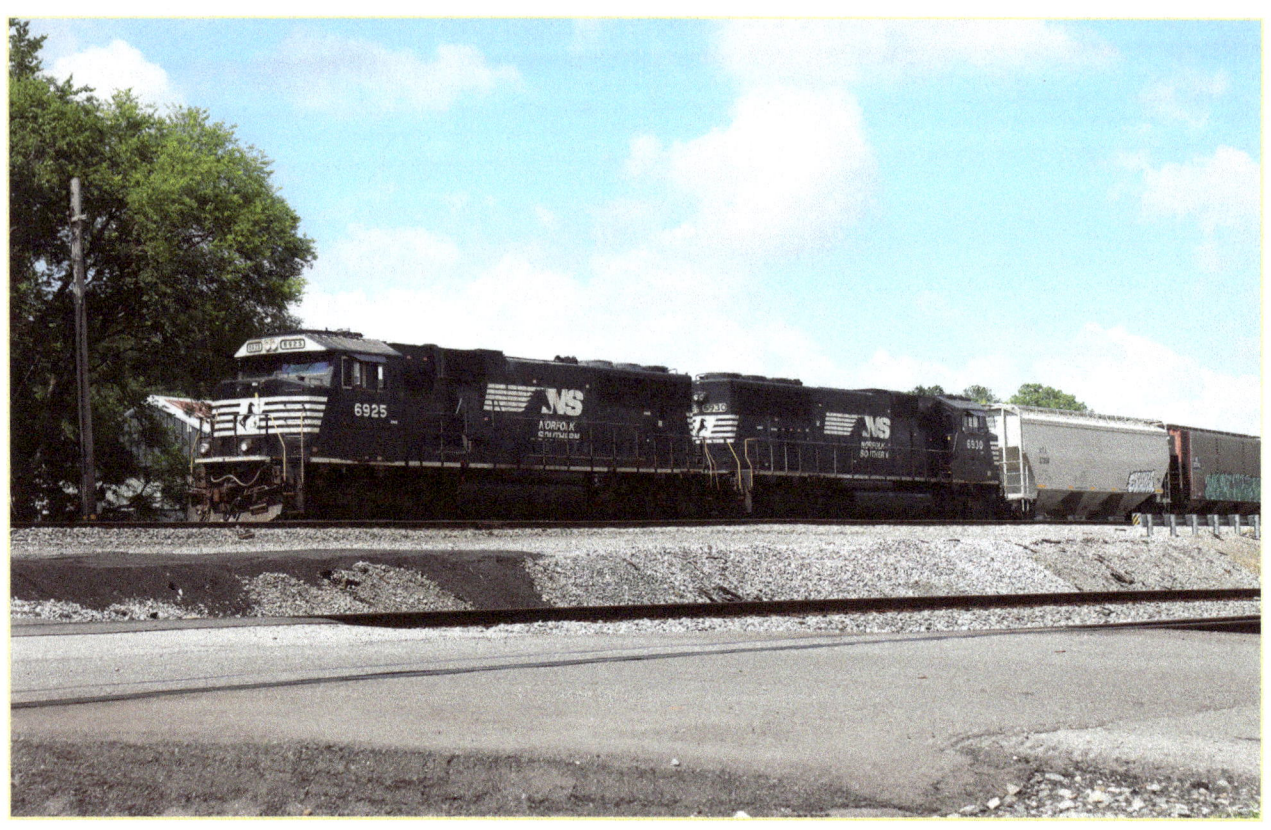

A pair of Norfolk Southern SD60s leads a mixed-freight out of Irondale as the Union Pacific engine still waits for a crew after two hours.

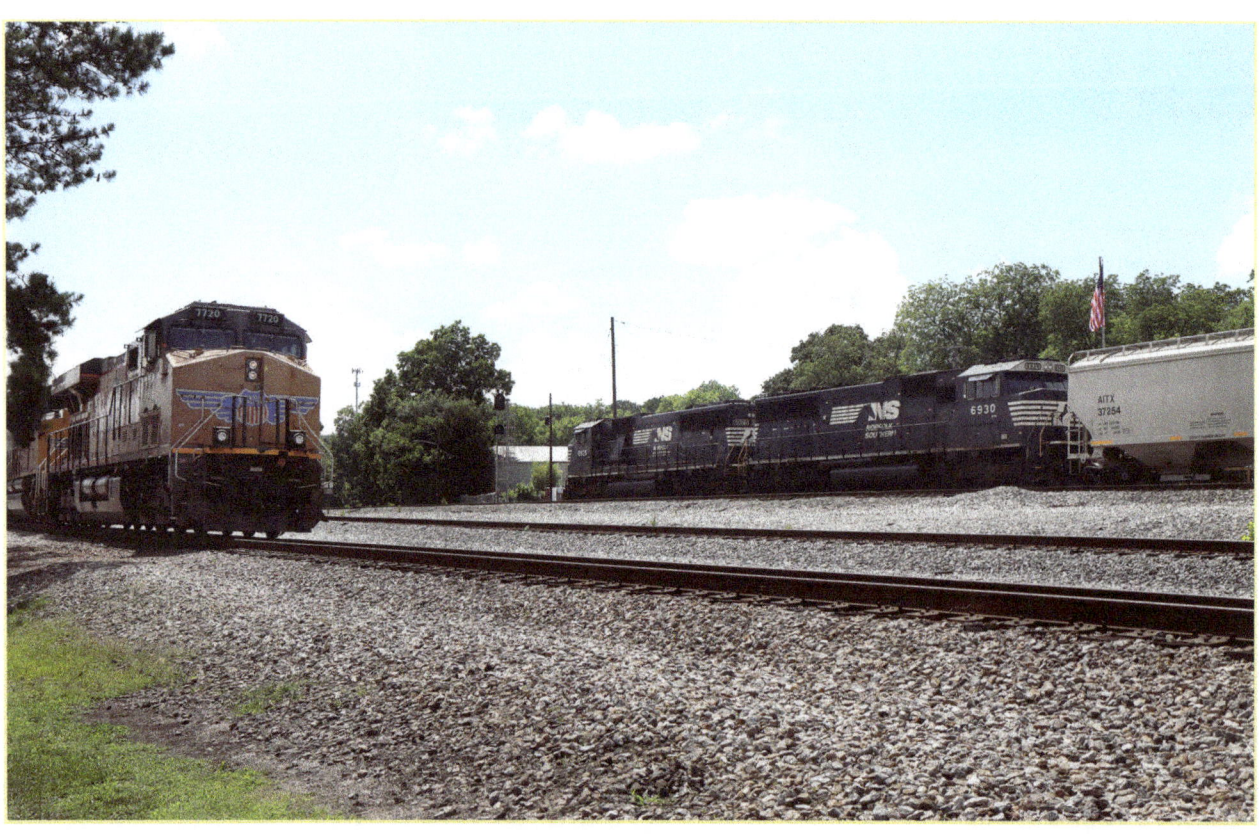

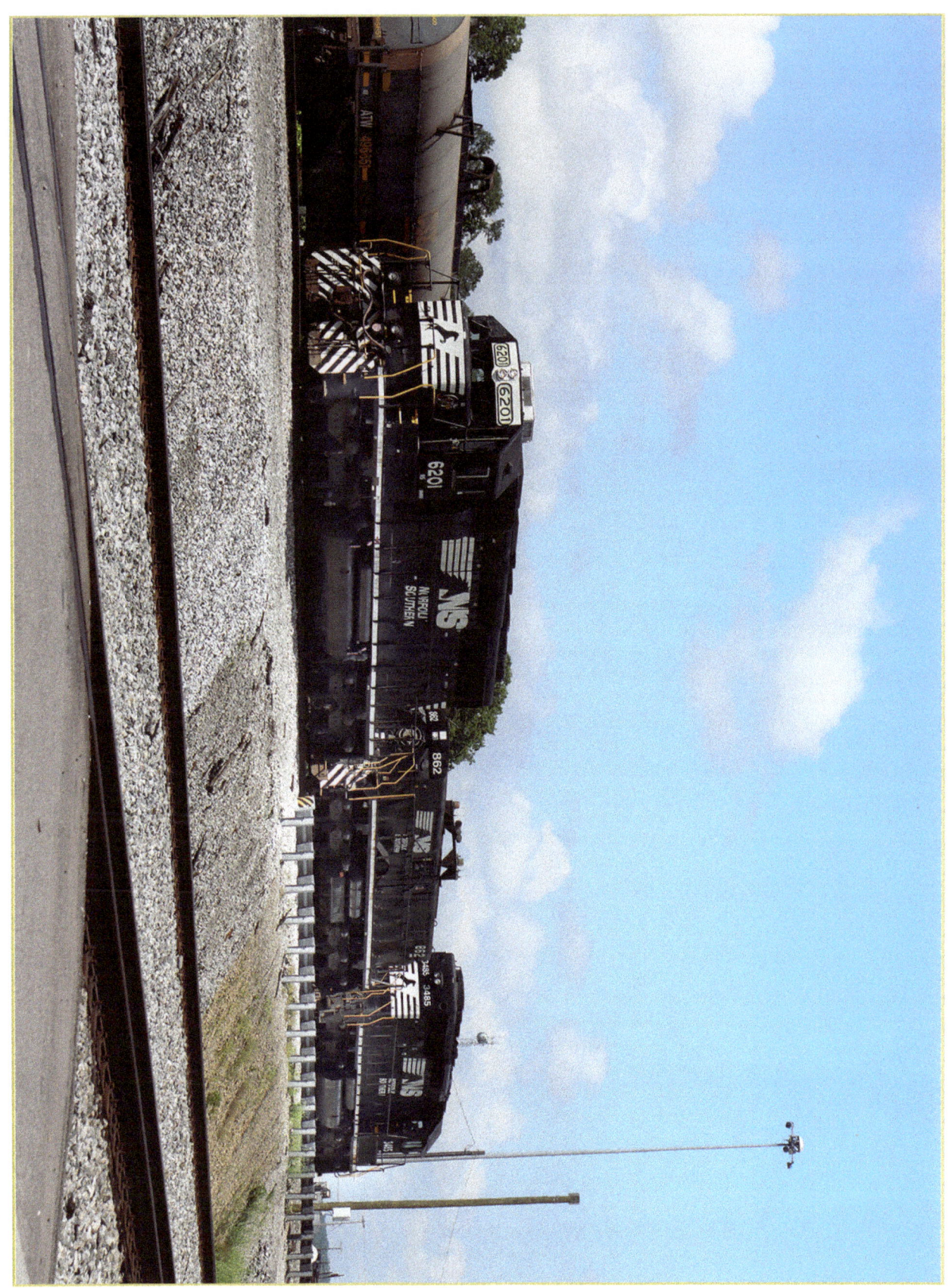

Two Norfolk Southern SD40s with a slug between them are in charge of moving cars from trains to the tracks where they are needed.

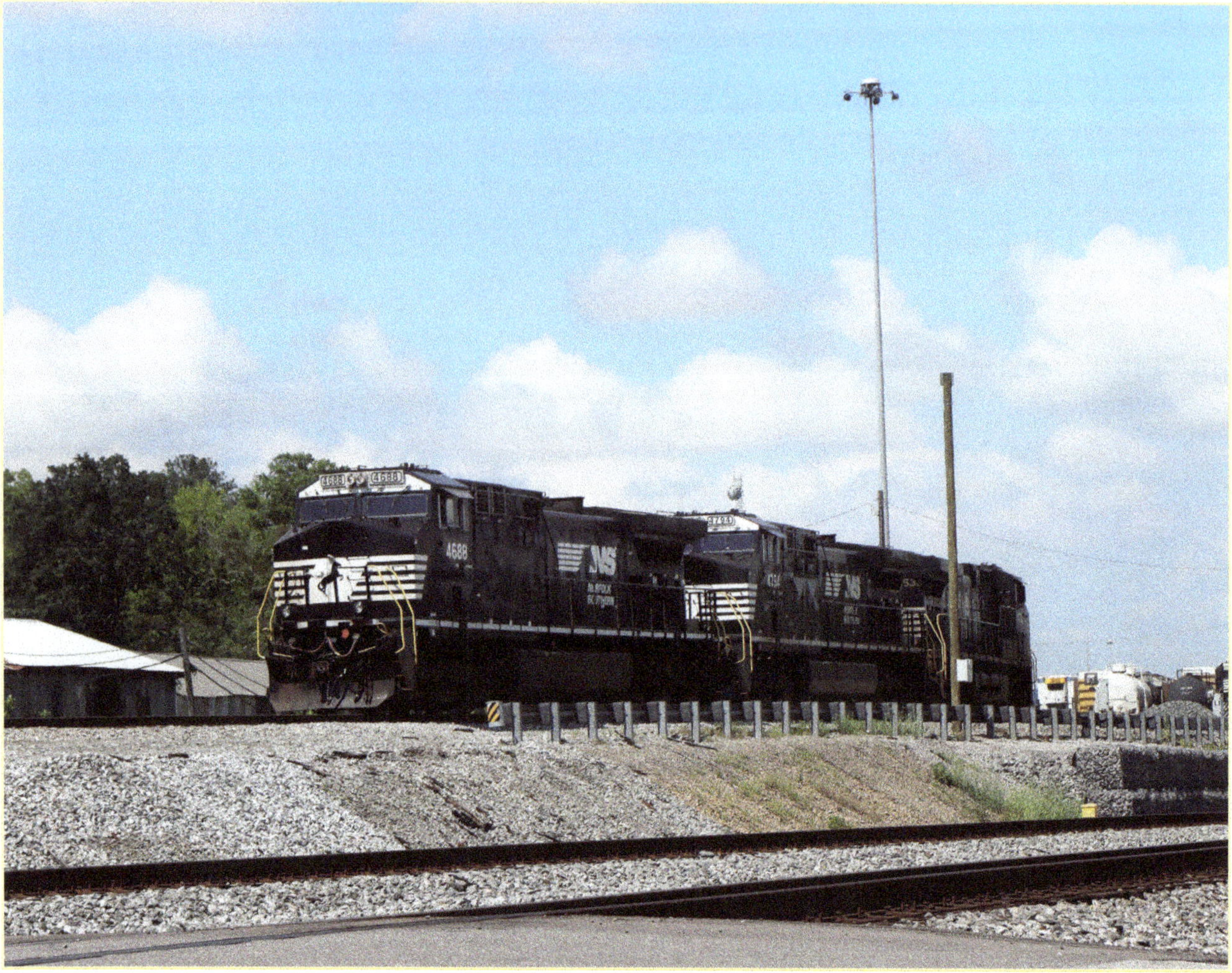

Three brand new AC44s prepare to pull a train out of Irondale.

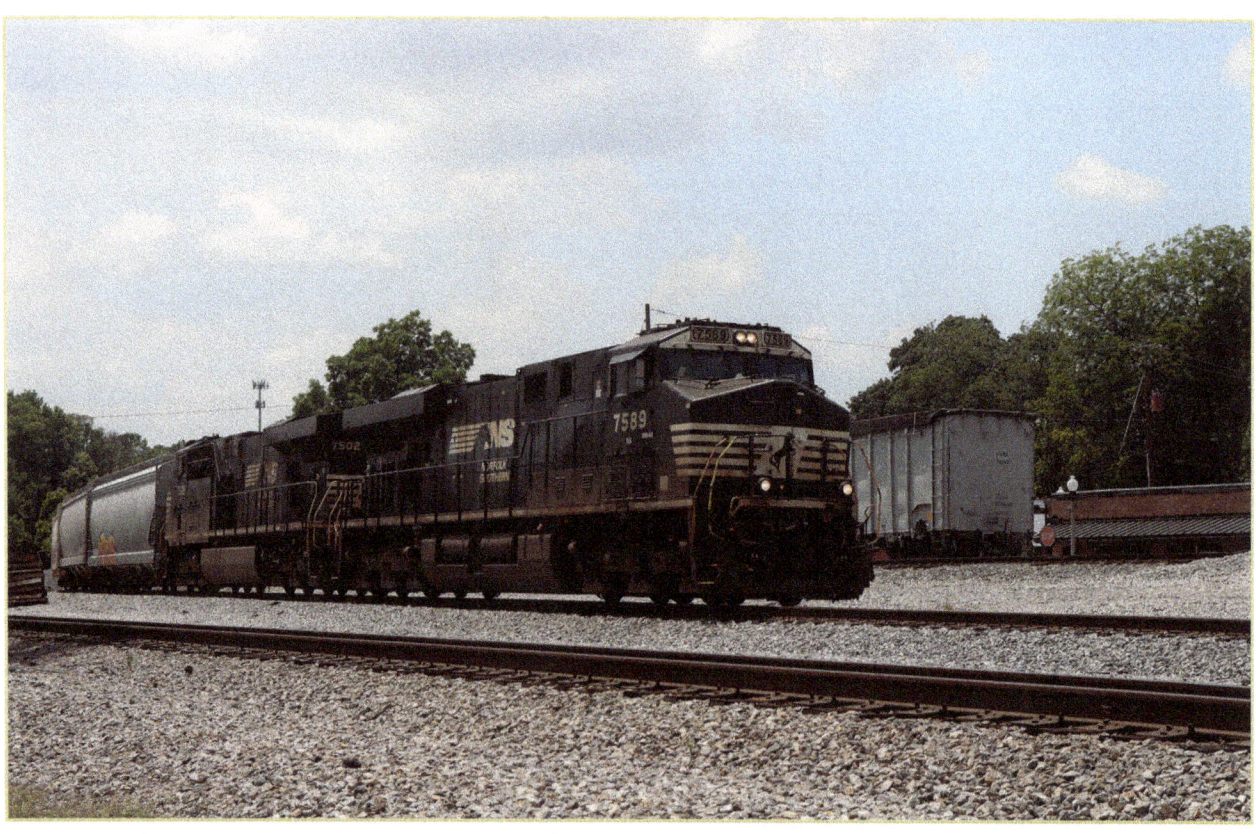

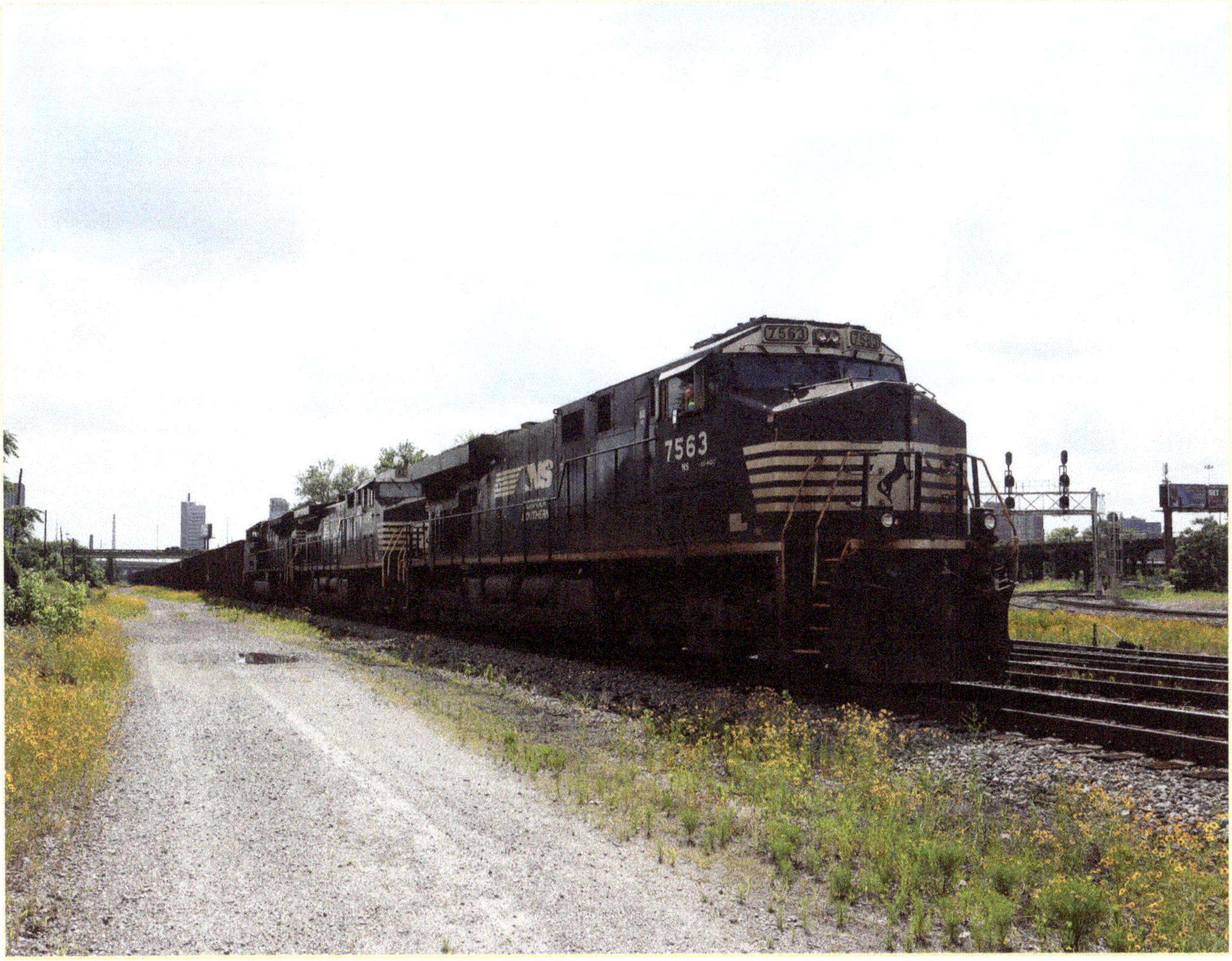

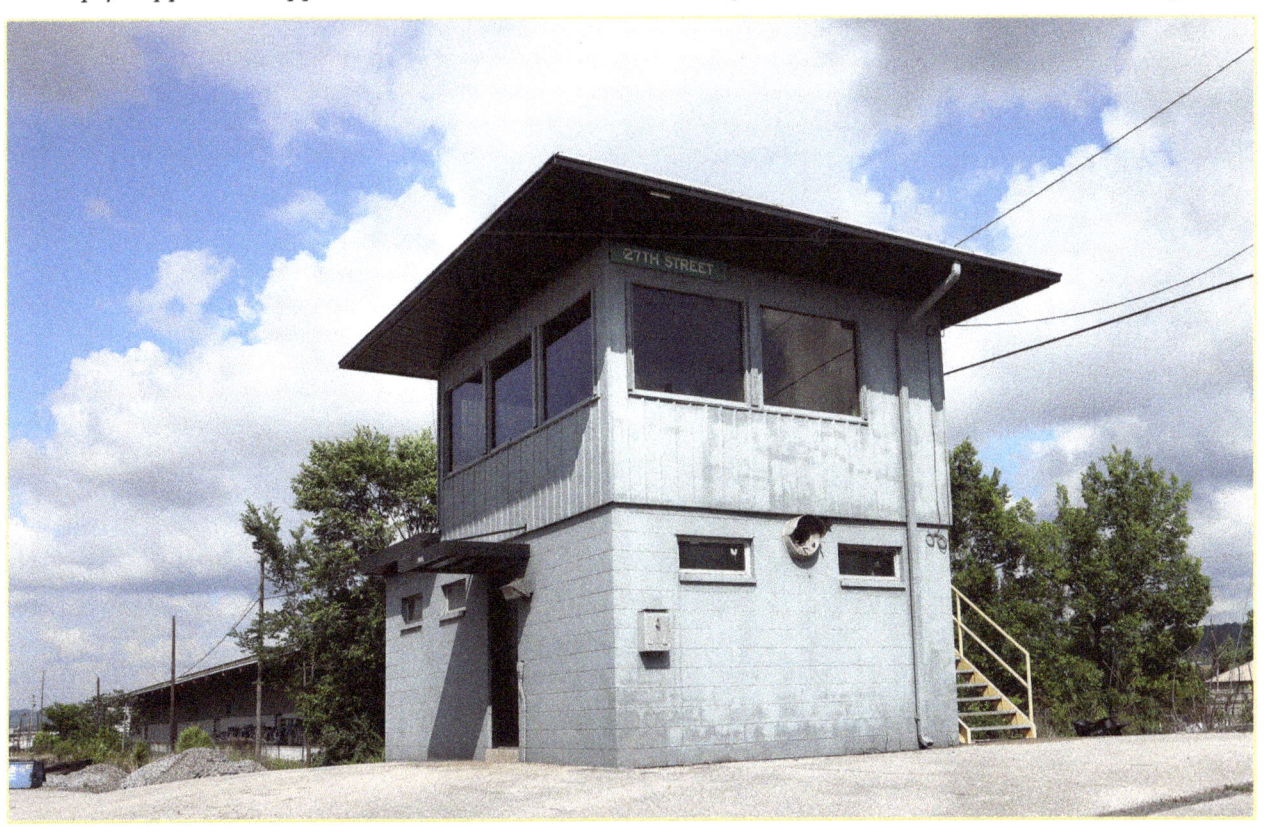

An empty hopper train approaches Sloss Furnaces from Birmingham. The CSX tracks are in the background.

An old railroad tower sits across from Sloss Furnaces.

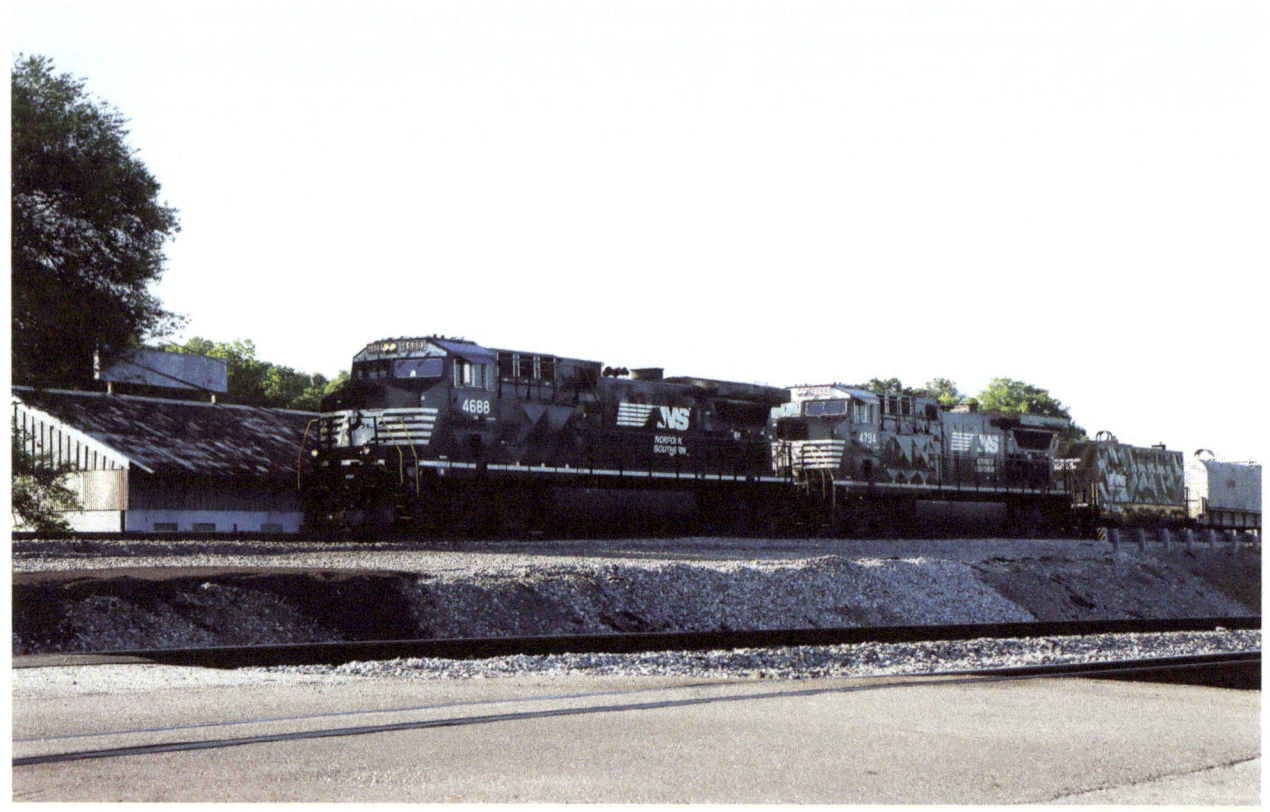
A pair of shiny new locomotives lead steel-coil cars out of Irondale.

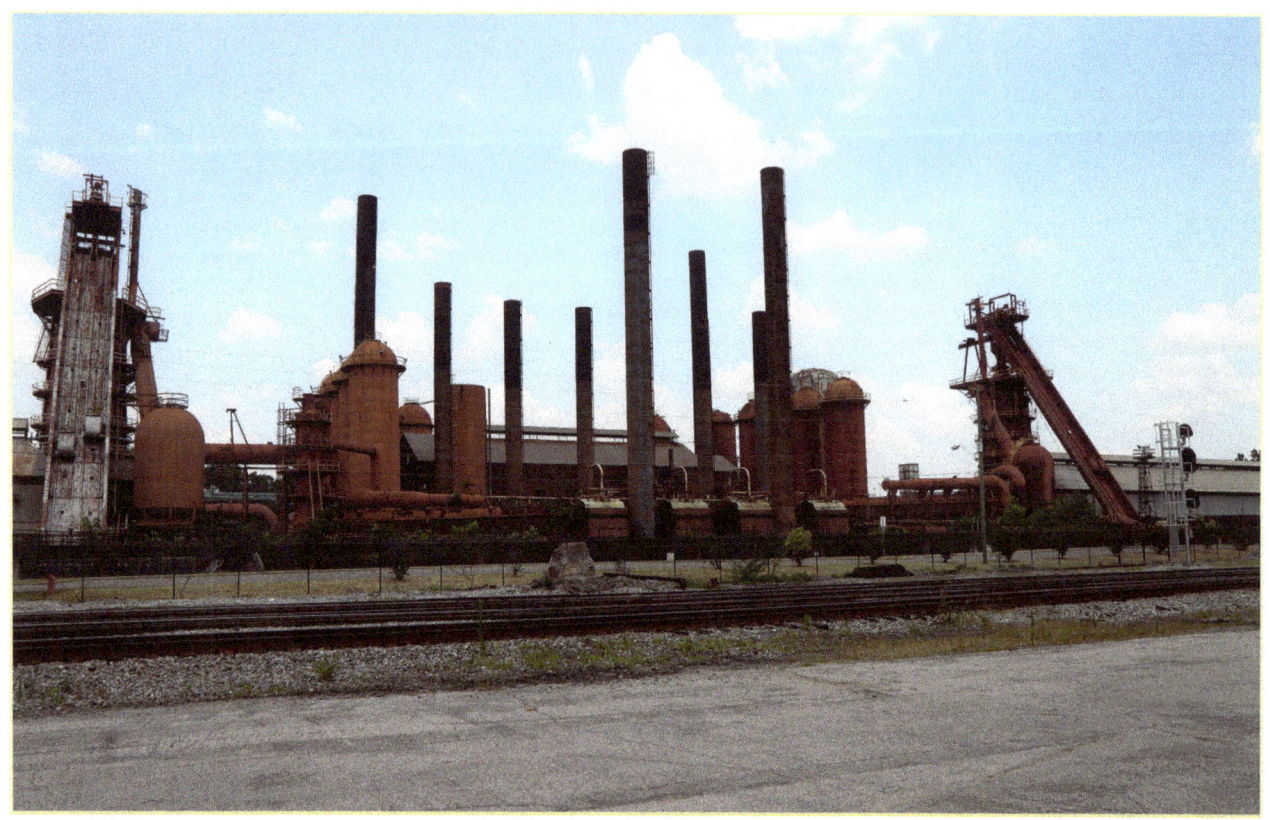
Norfolk Southern's AGS South mainline passes by the Sloss Blast Furnaces in Birmingham. Originally operated from 1882 to 1971, Sloss is the only preserved blast furnace in the United States.

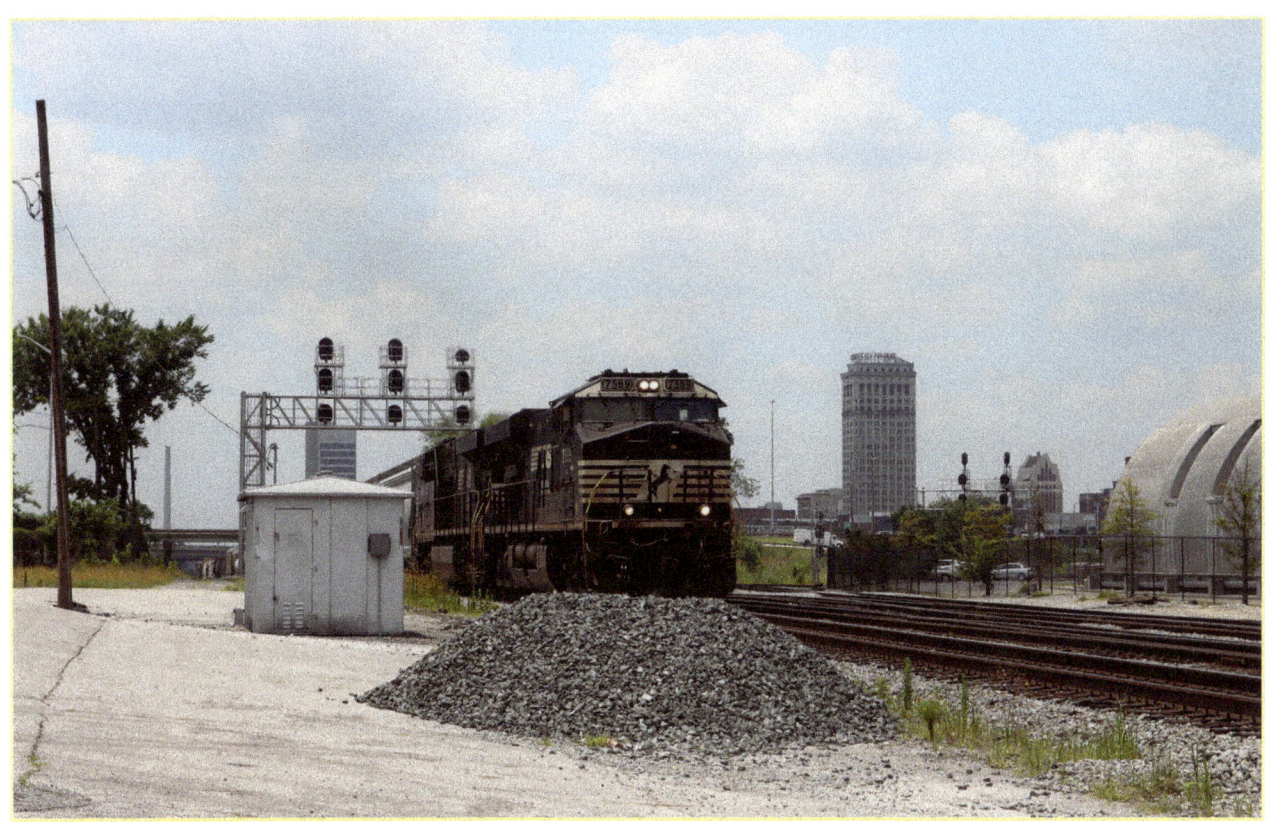
A Norfolk Southern mixed-freight speeds by Sloss Furnaces and arrive in Irondale a little later.

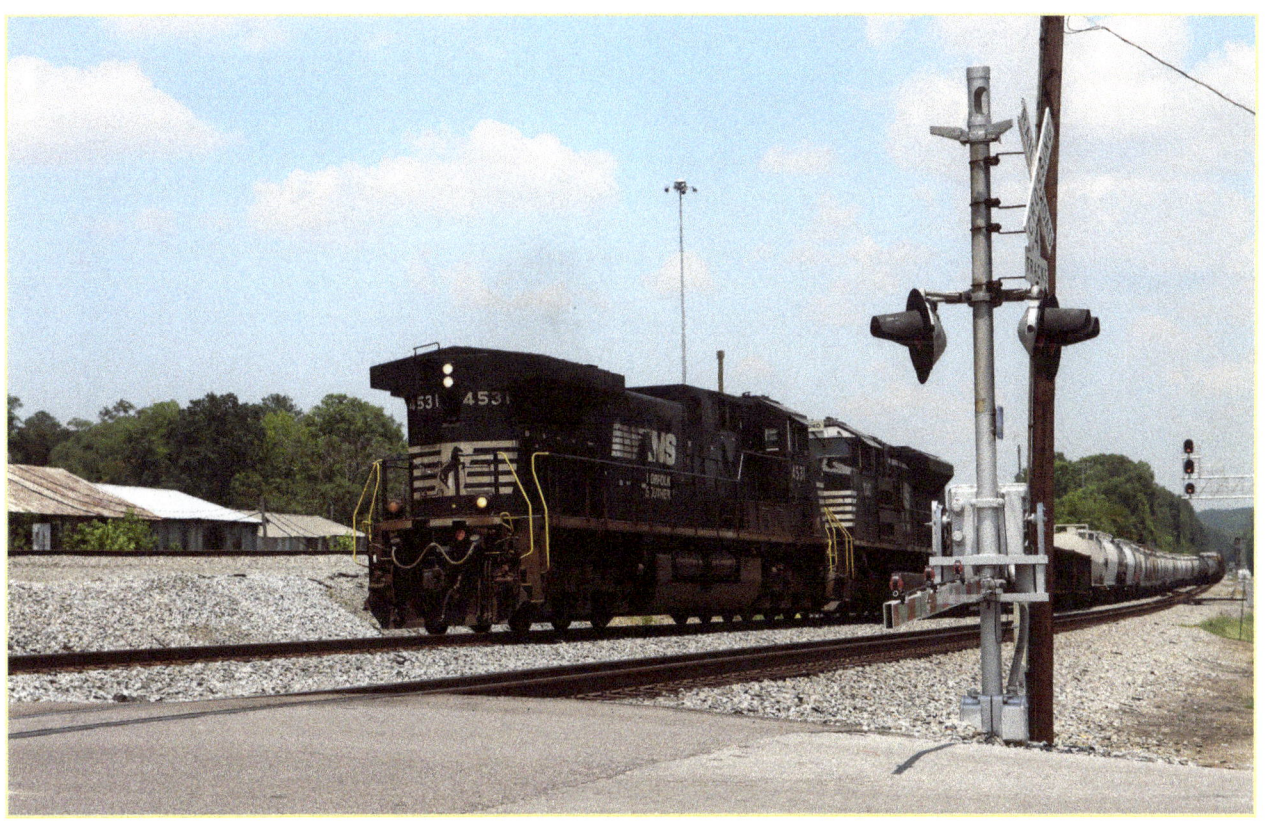
A Norfolk Southern GEVO leads a train running backwards.

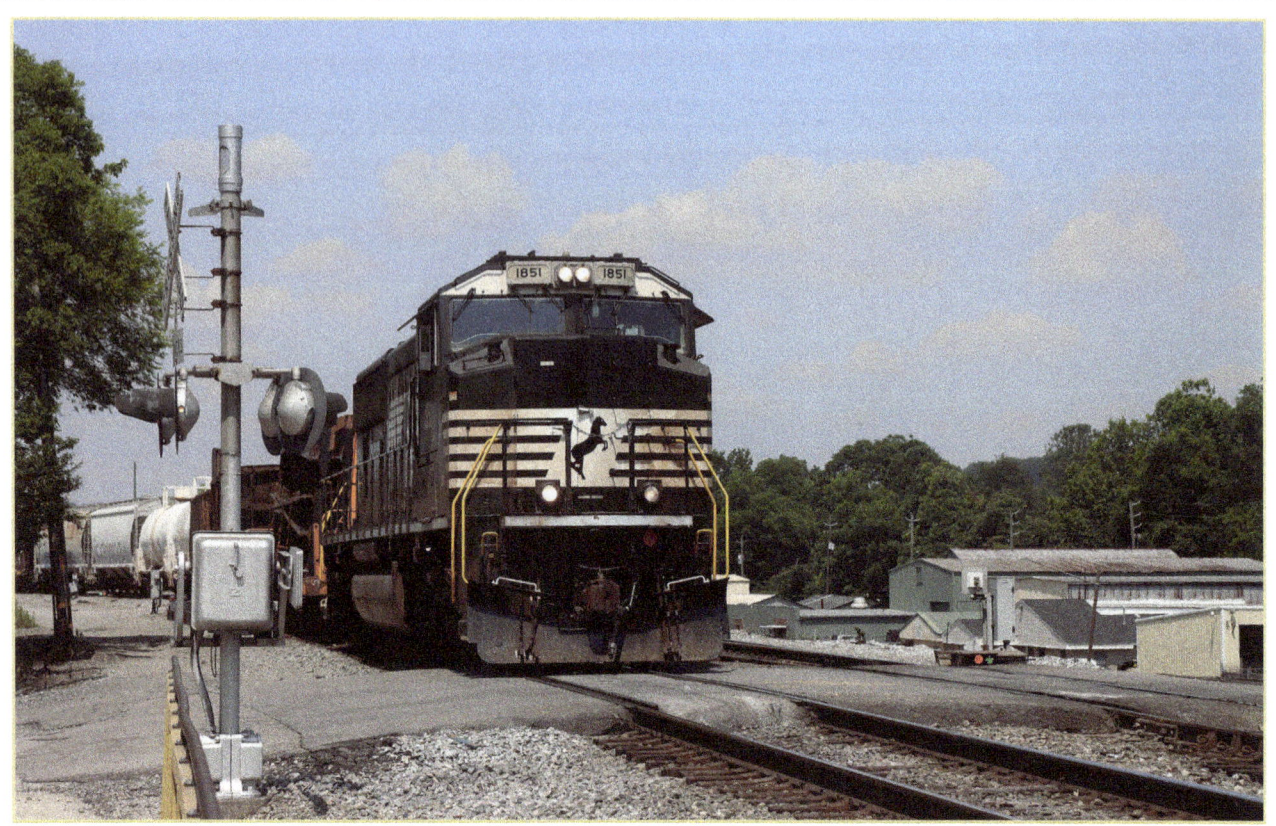

Norfolk Southern 1851, an SD70ACC, leads a flatbed while carrying an entire section of track.

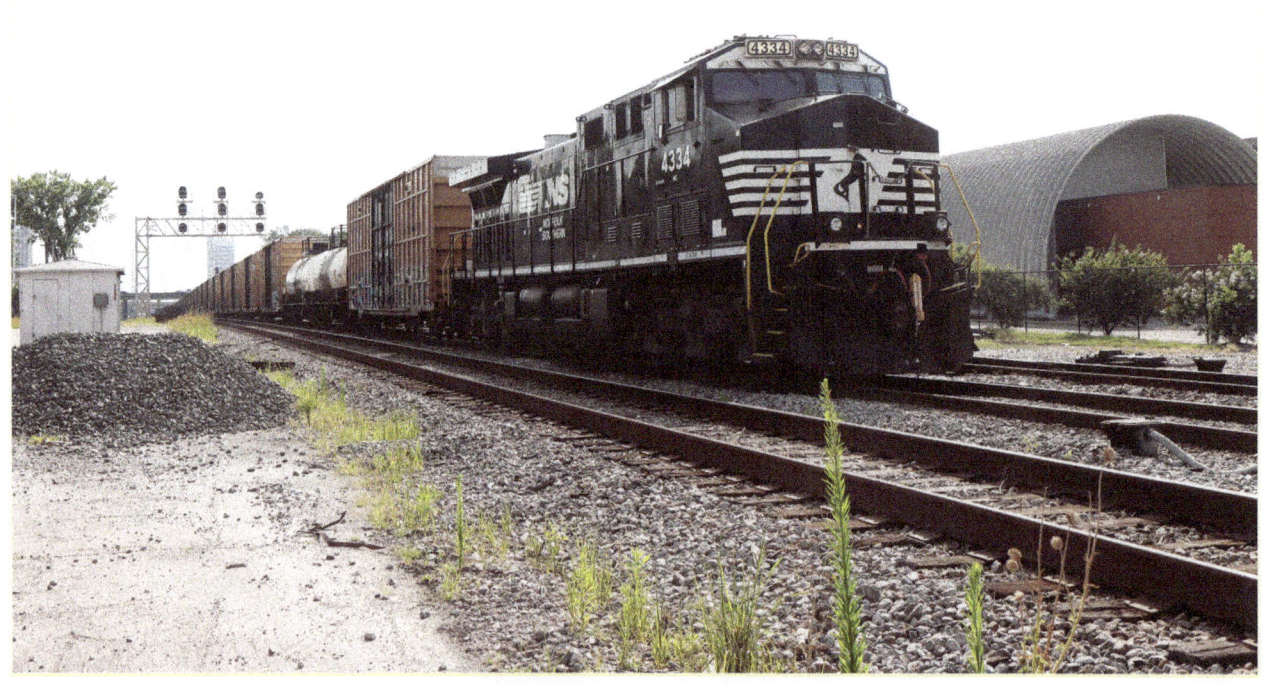

A brand new AC44 hauls a mixed-freight train past Sloss.

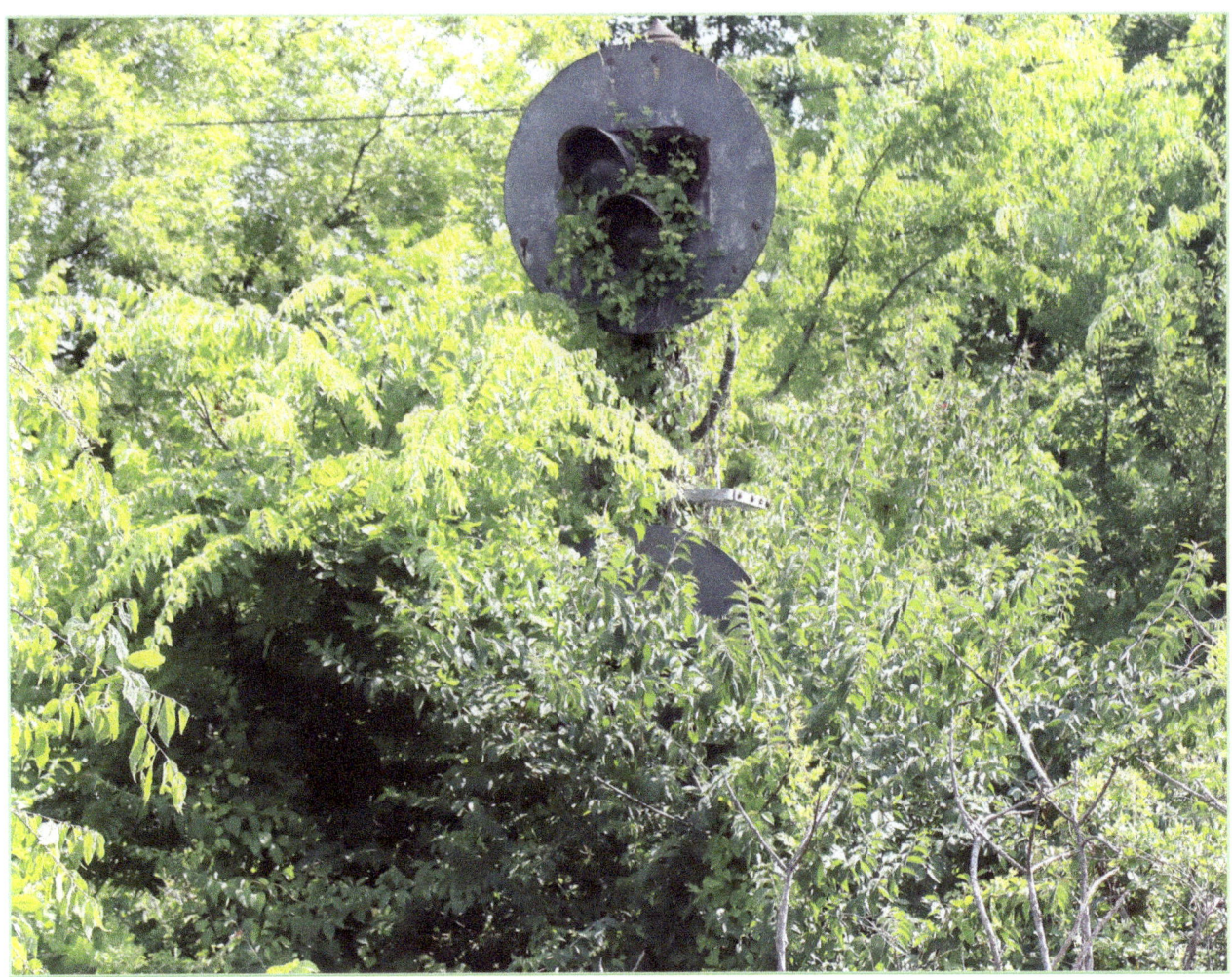
This overgrown signal near Sloss most likely goes back to the 1950s and '60s. My best guess about the owner would be Seaboard Air Line.

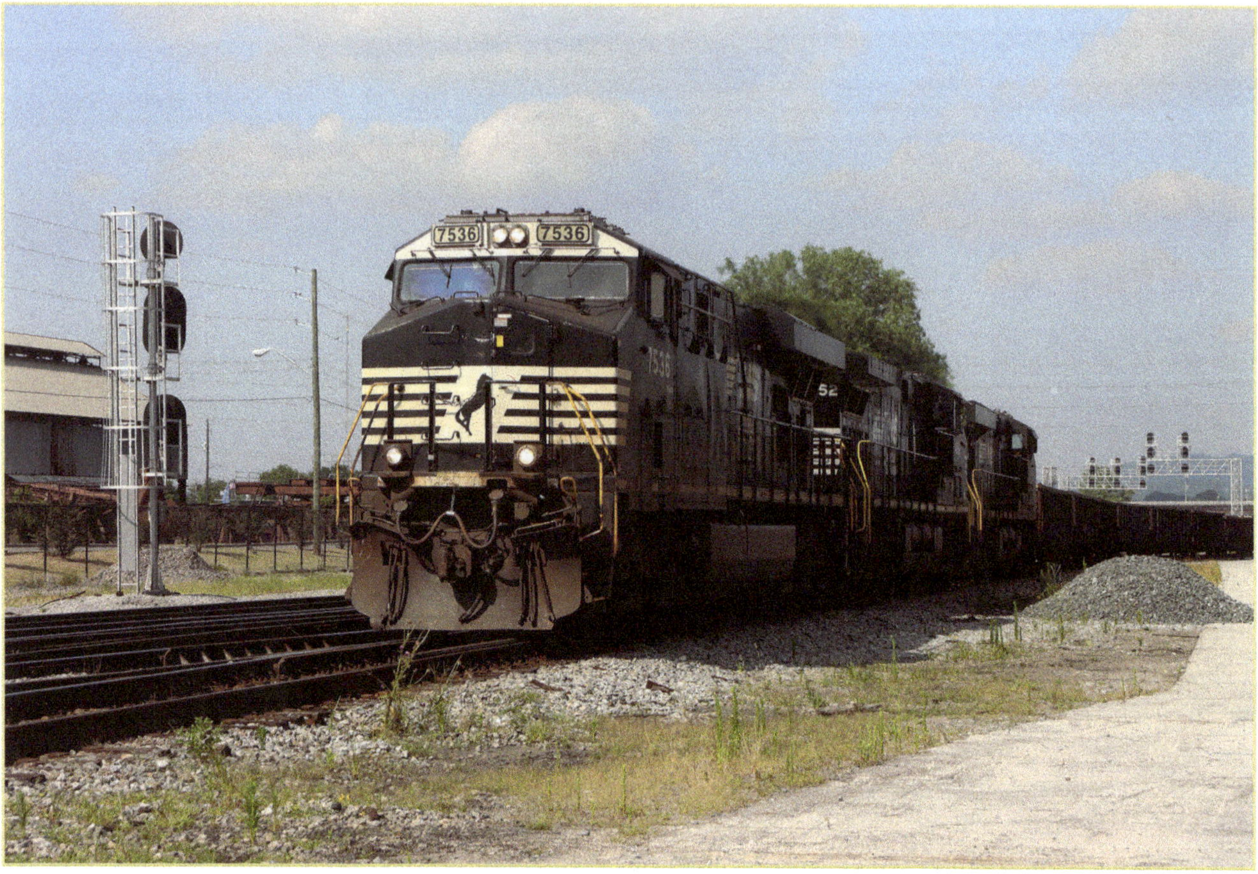

A Norfolk Southern locomotive leads a train full of empty gondolas past Sloss.

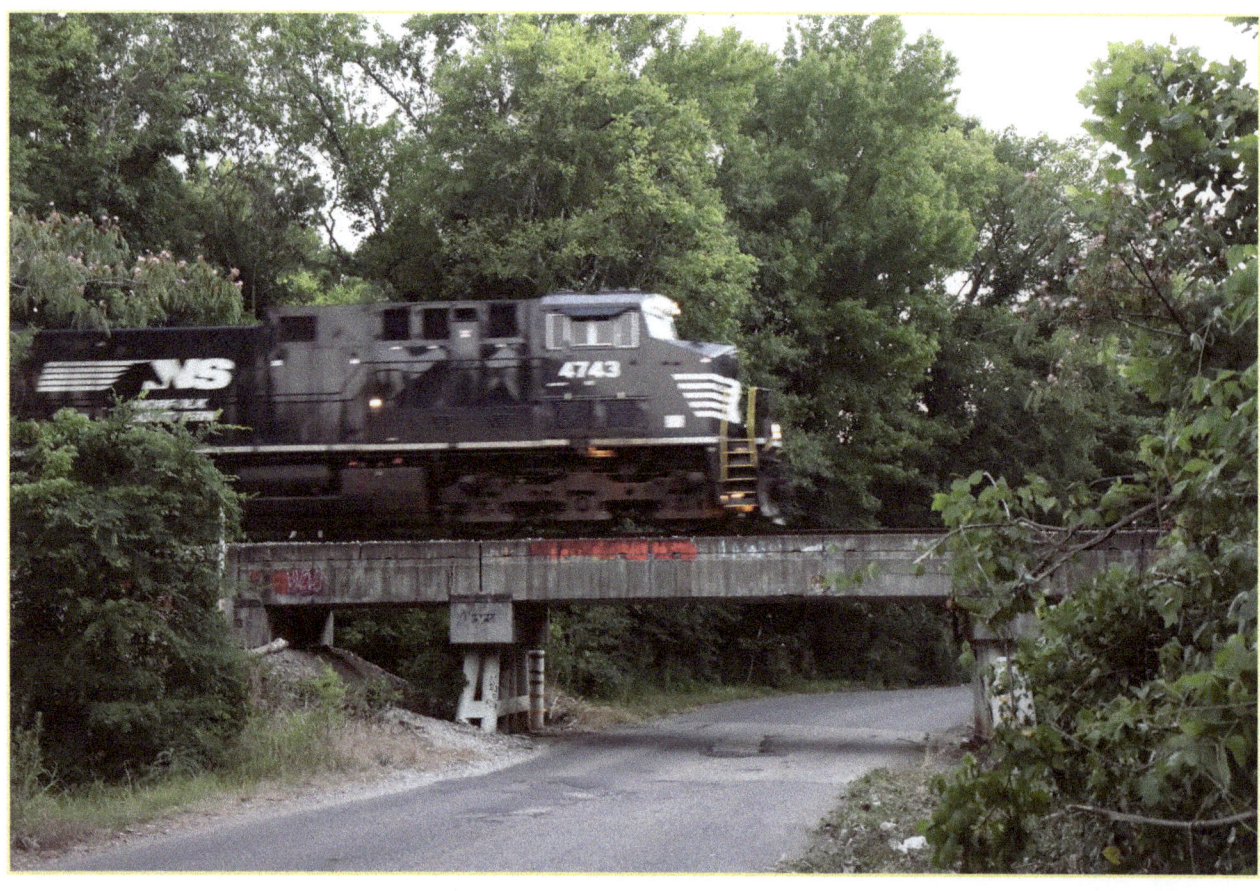

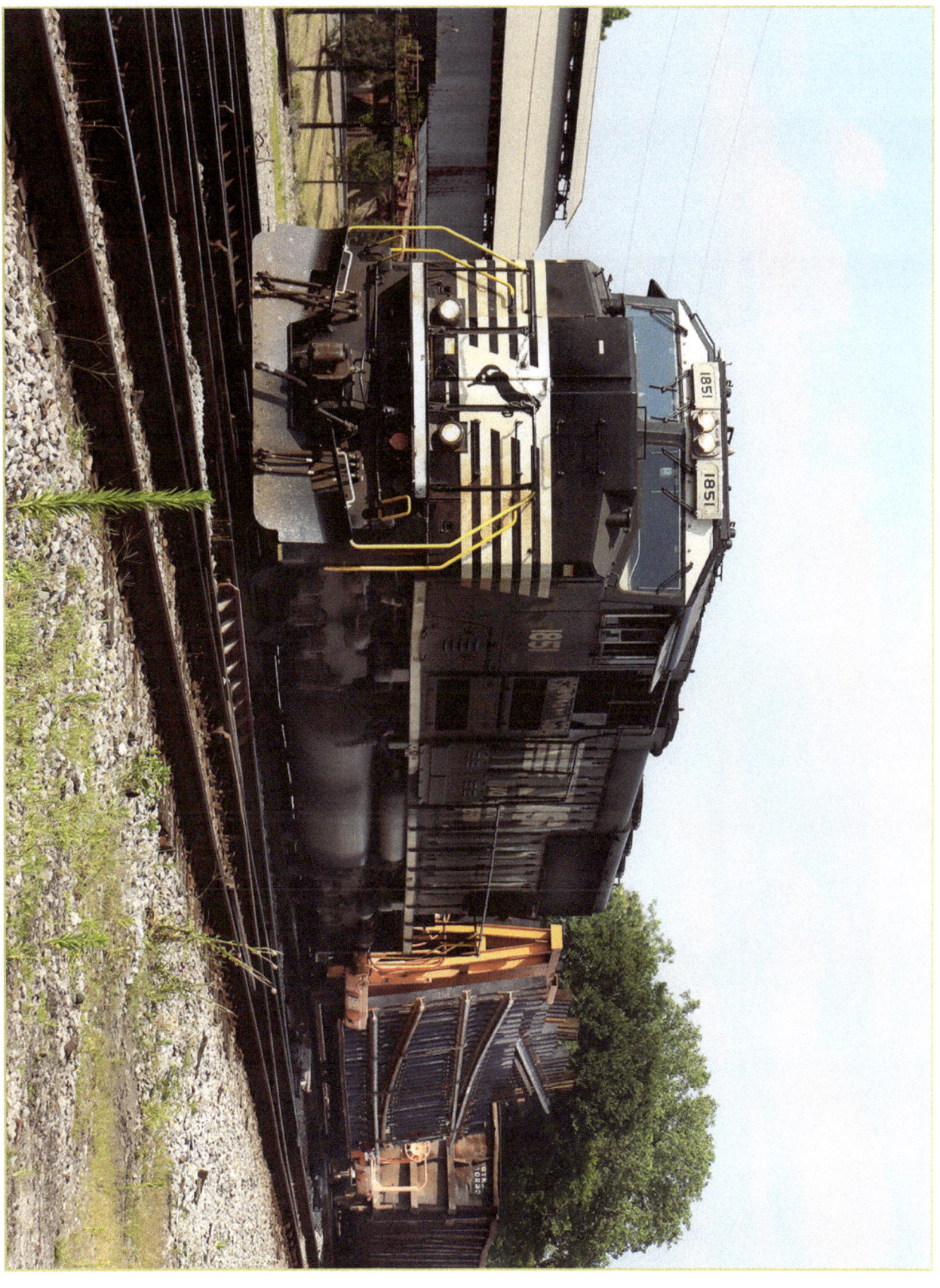

1851 continues past Sloss with the switch.

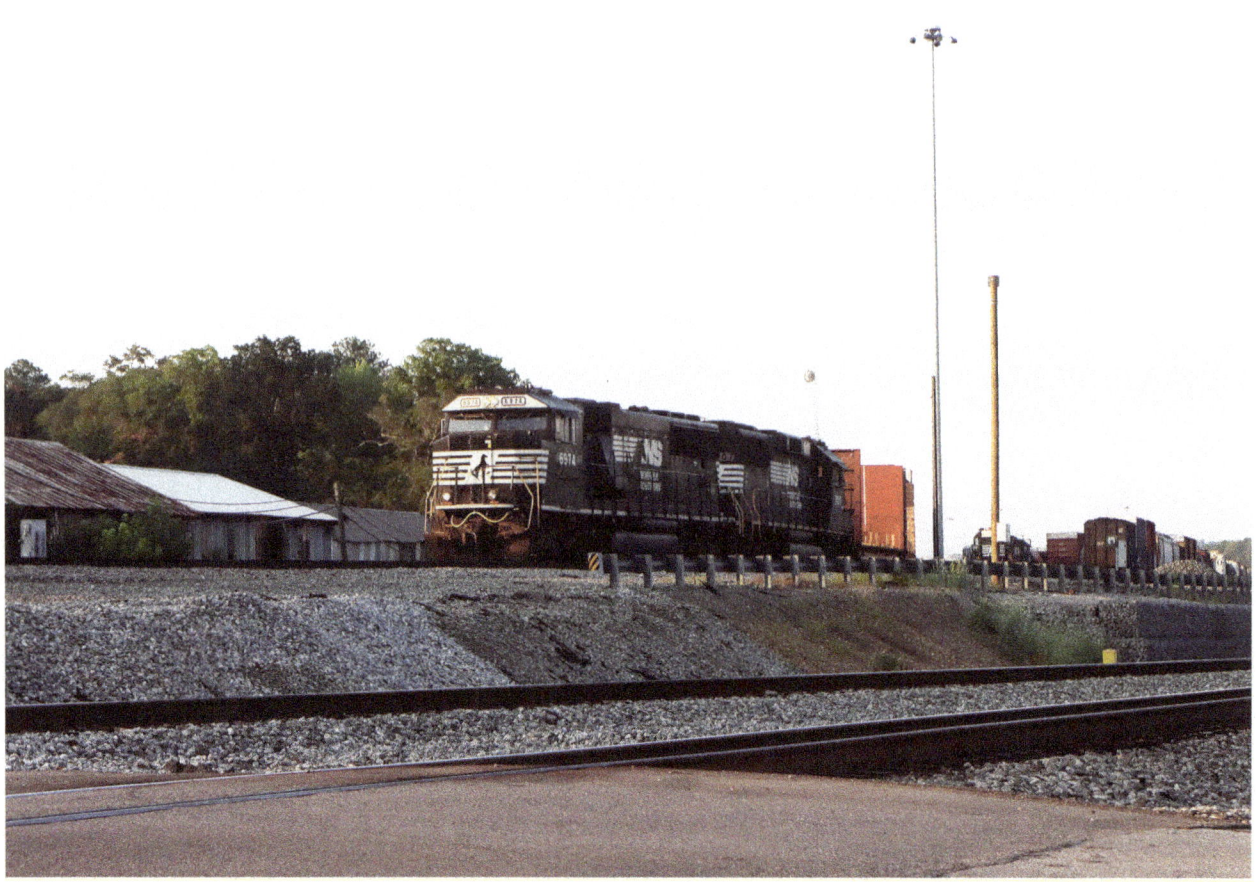
An SD60 departs Irondale with the evening local headed toward Birmingham.

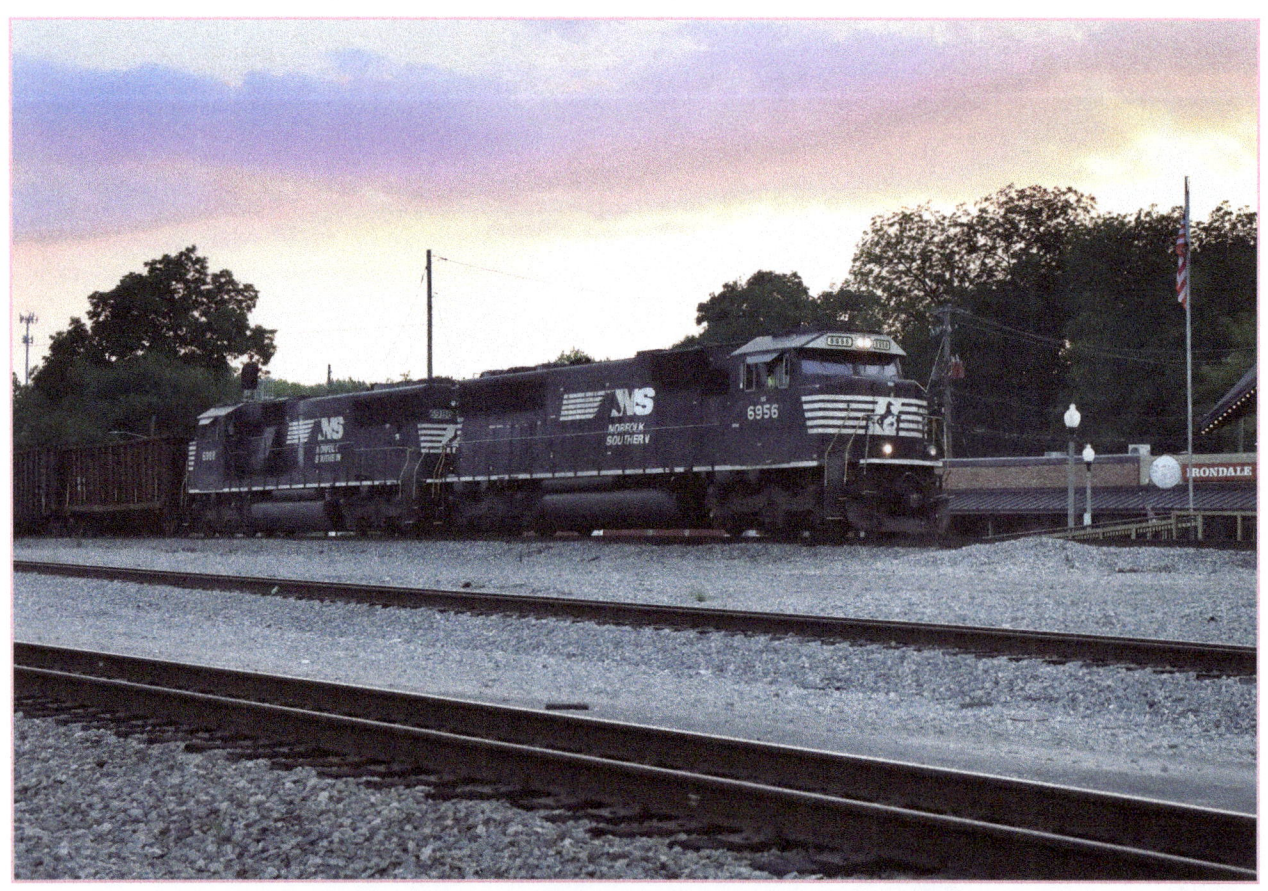
A pair of SD60s pulls rusty hoppers toward Irondale.

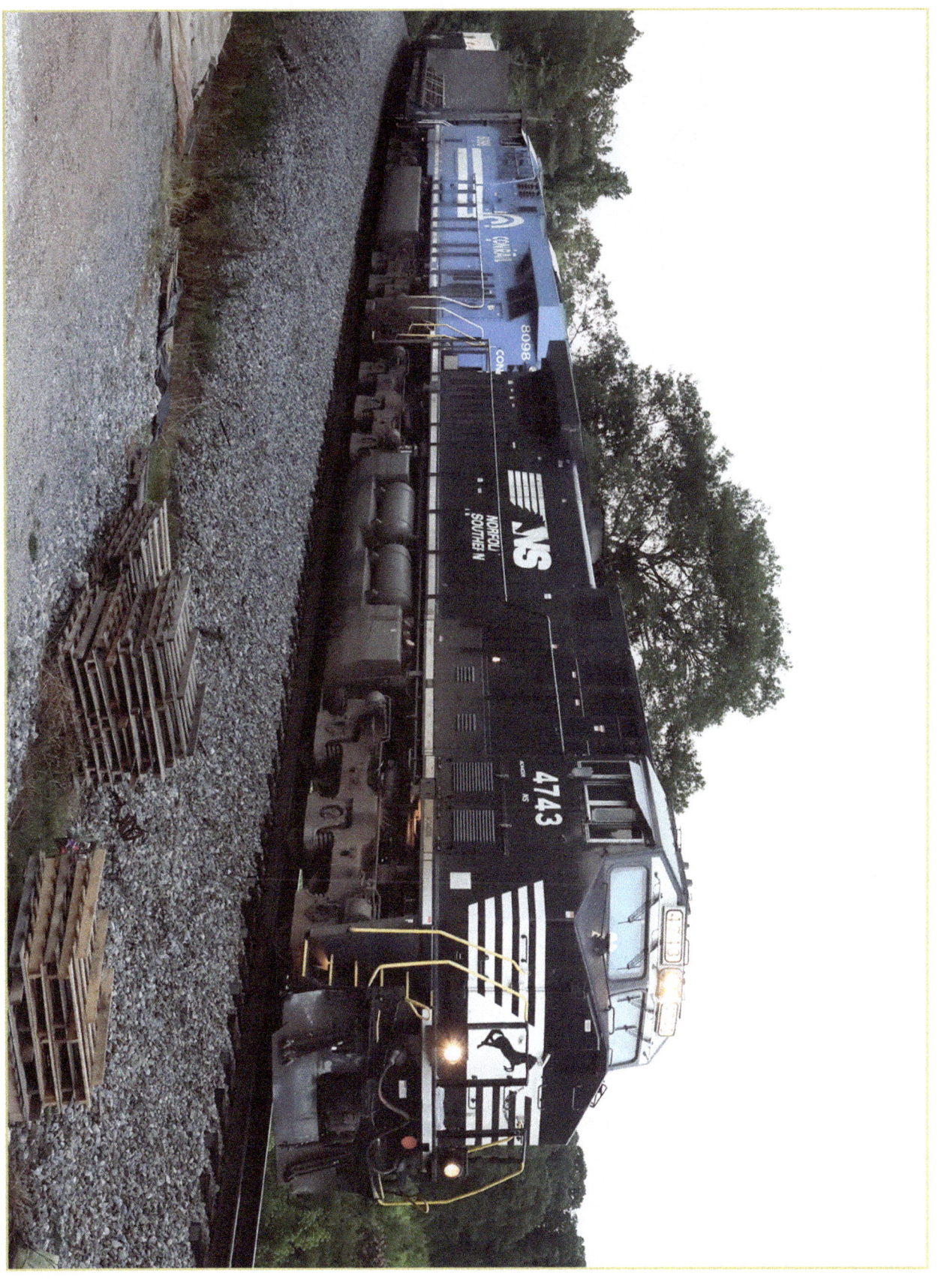

The sole Conrail Heritage Unit trails on a mixed-freight, heading toward Bessemer on the AGS South.

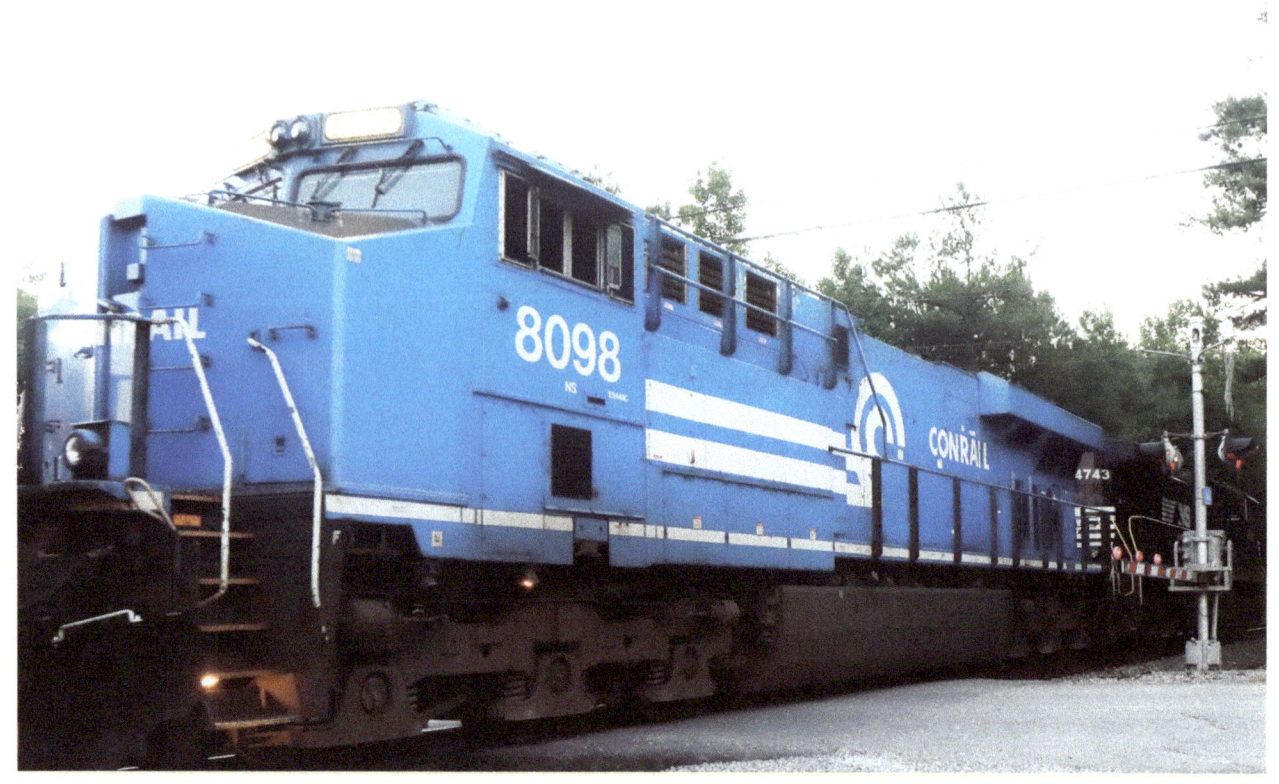

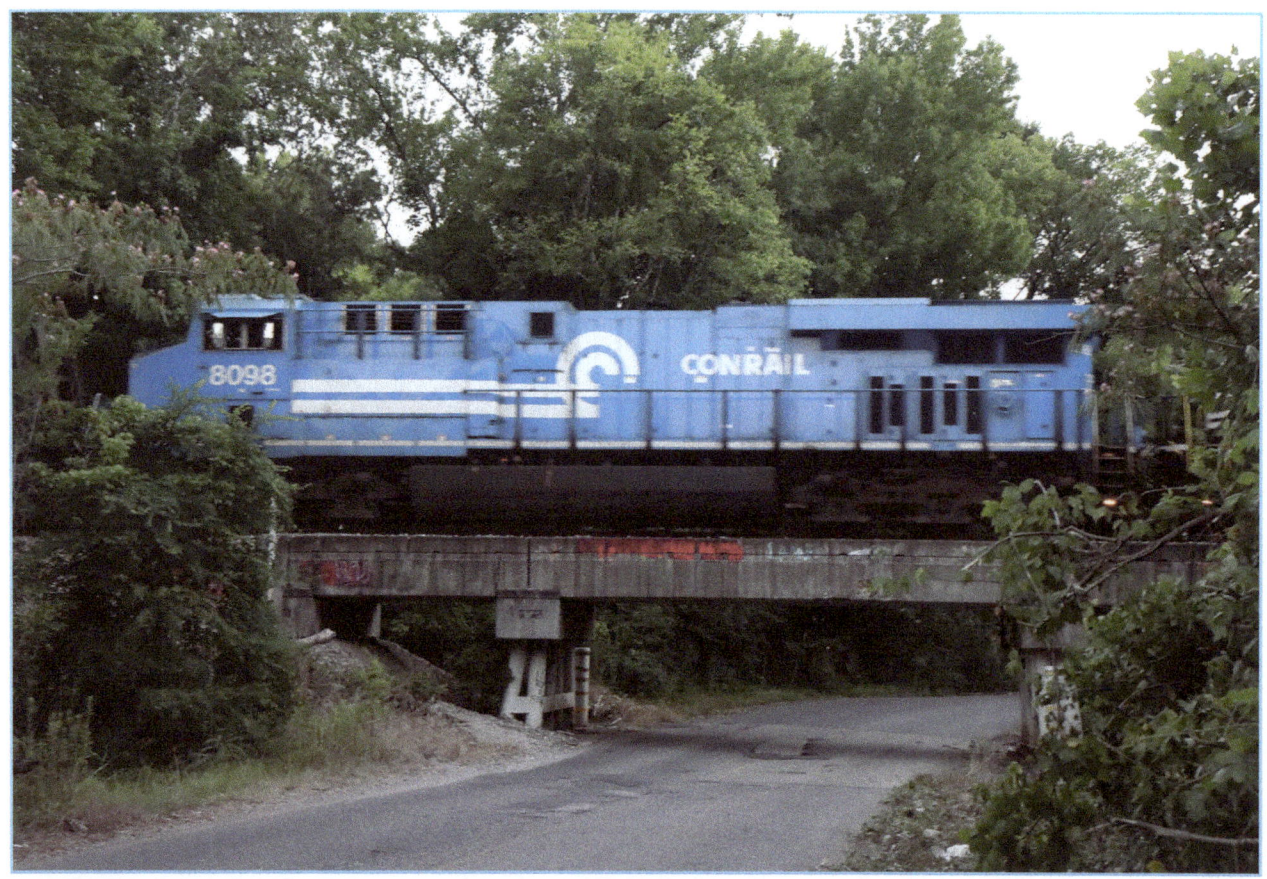

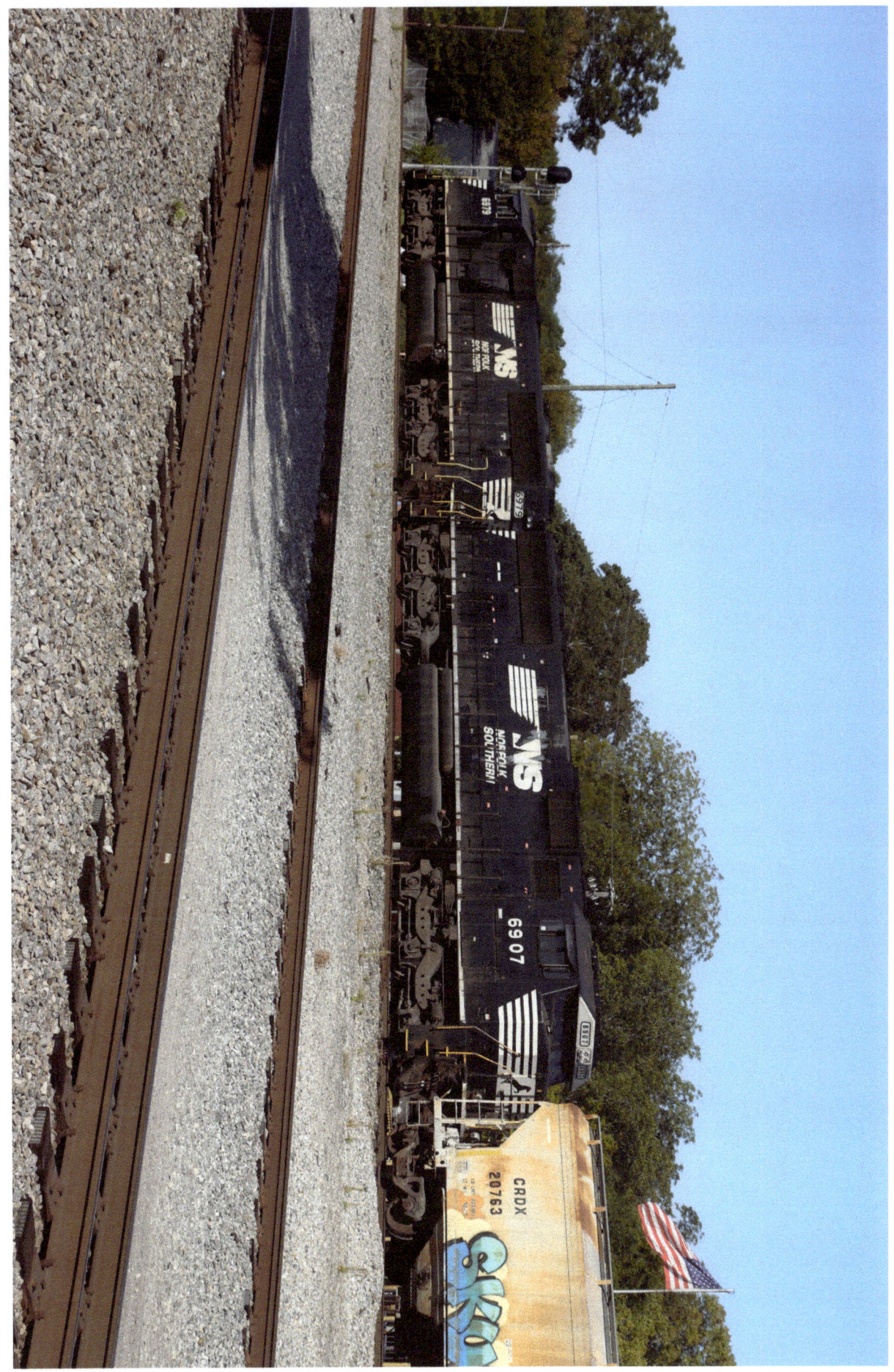

Two Norfolk Southern SD60s shove a train into Norris Yard.

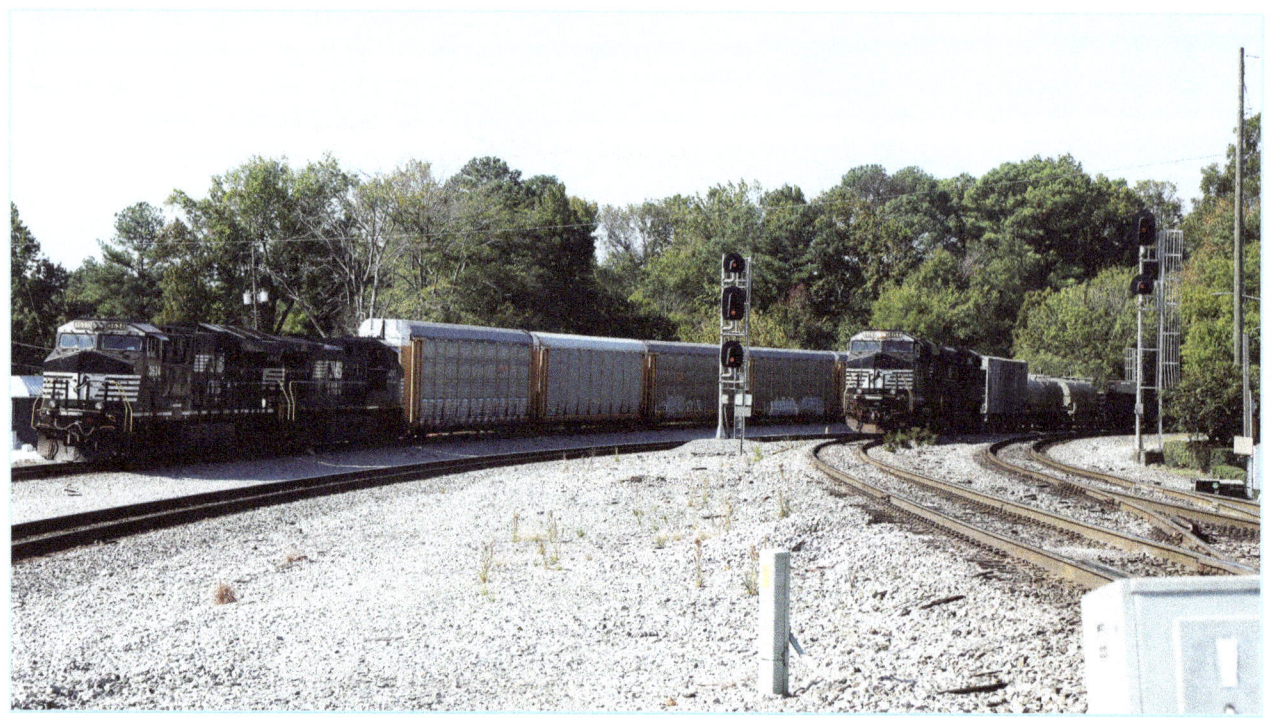

A Norfolk Southern AC44 pulls a train into Norris Yard while another sits idle on the Atlanta East End main line.

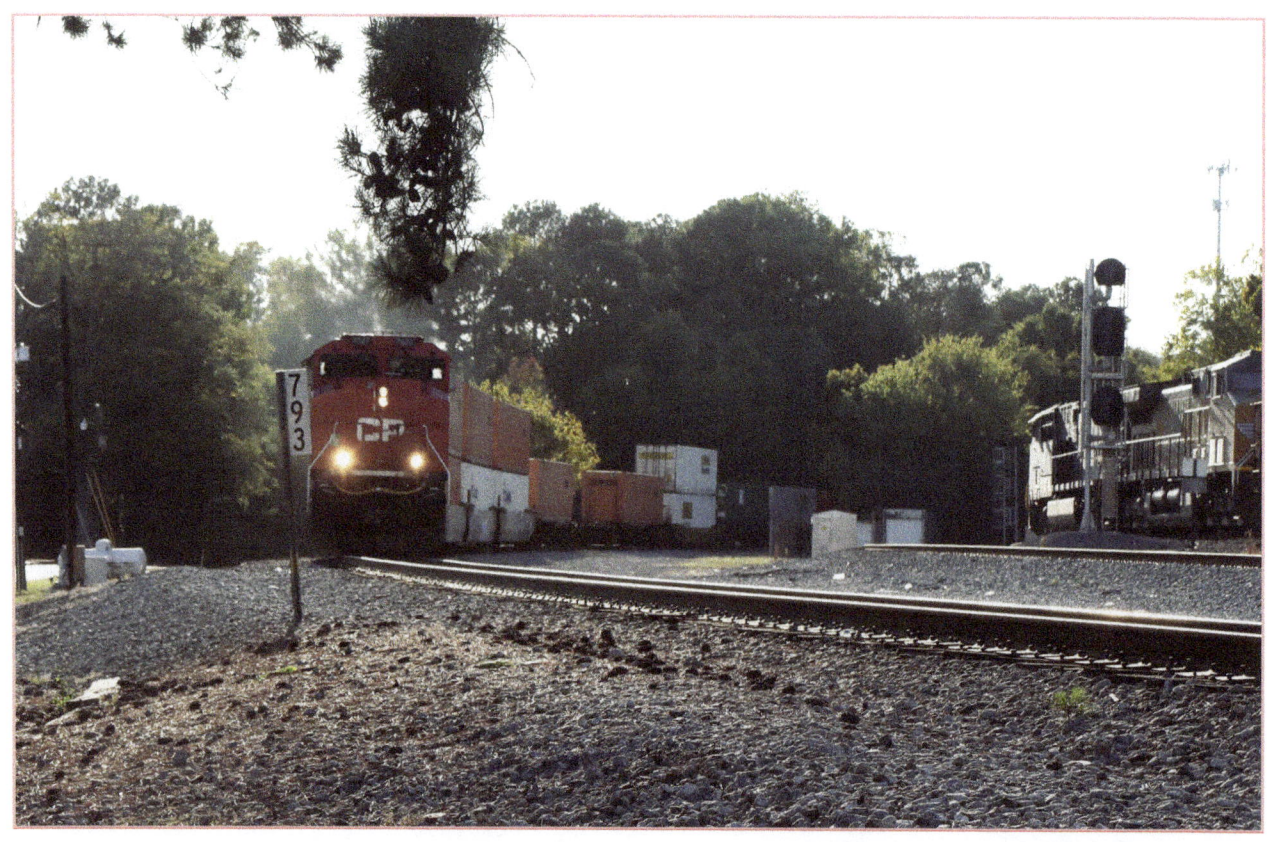

A CPKC locomotive pair, still in original CP paint, brings a run-through train from Meridian, Mississippi, into Norris Yard to have a crew change.

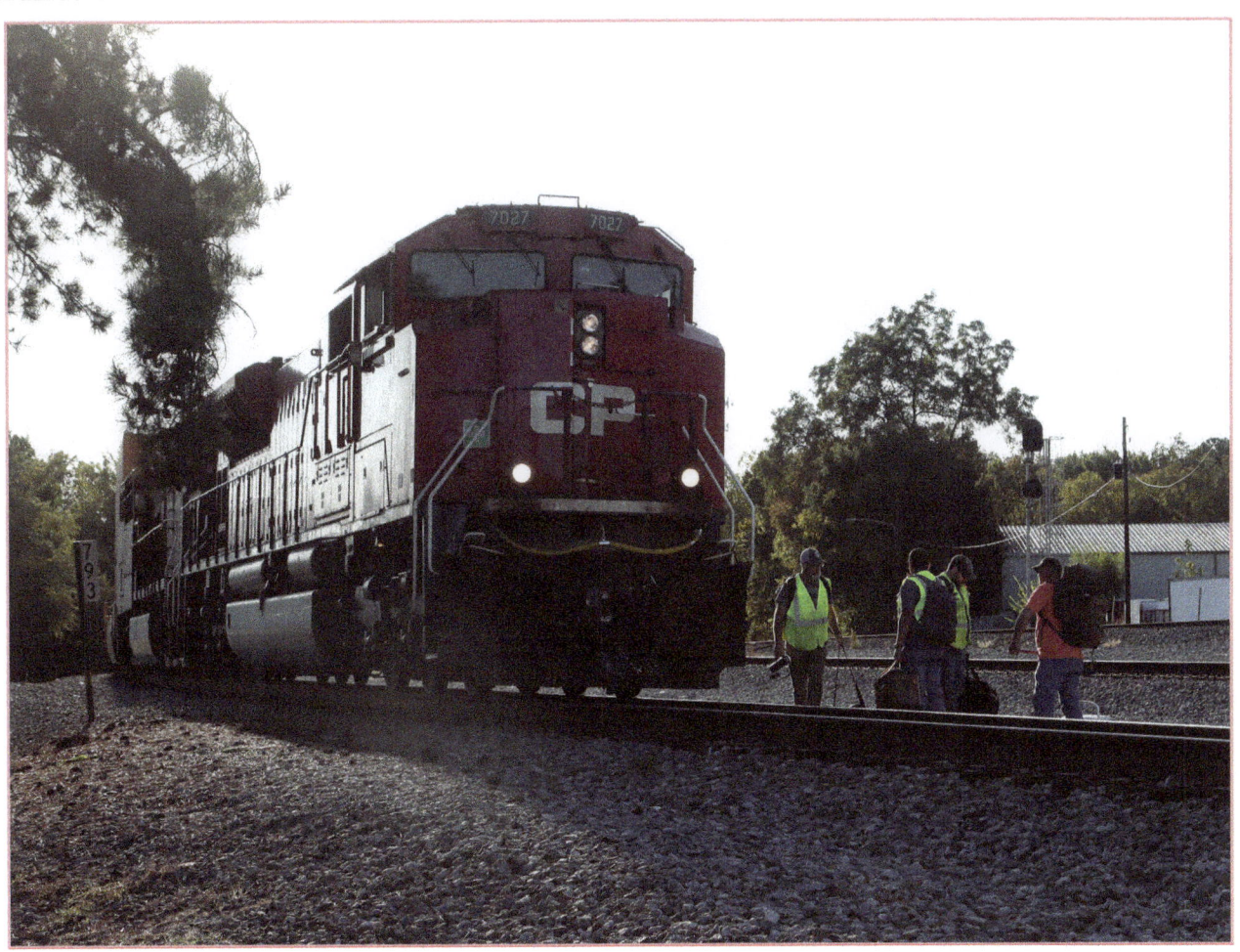

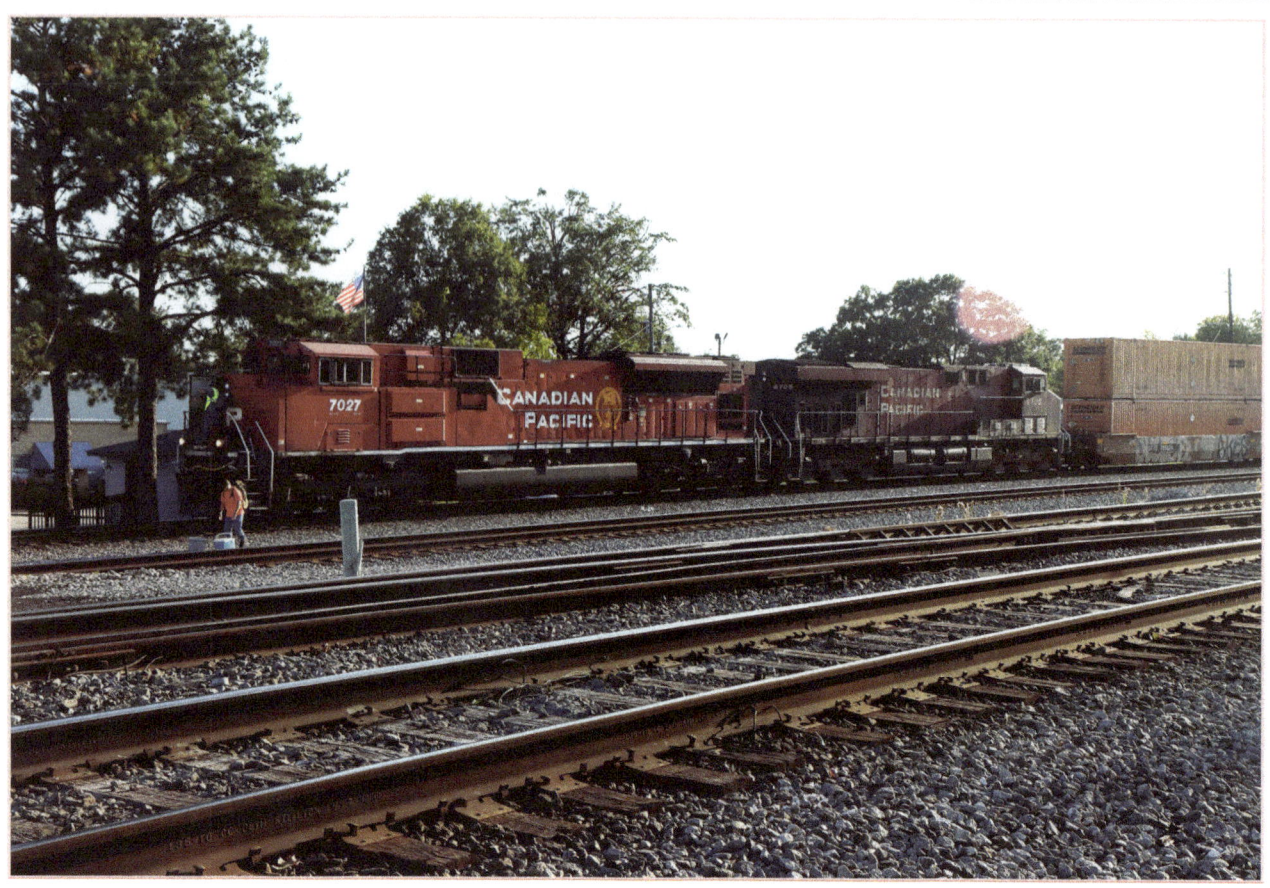

The locomotive in charge of this train is **CPKC 7027**, an **SD70ACU** that is part of a new rebuild program by **CPKC** using the remains of the extinct **SD9043MAC** series of locomotives. Notice the rear in the next picture.

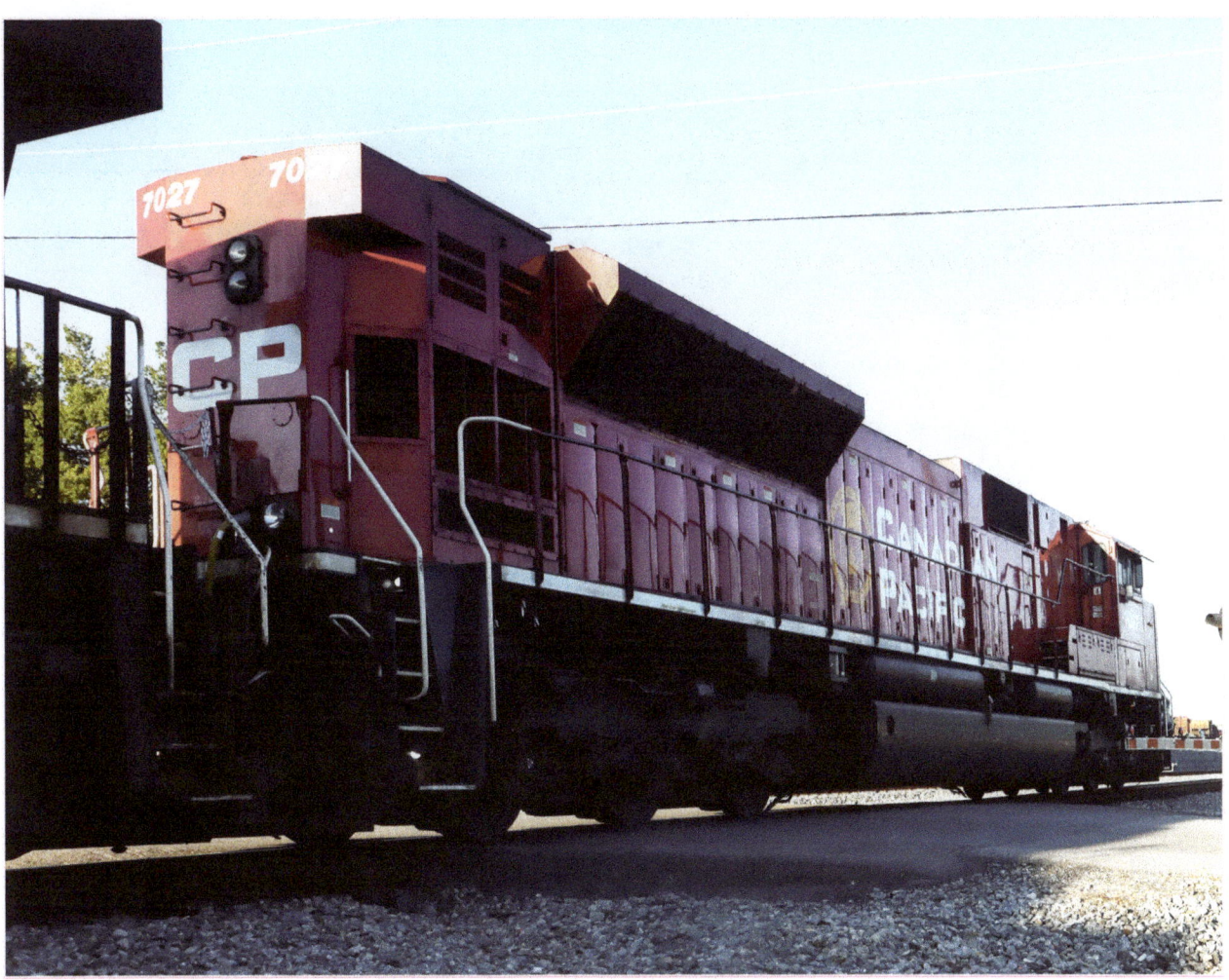

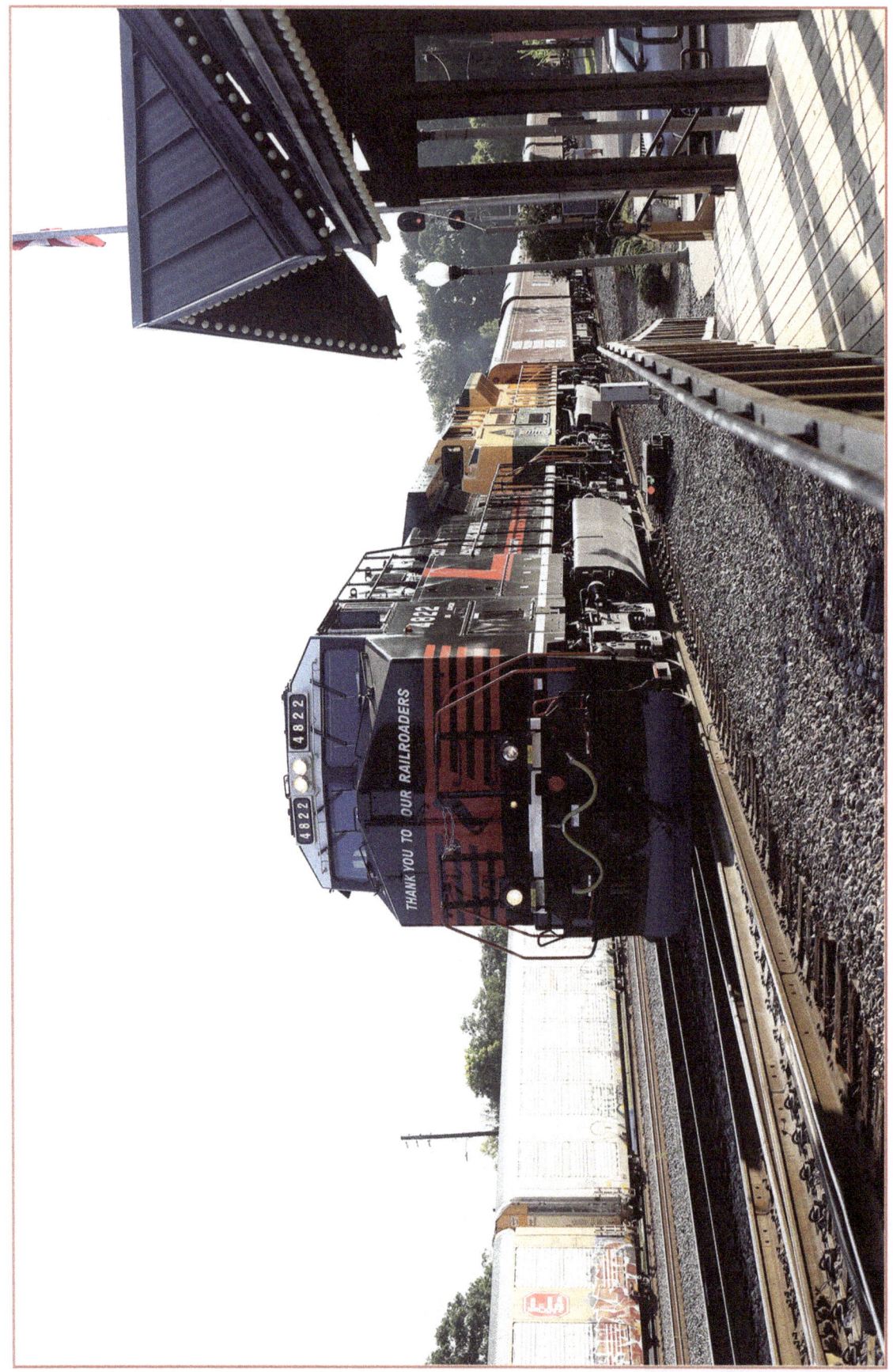

Norfolk Southern 4822, the newest special unit, leads the corporate train into Irondale with the Reading Heritage Unit trailing.

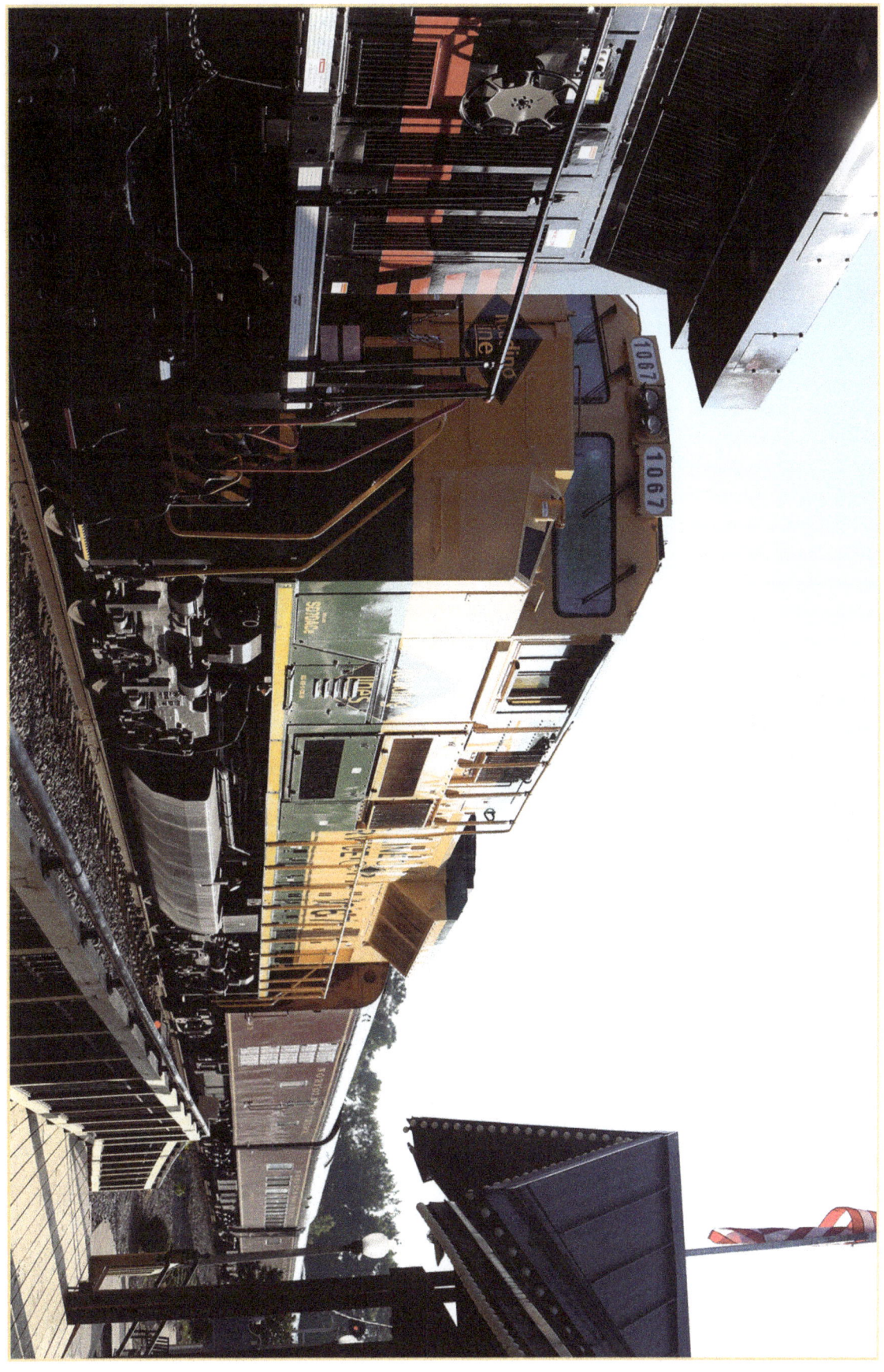

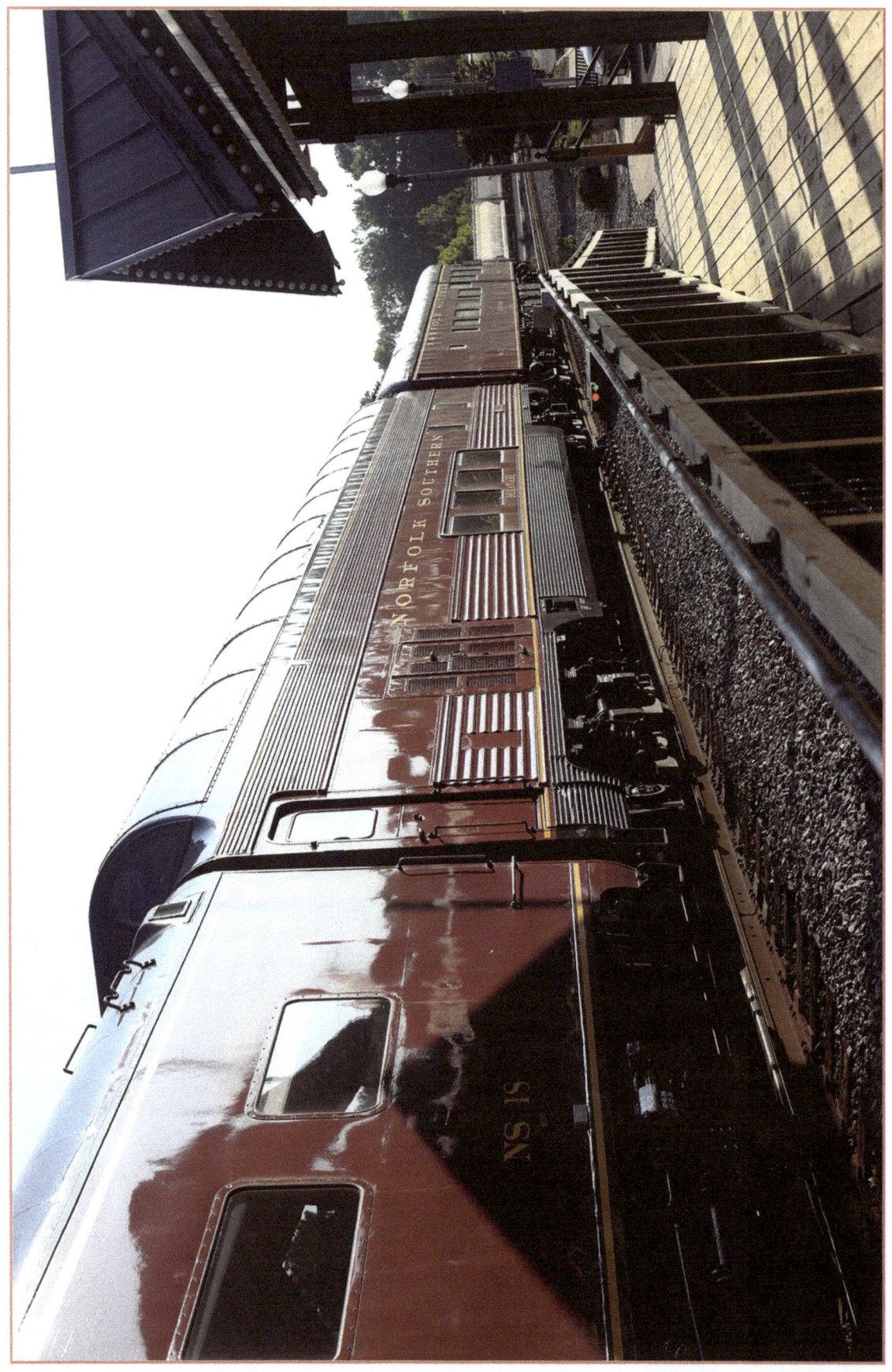

The dome car on the Norfolk Southern corporate train

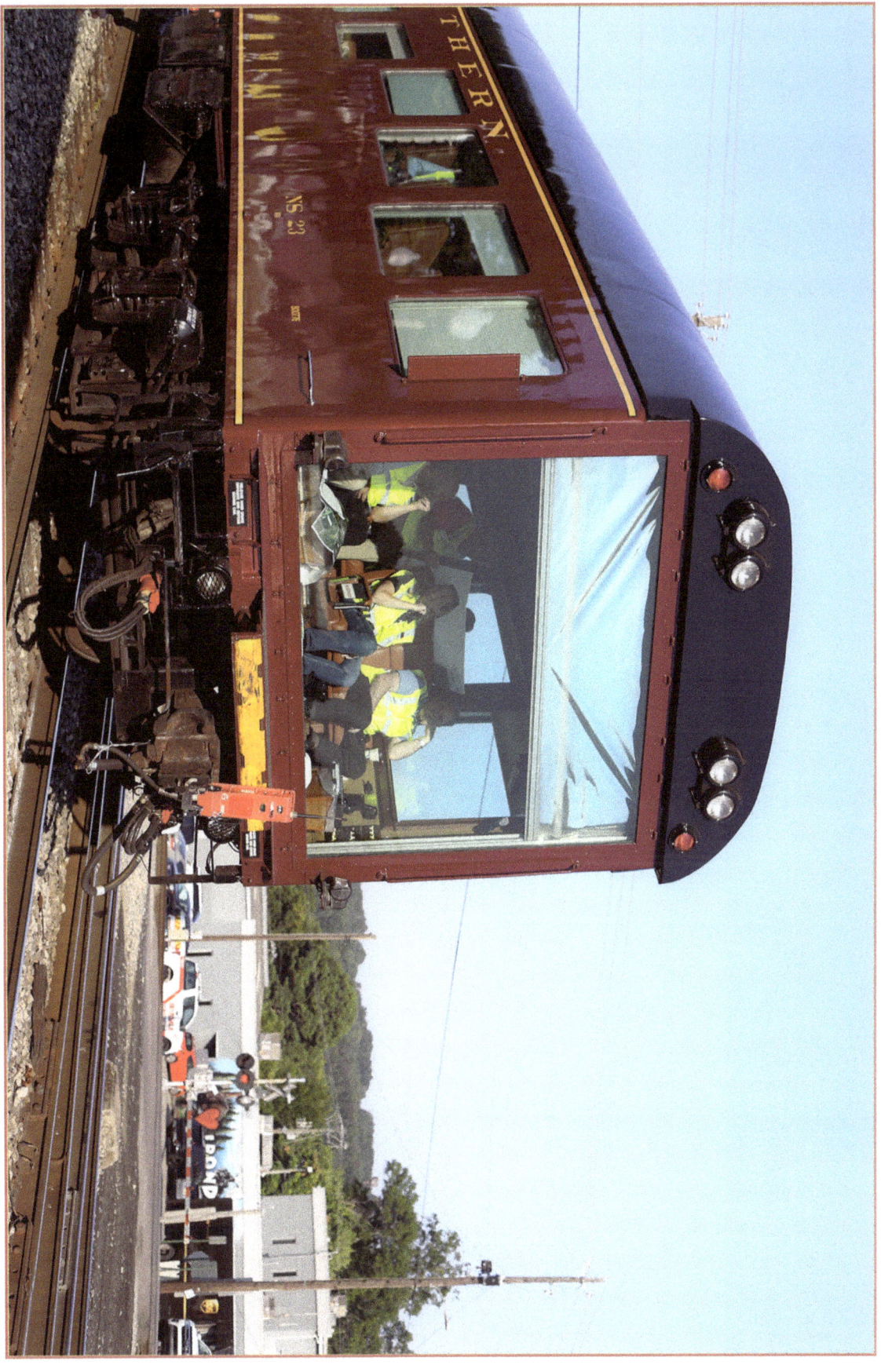

The rear observation car on the corporate train

CSX

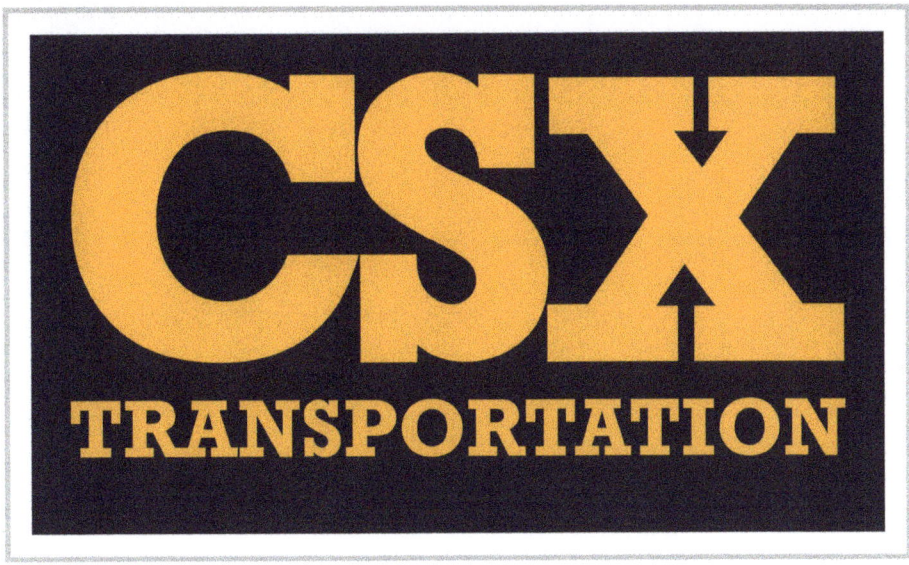

B oyles Yard is CSX's yard in Birmingham and is located north of the city in Tarrant, Alabama. The yard itself was originally developed in 1909 and continues to serve with CSX. The BNSF interchanges with them at a wye near the edge of the yard daily, and the ATN interchanges with them deeper within the yard. The operations within the yard are done with pairs of the newly rebuilt SD40-3 locomotives, which you can actually see from the fish market located on Vanderbilt Road.

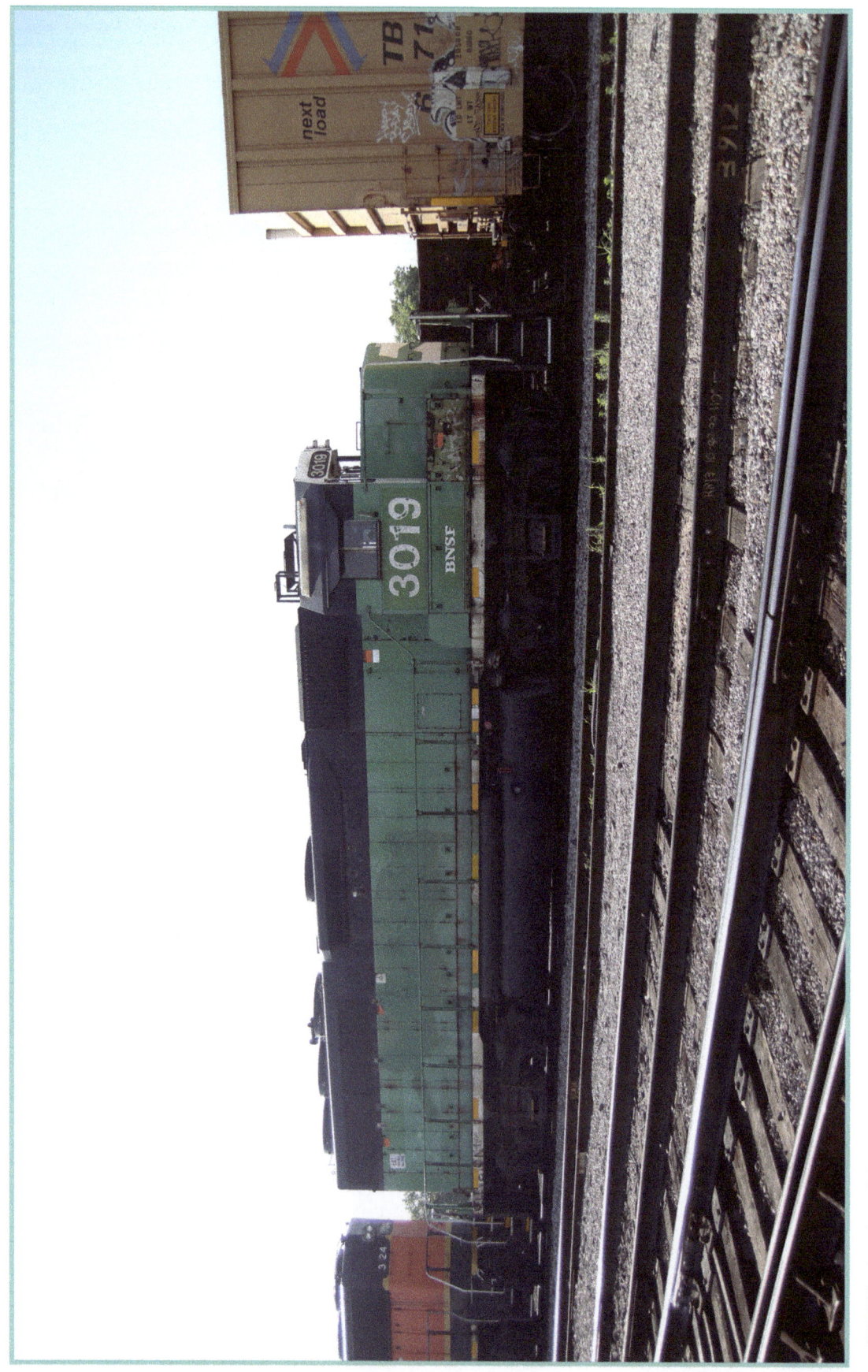

BNSF 3019 is a GP40M still in its original Burlington Northern livery. Originally ordered by the Chicago, Burlington and Quincy Railroad in the 1960s, it continued service even after the merger that resulted in it being painted in this green livery. After this, it served with the Burlington Northern Railroad until 1995 when Burlington Northern merged with Santa Fe to form BNSF. Today it serves BNSF on its Birmingham Subdivision, performing switching duties and occasionally running locals.

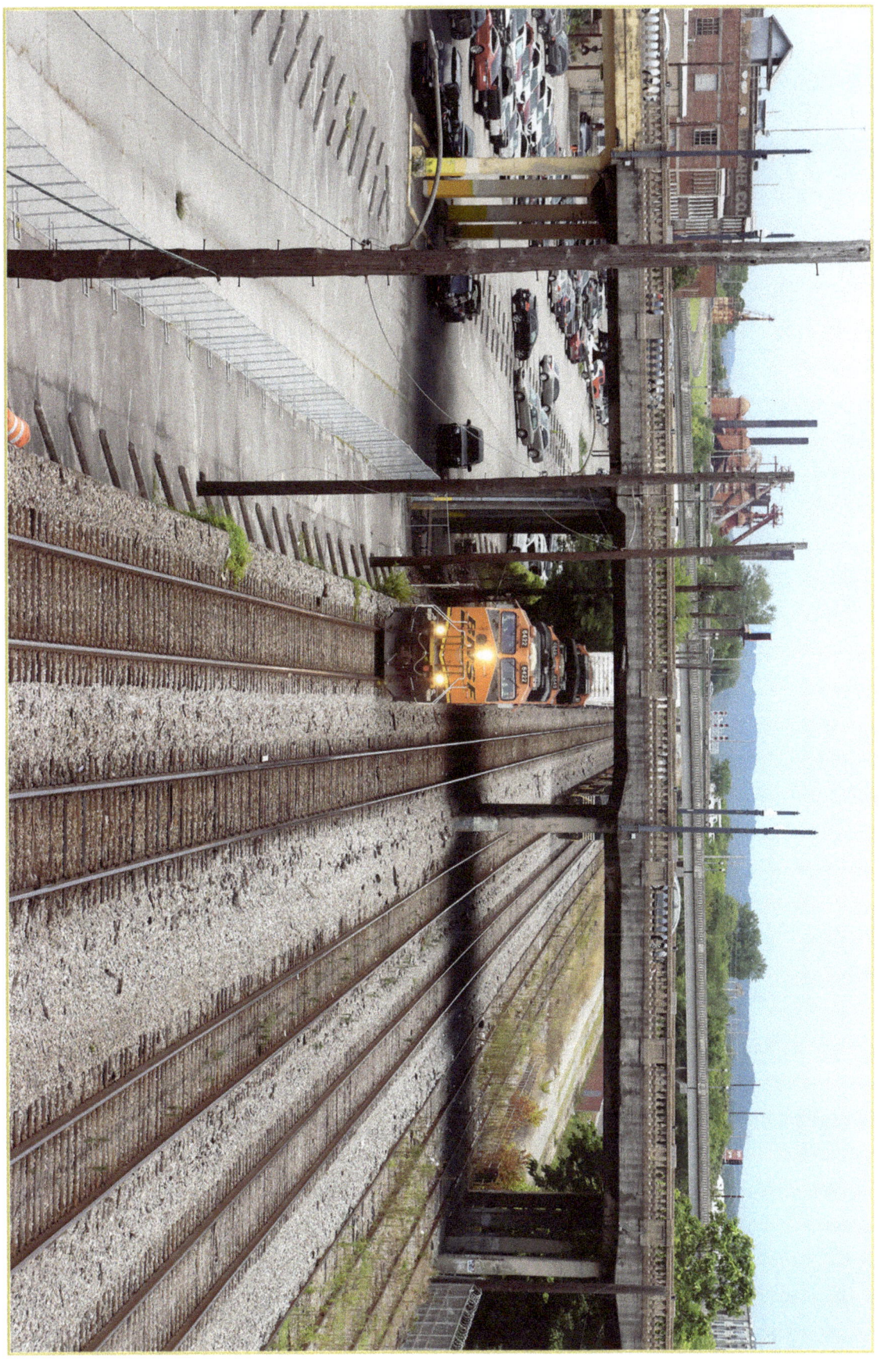

A BNSF container train emerges from the CSX track that the railroad has rights to use.

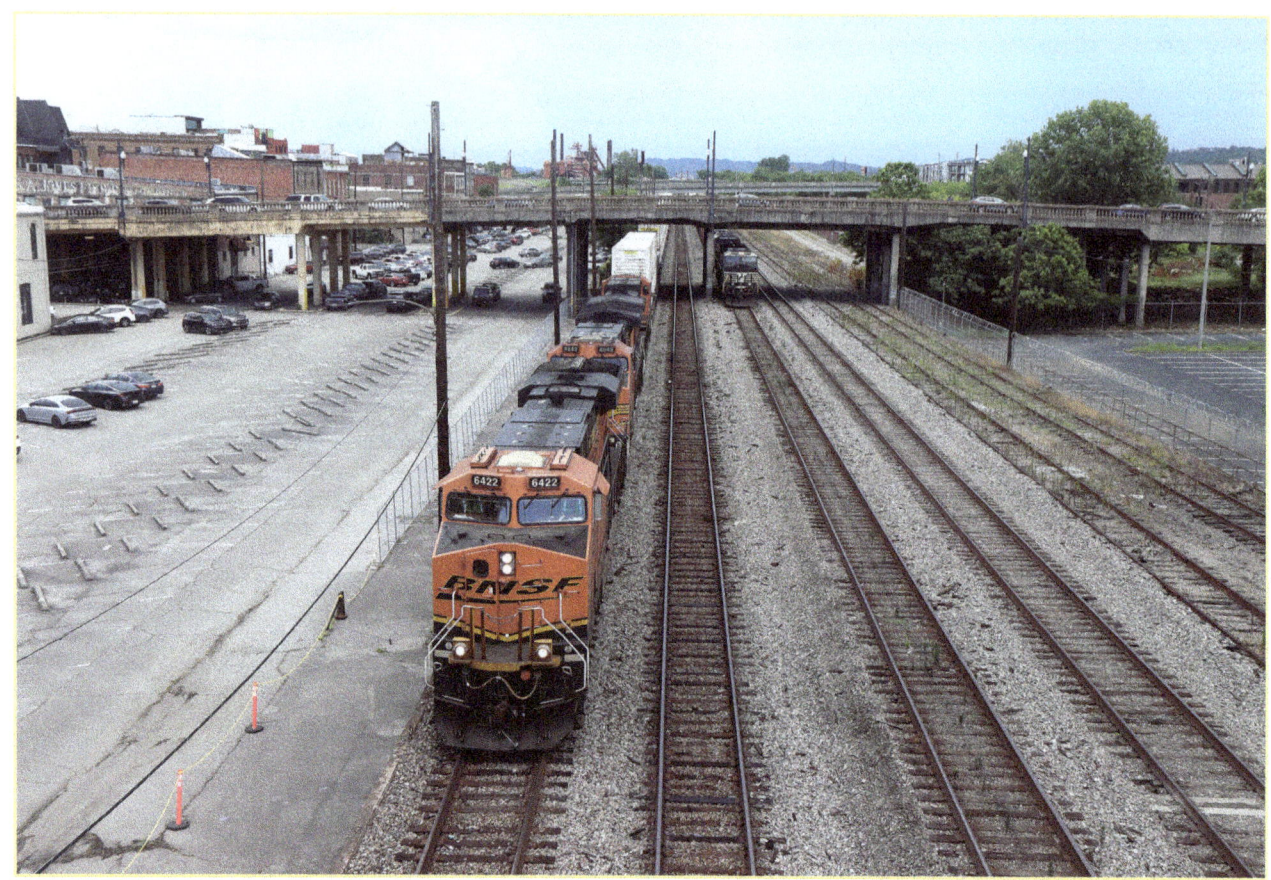

The BNSF container train races a Norfolk Southern manifest.

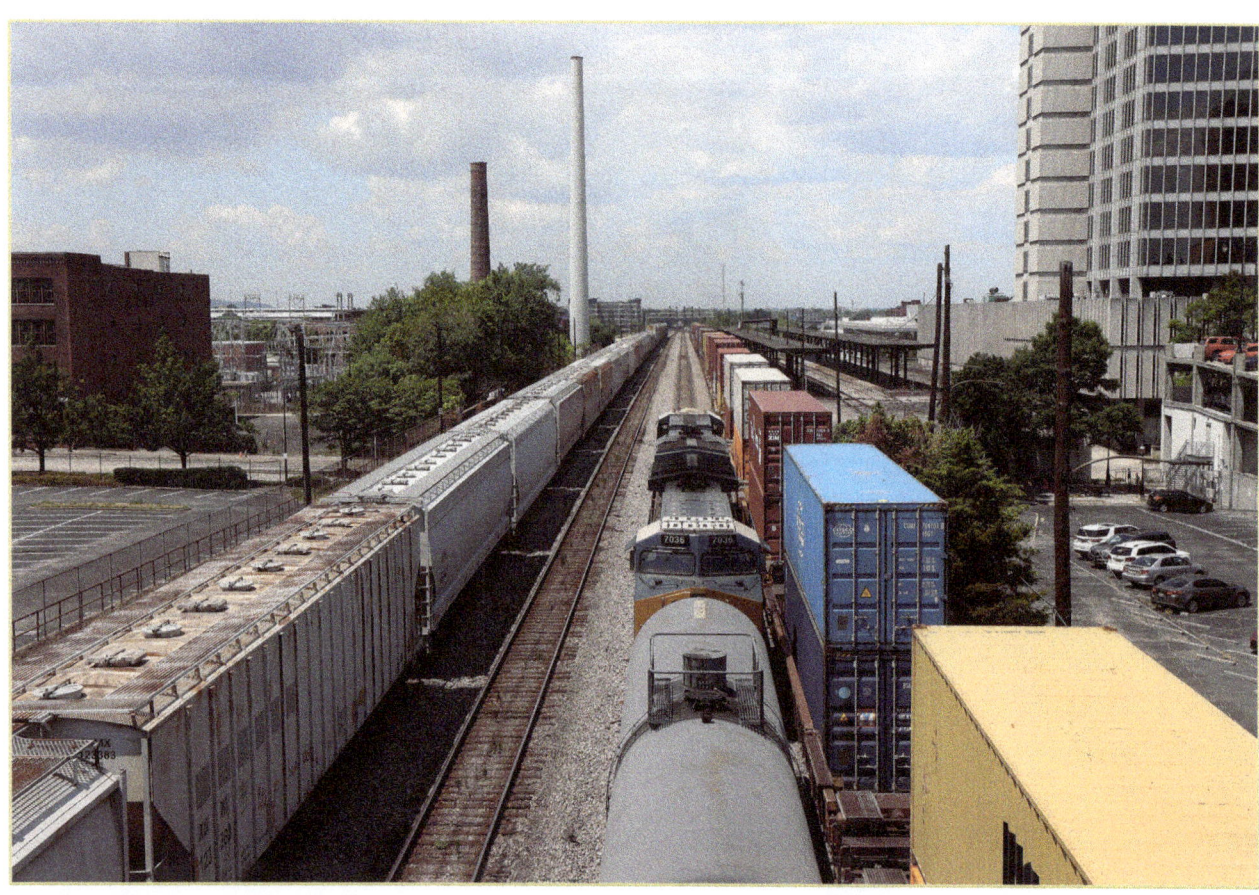

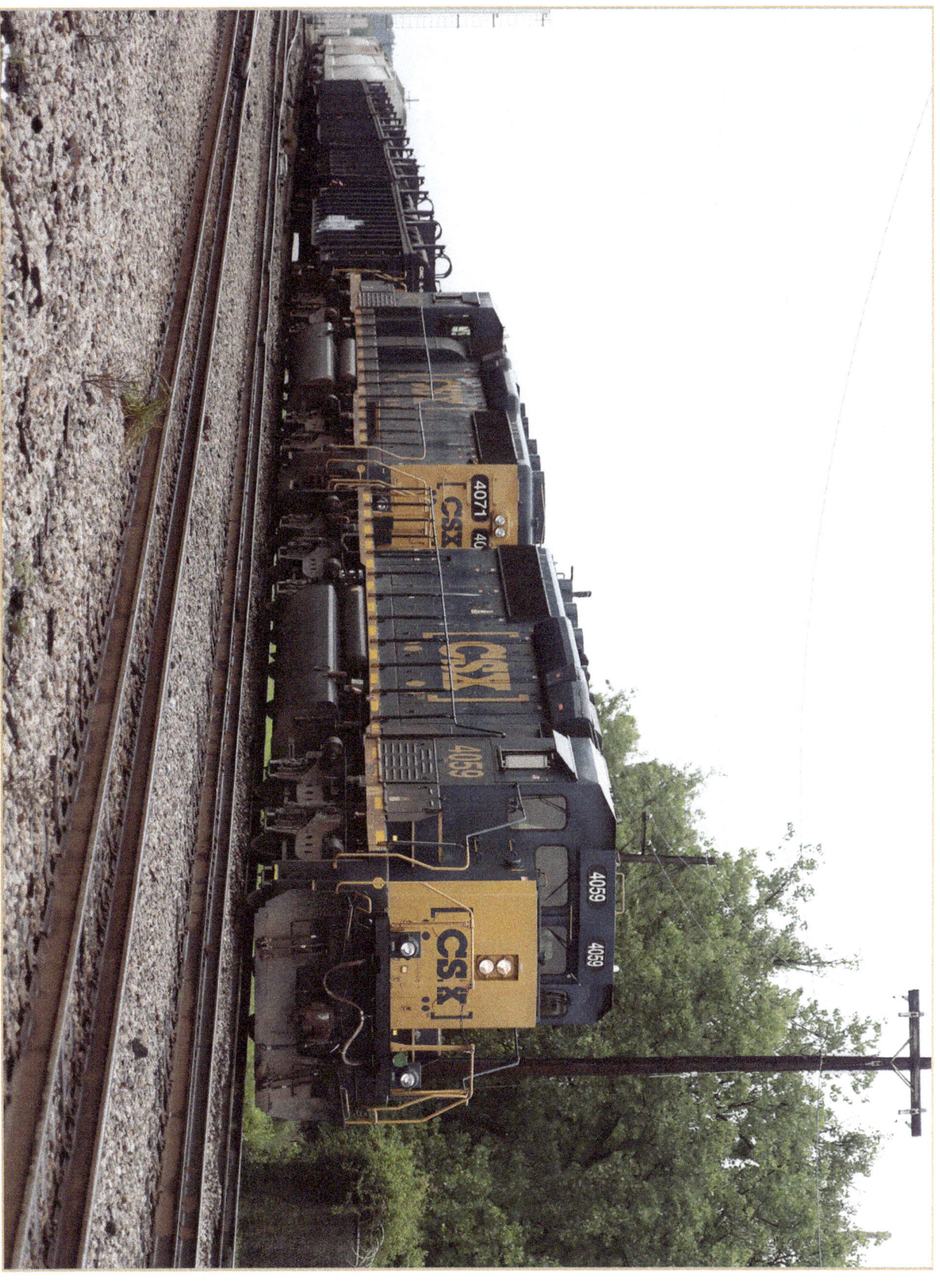
CSX 4059 leads the local to Norris Yard on a gloomy day.

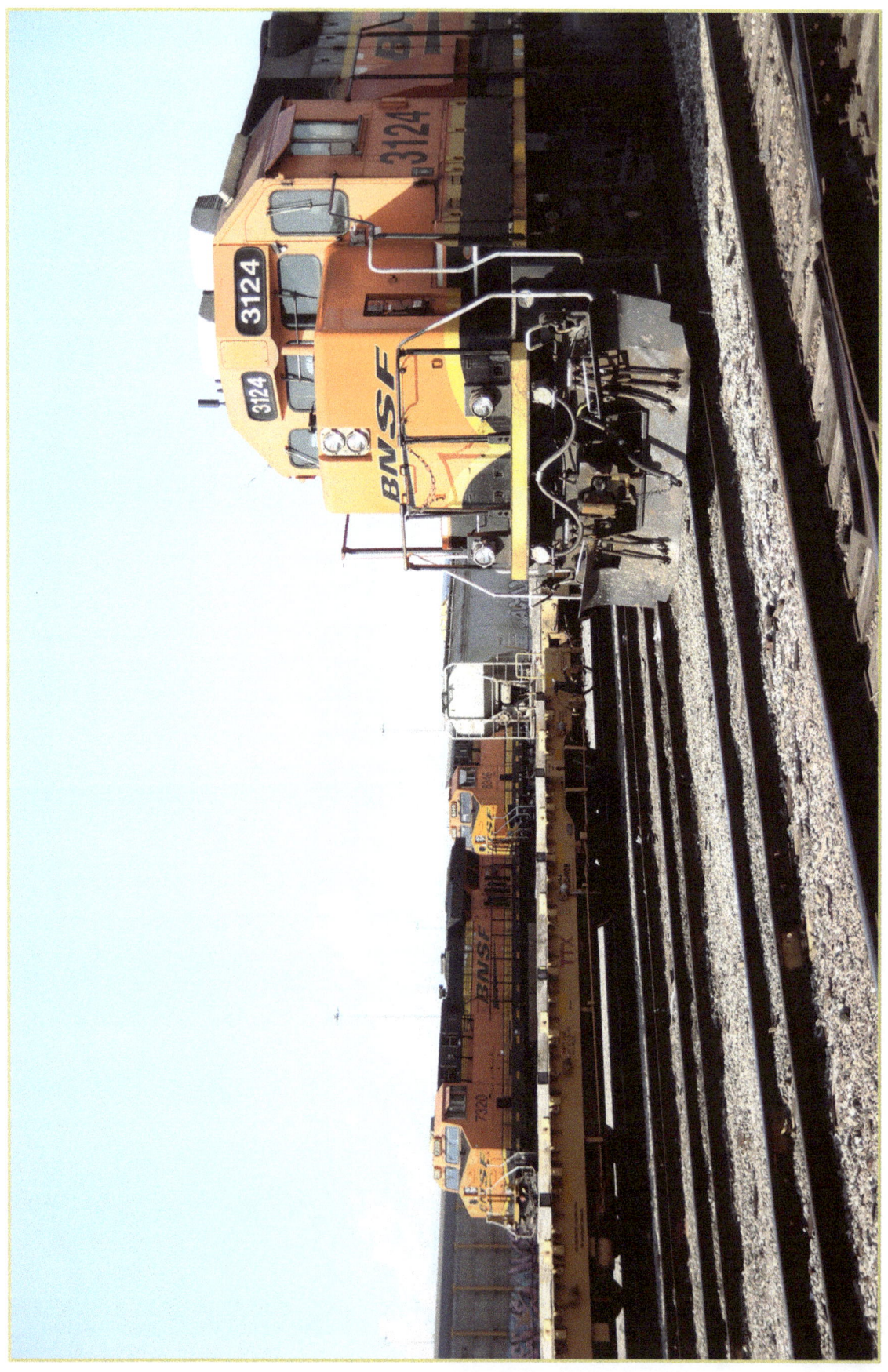

A BNSF GP38-2 sits in the yard while two GEVOs are hooked up to a train.

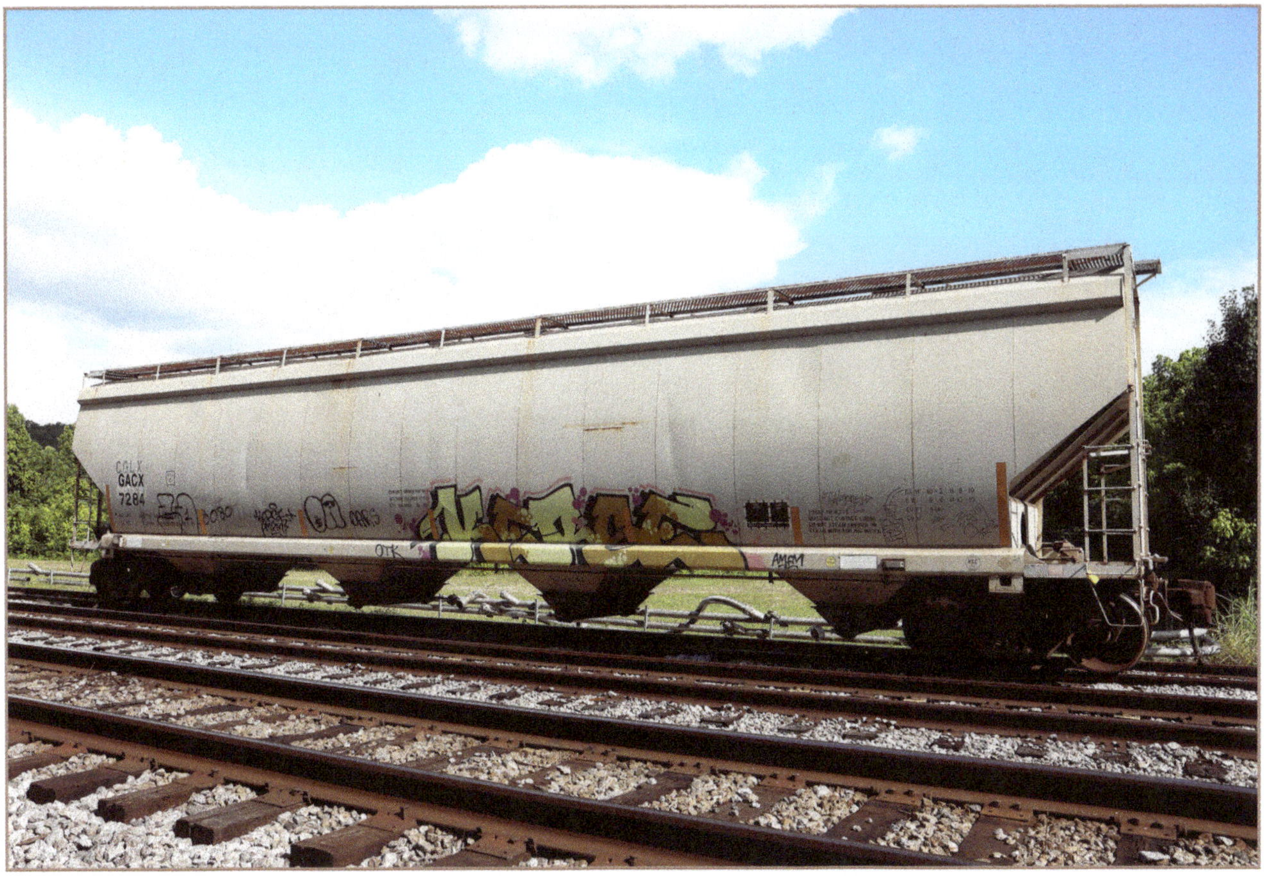

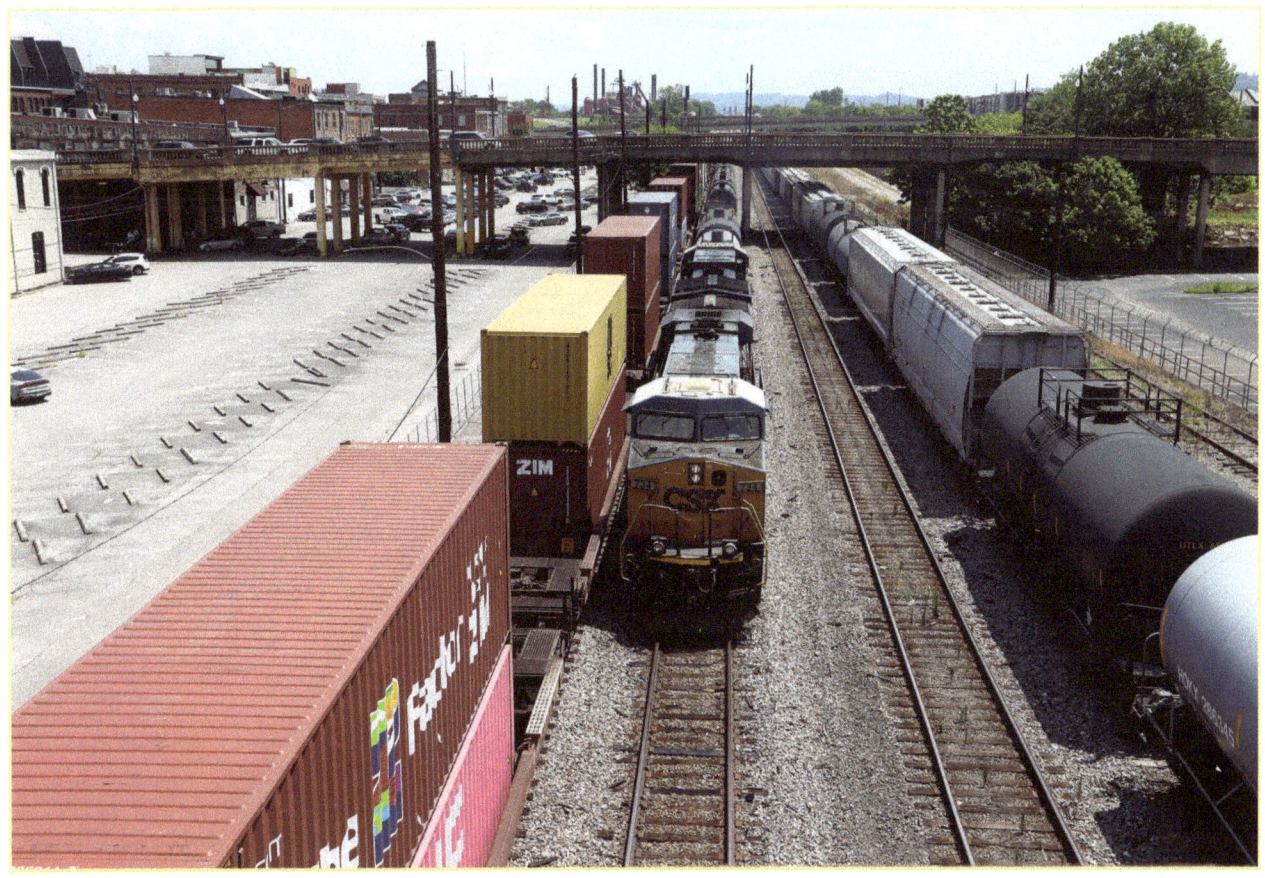

A covered hopper sits alone at a long-abandoned industry in Helena.

A CSX mixed-freight passes a container train on its way out of Boyles Yard.

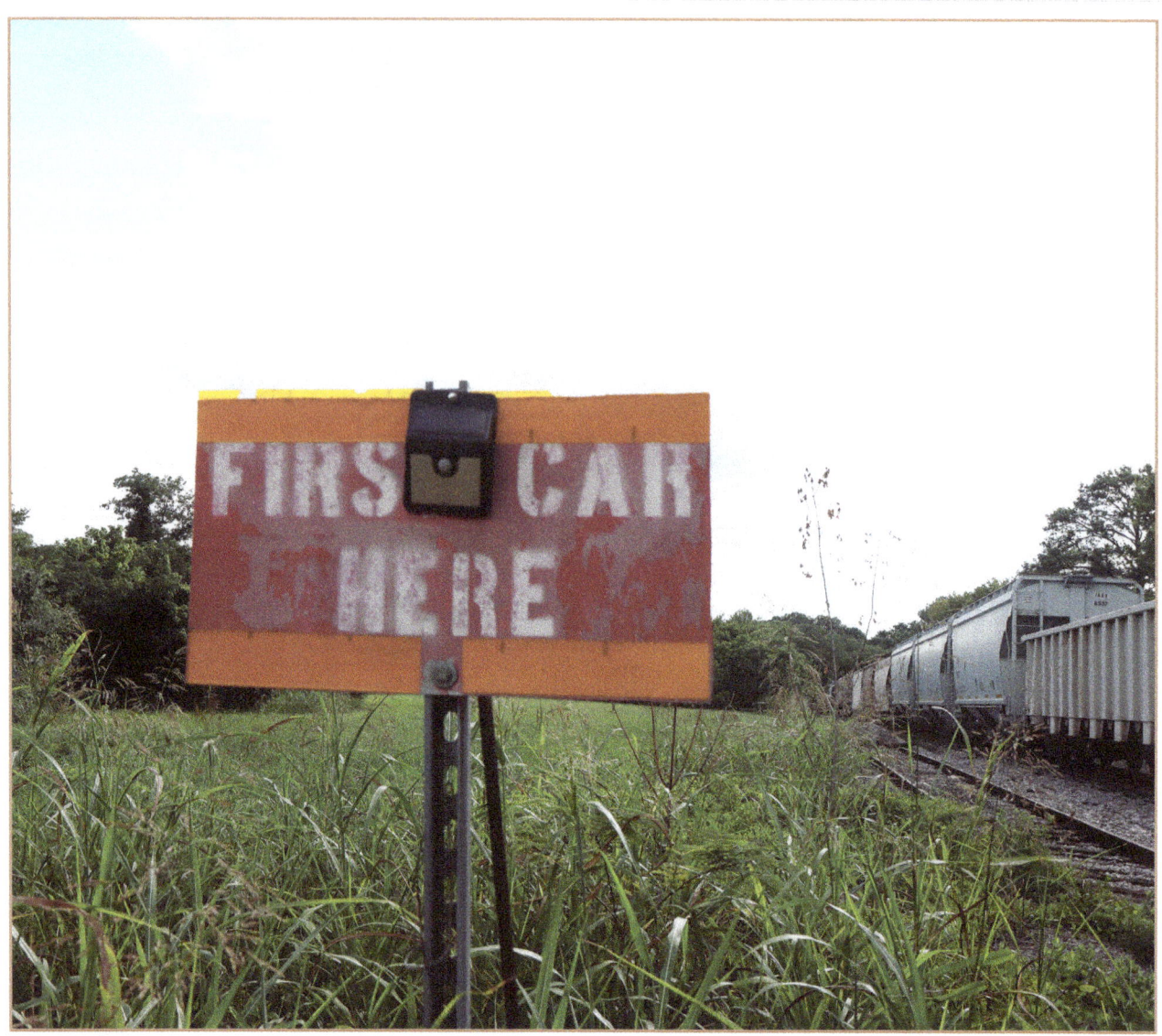

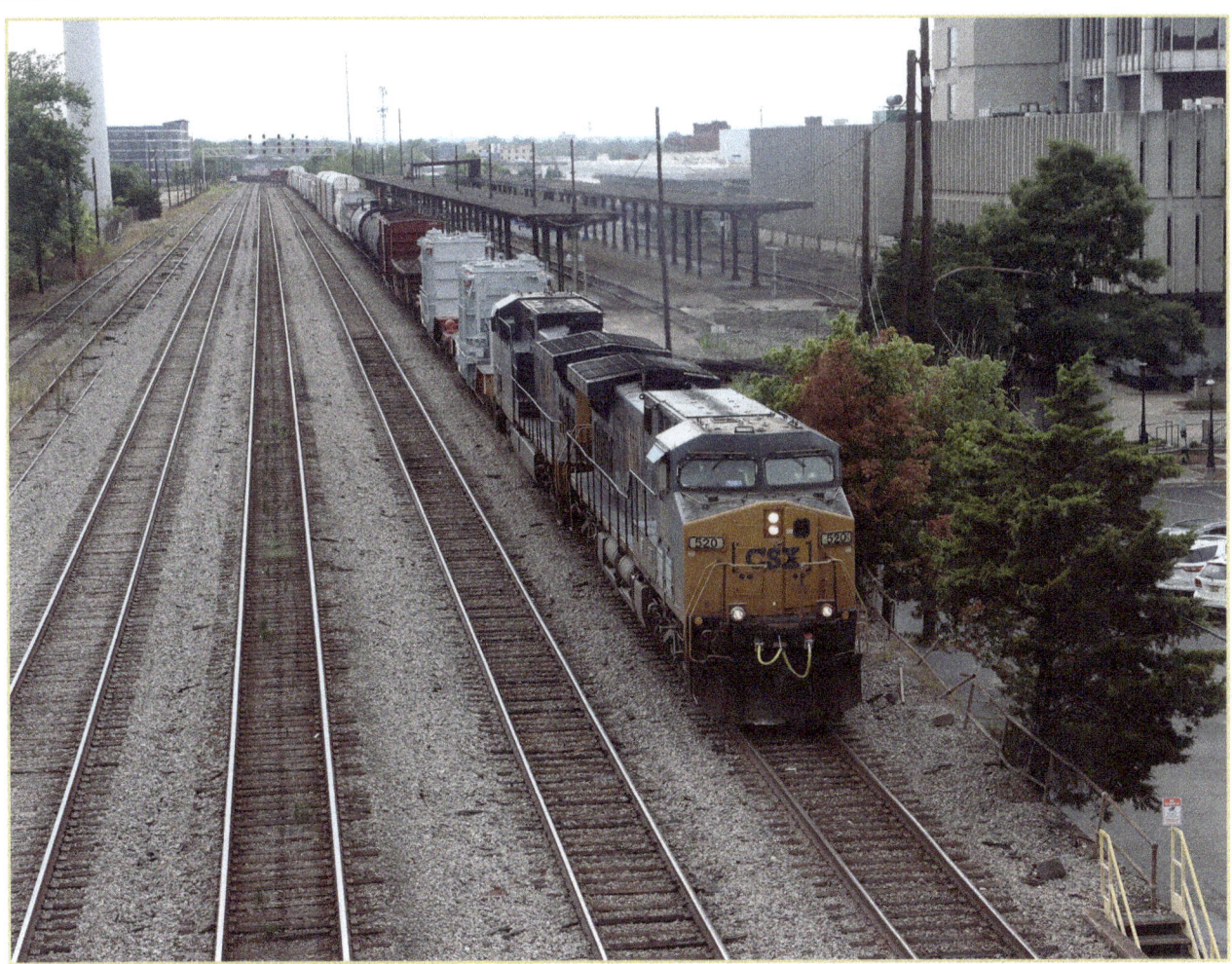
Two CSX locomotives pull heavy industrial equipment toward Boyles Yard in Tarrant.

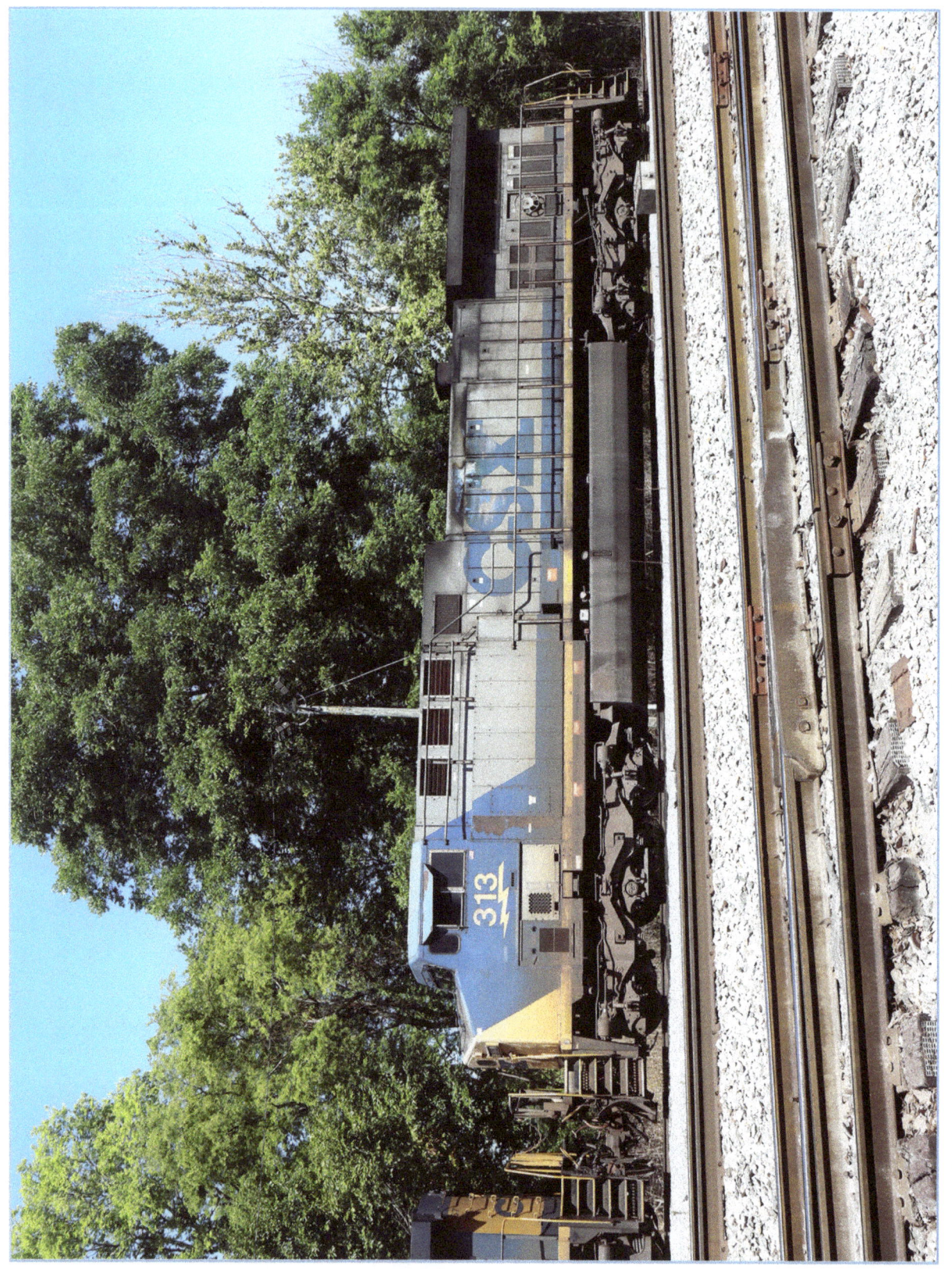

CSX AC44CW 313 idles in Calera Yard. 313 is painted in an older CSX paint scheme, and the lightning bolt on the front shows it has been converted from DC to AC traction motors.

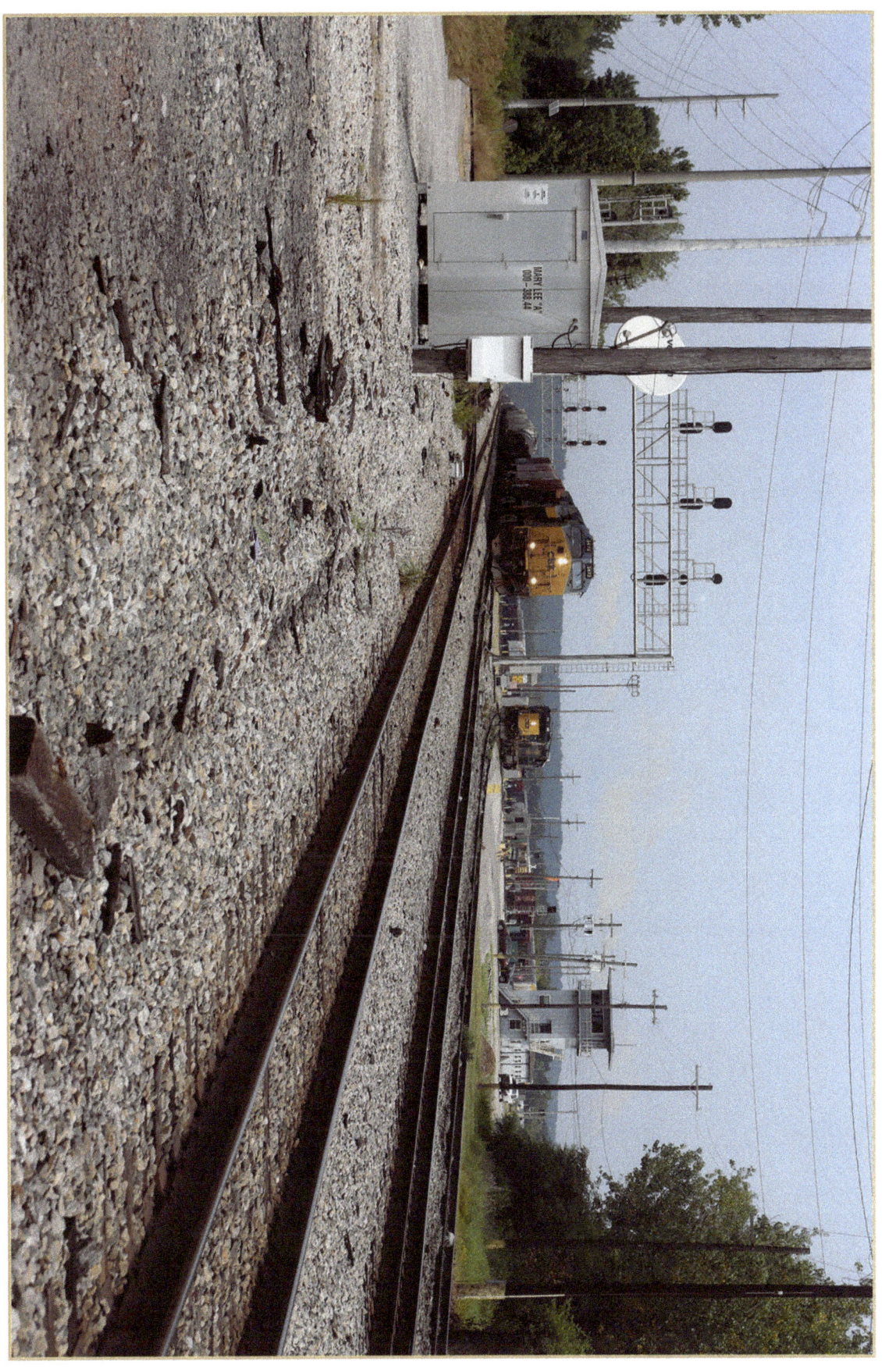

A CSX mixed-freight leaves Boyles Yard as two SD40-3s are "humping" cars. Humping is sending cars down a hill to the tracks where they are needed.

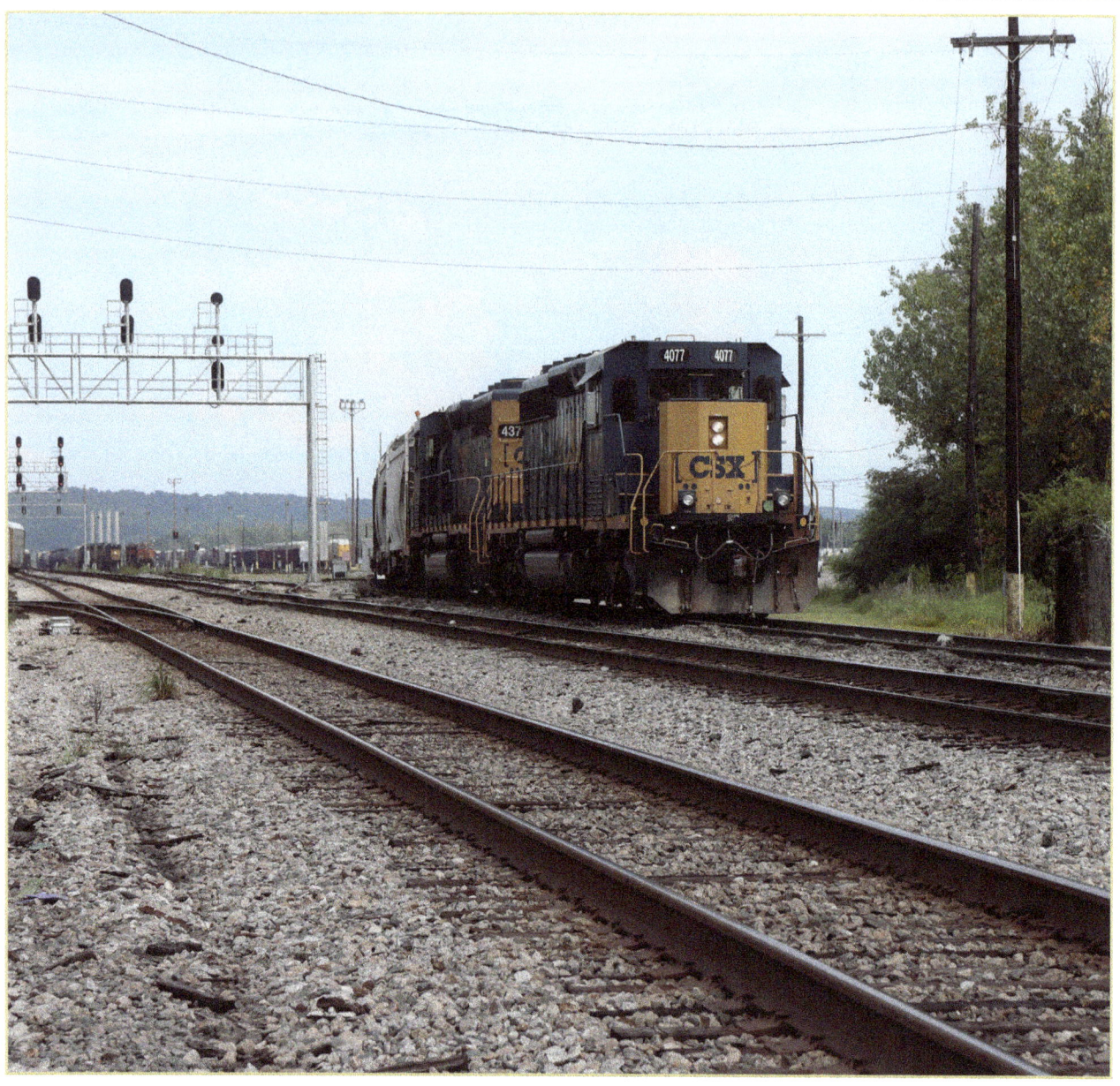
A pair of CSX SD40-3s exit Boyles Yard with a cut of cars that need to be classified.

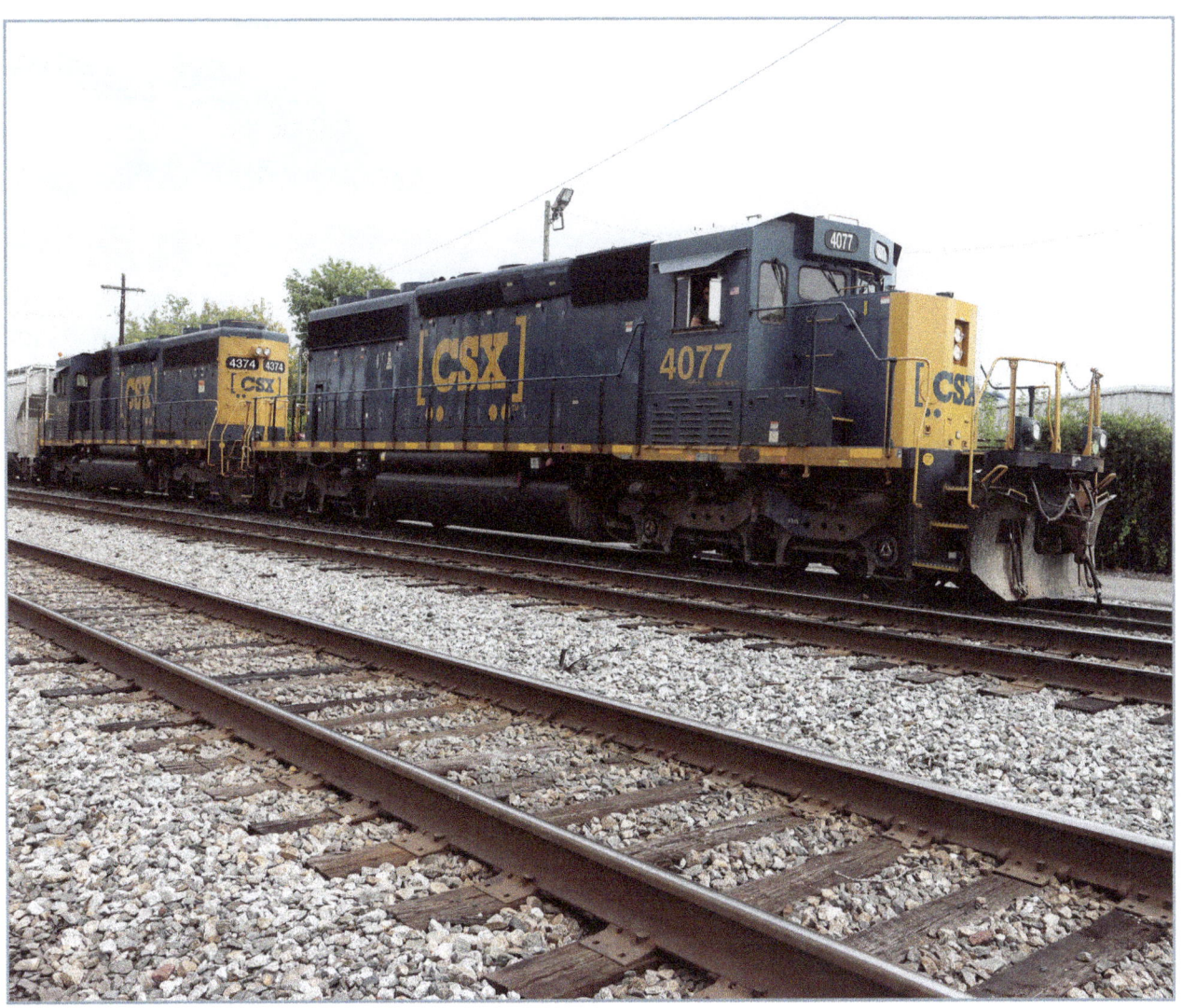

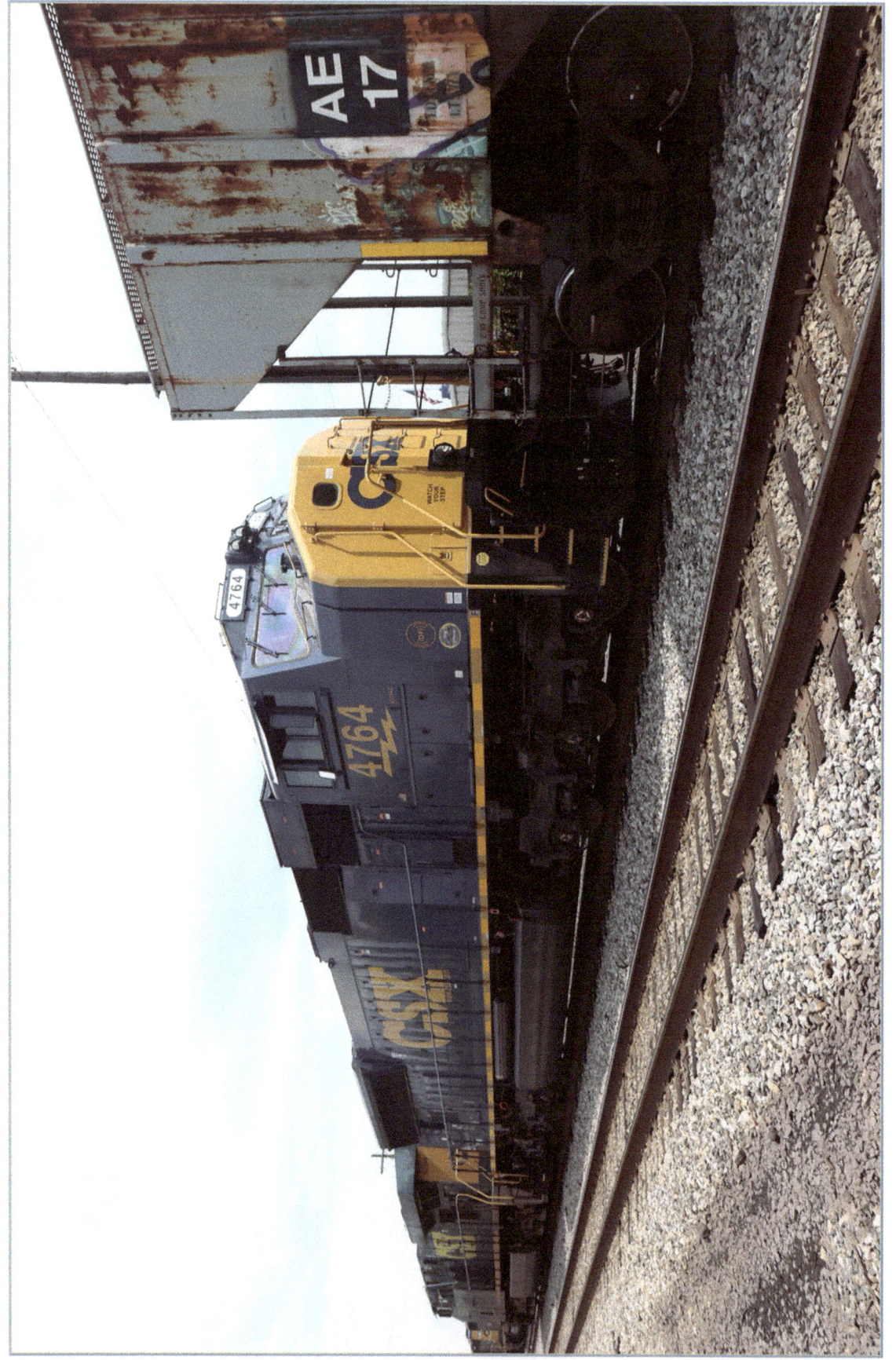

A CSX SD70MAC trails on a mixed-freight entering Boyles Yard.

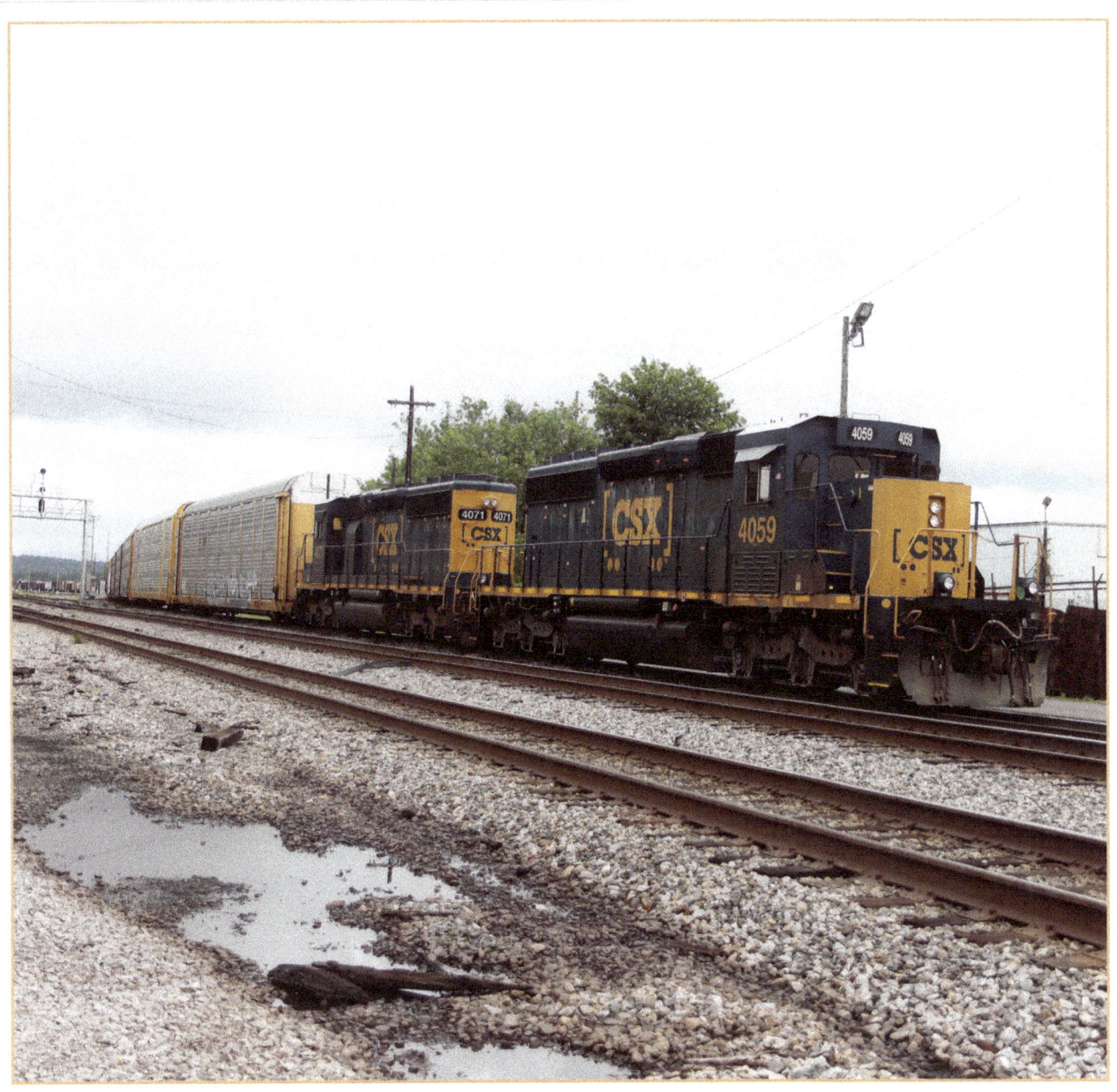

CSX 4059 leads the local to Norris Yard.

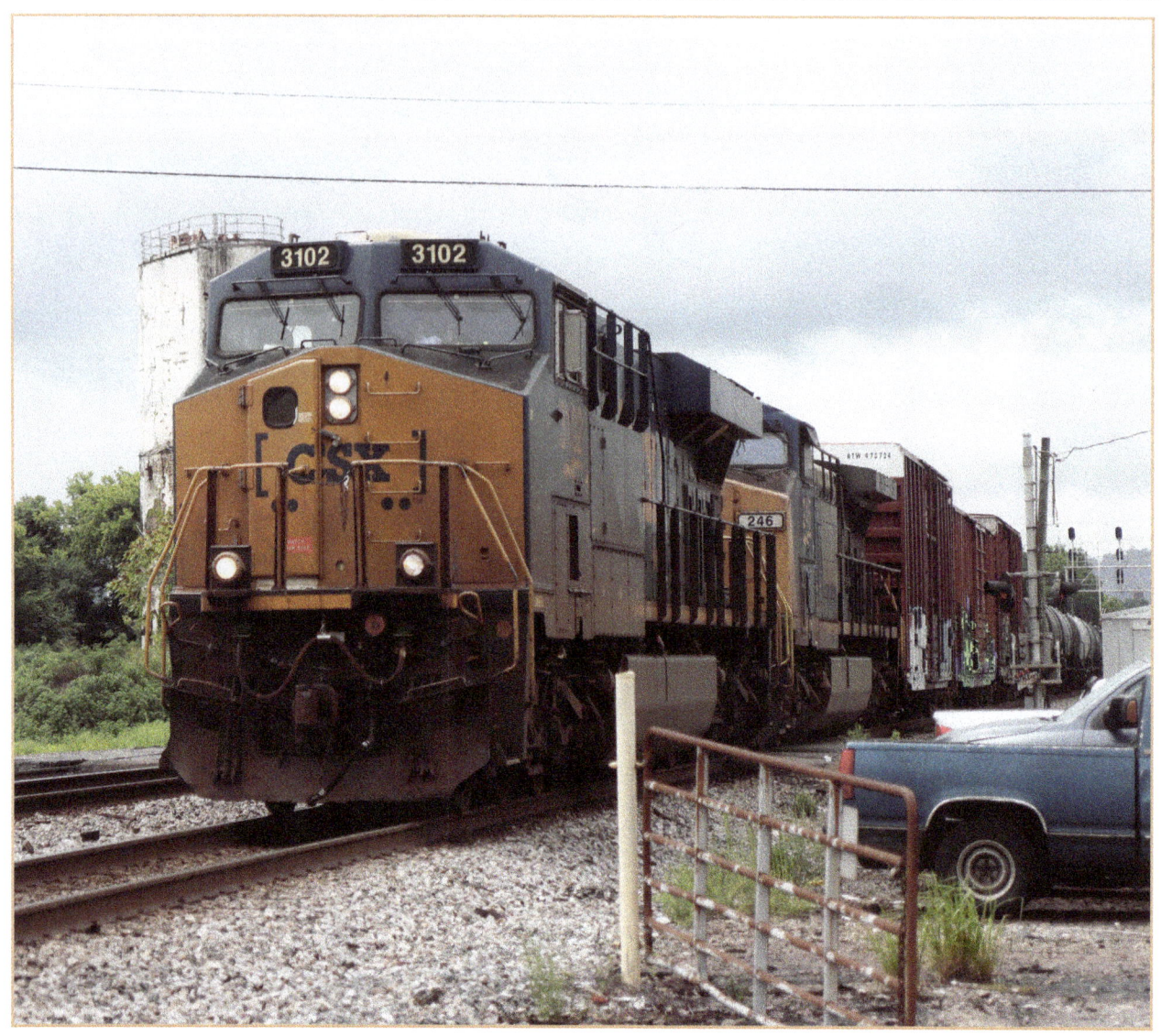

A CSX mixed-freight enters Boyles Yard at a high speed.

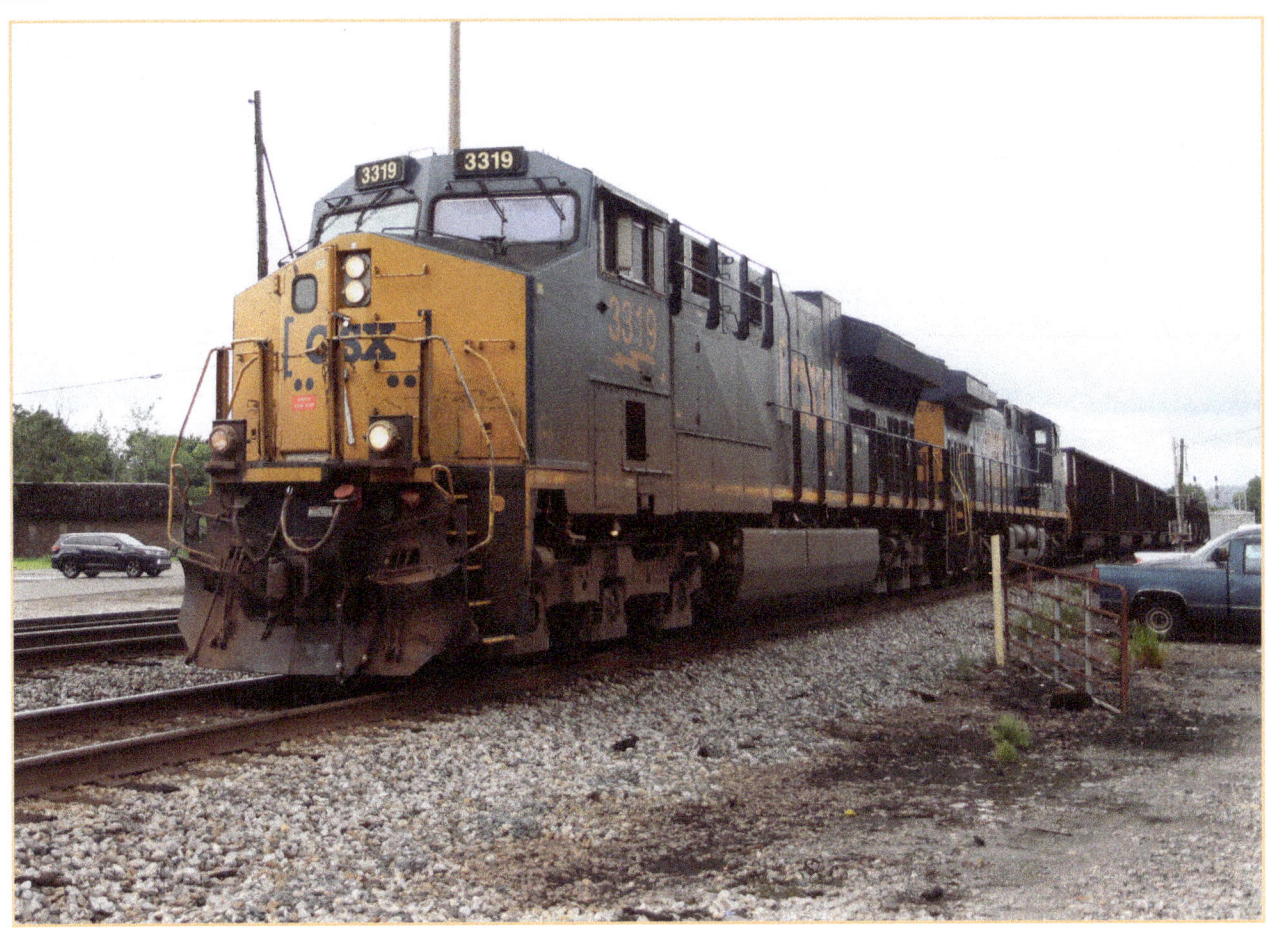

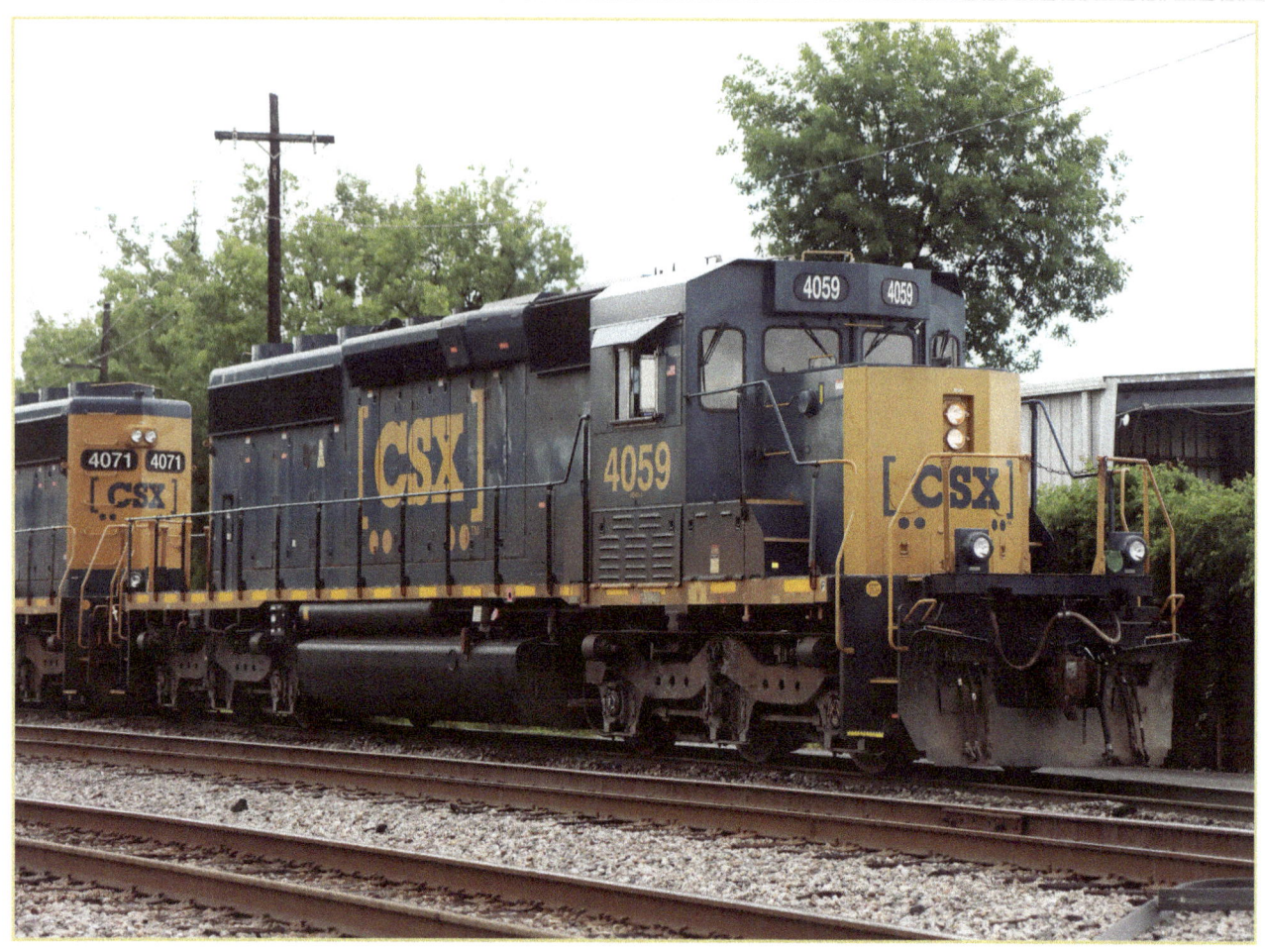

CSX SD40-3 4059 switches in Boyles Yard.

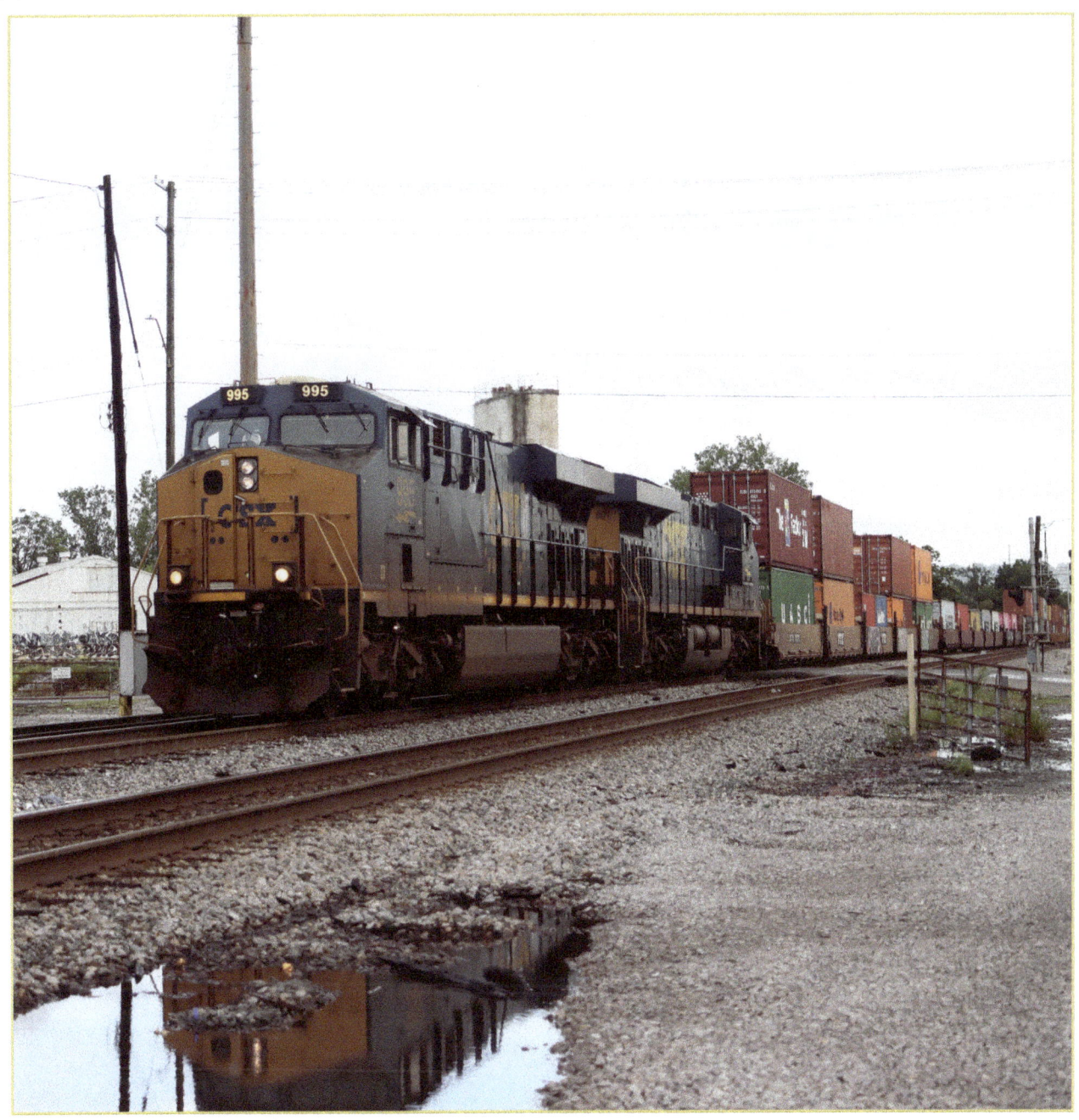

CSX 995 leads a container train into Boyles Yard with 513 as middle power.

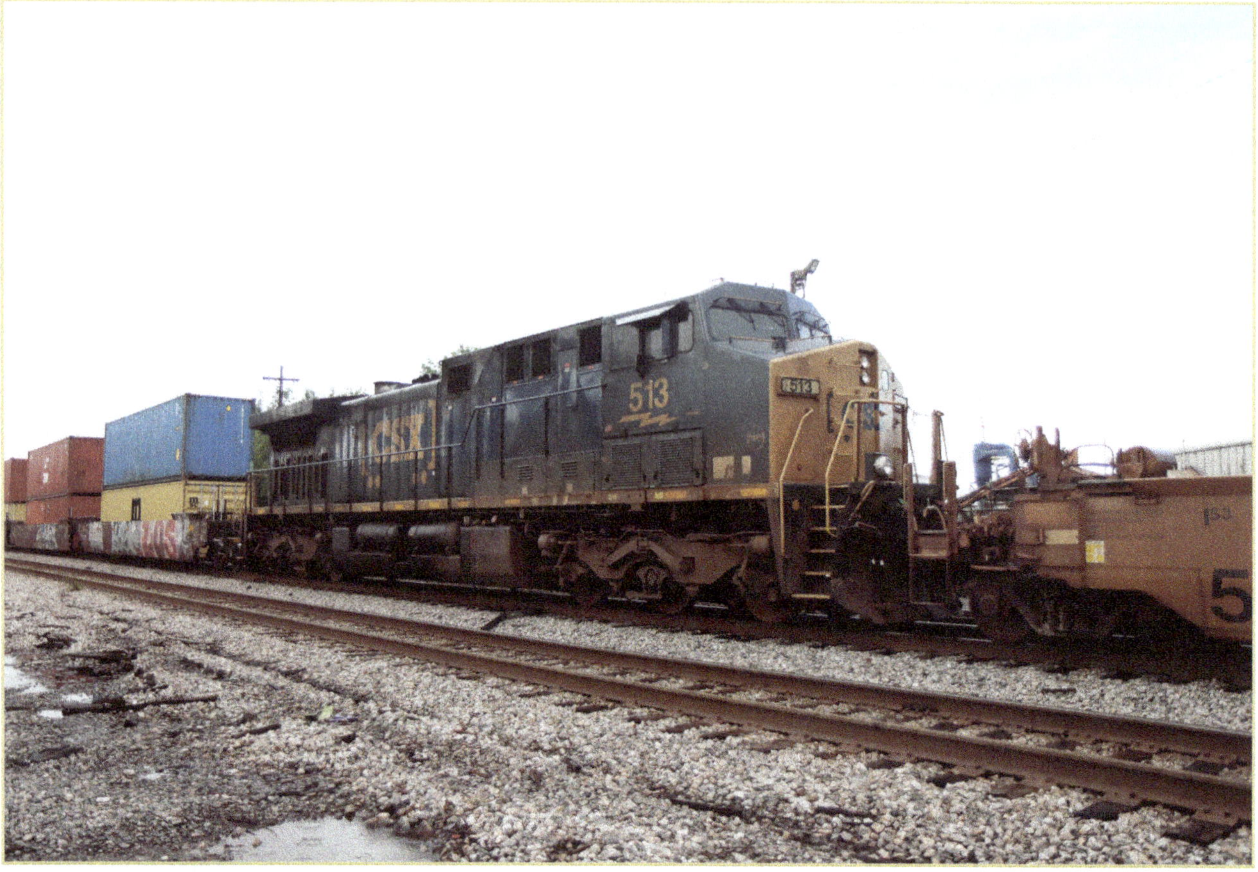

Trains of Alabama

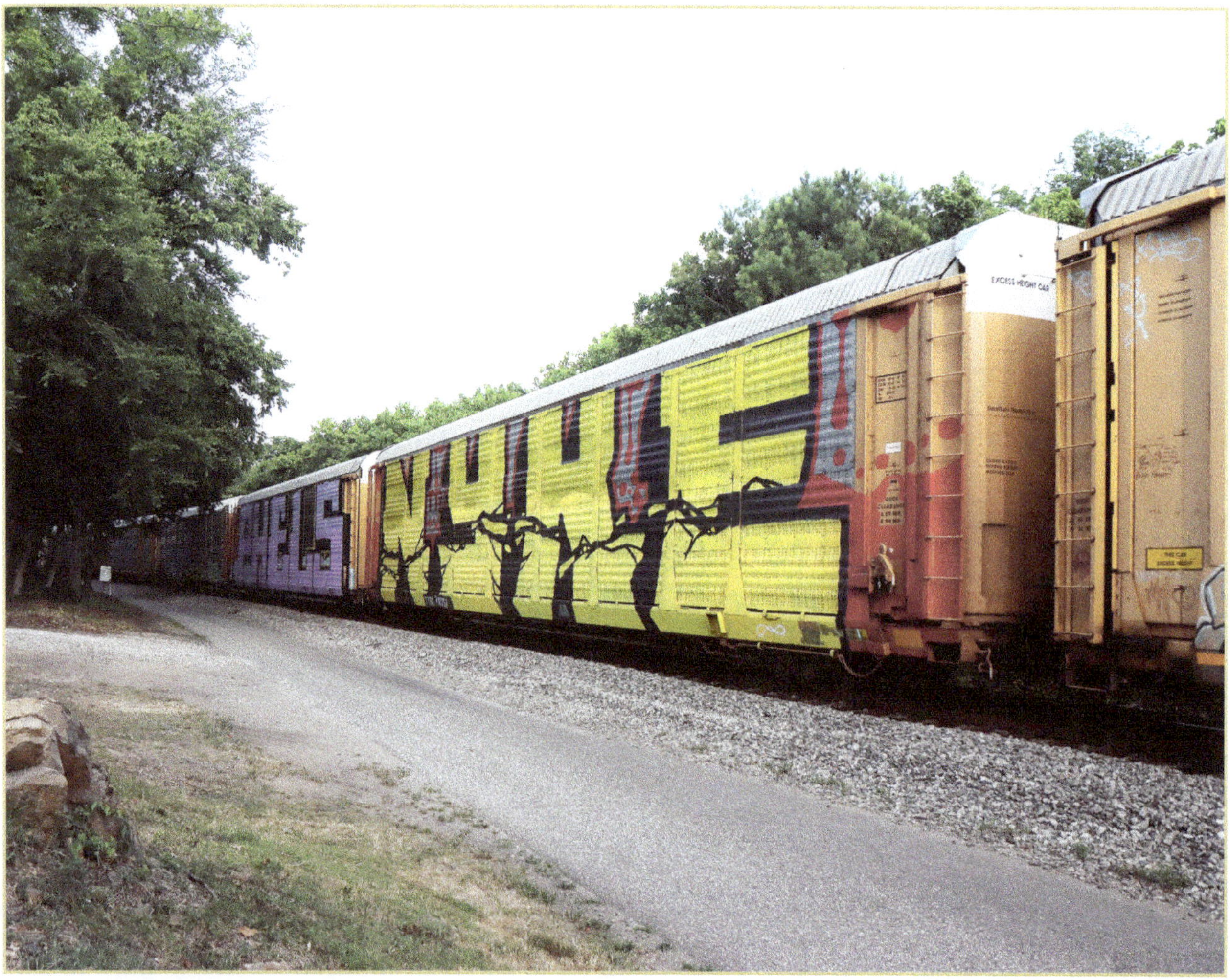

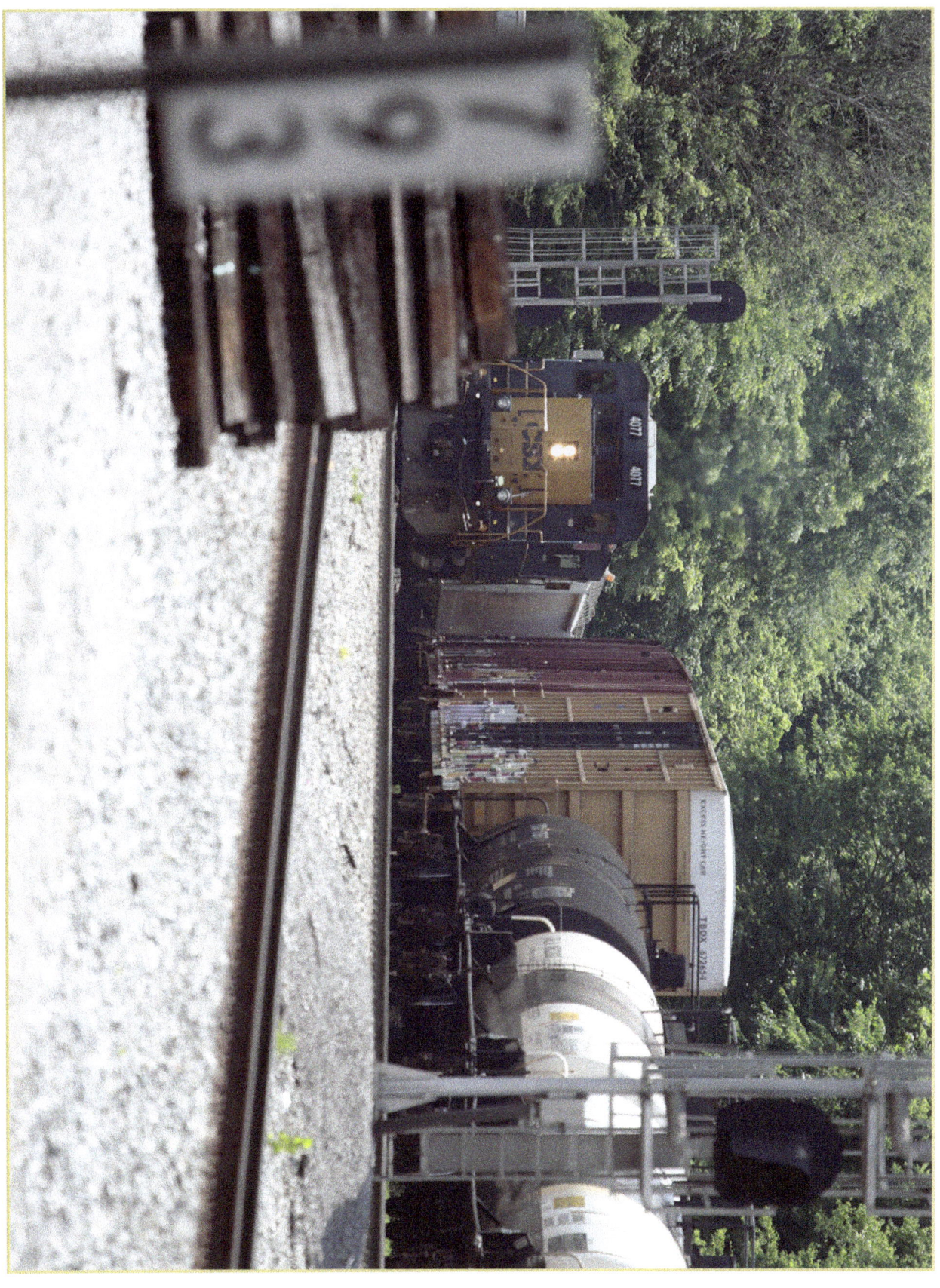

CSX 4077 enters Norris Yard pulling Y103, the local from Boyles Yard.

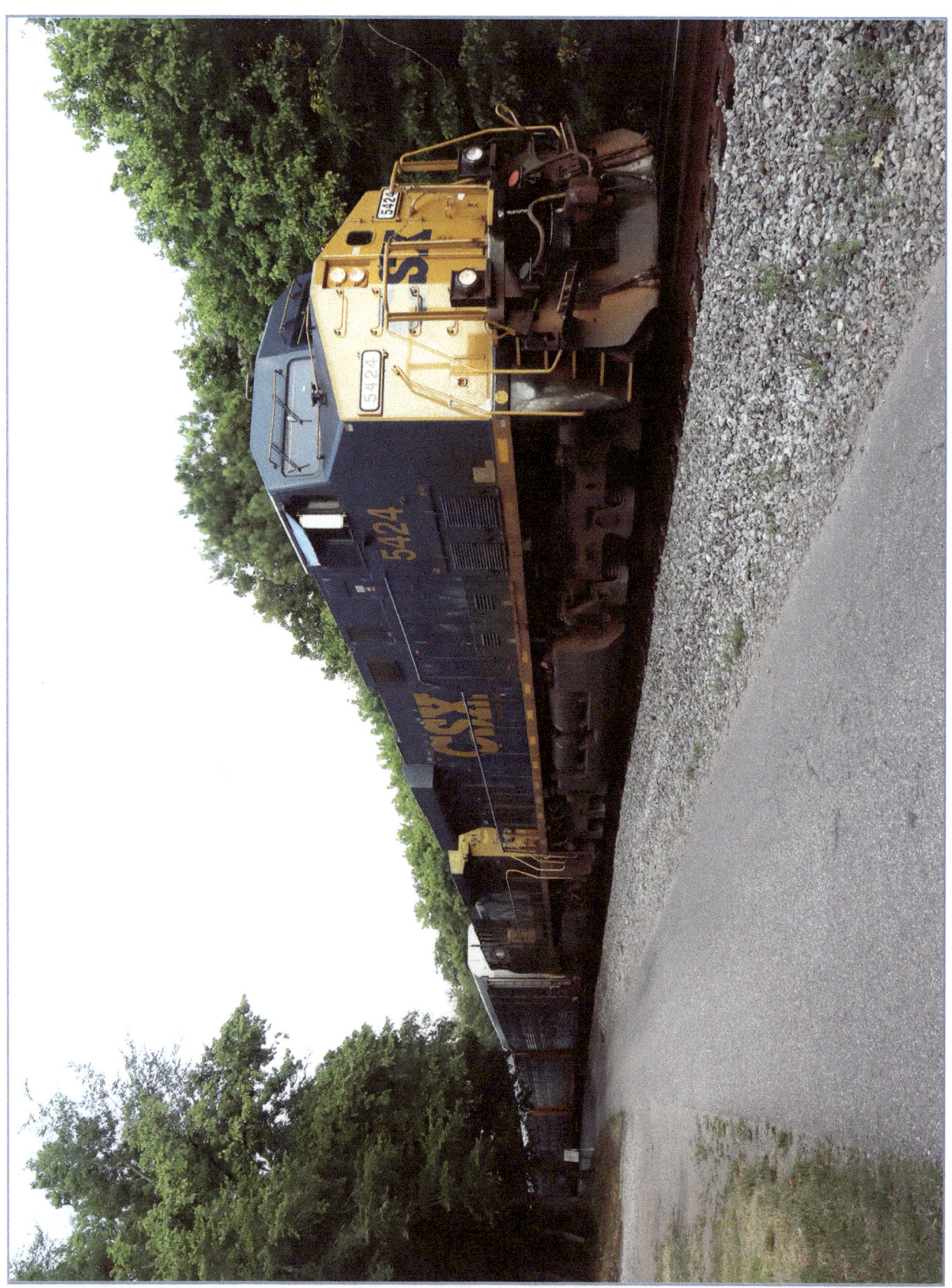

CSX 5424 races through Helena, pulling autoracks.

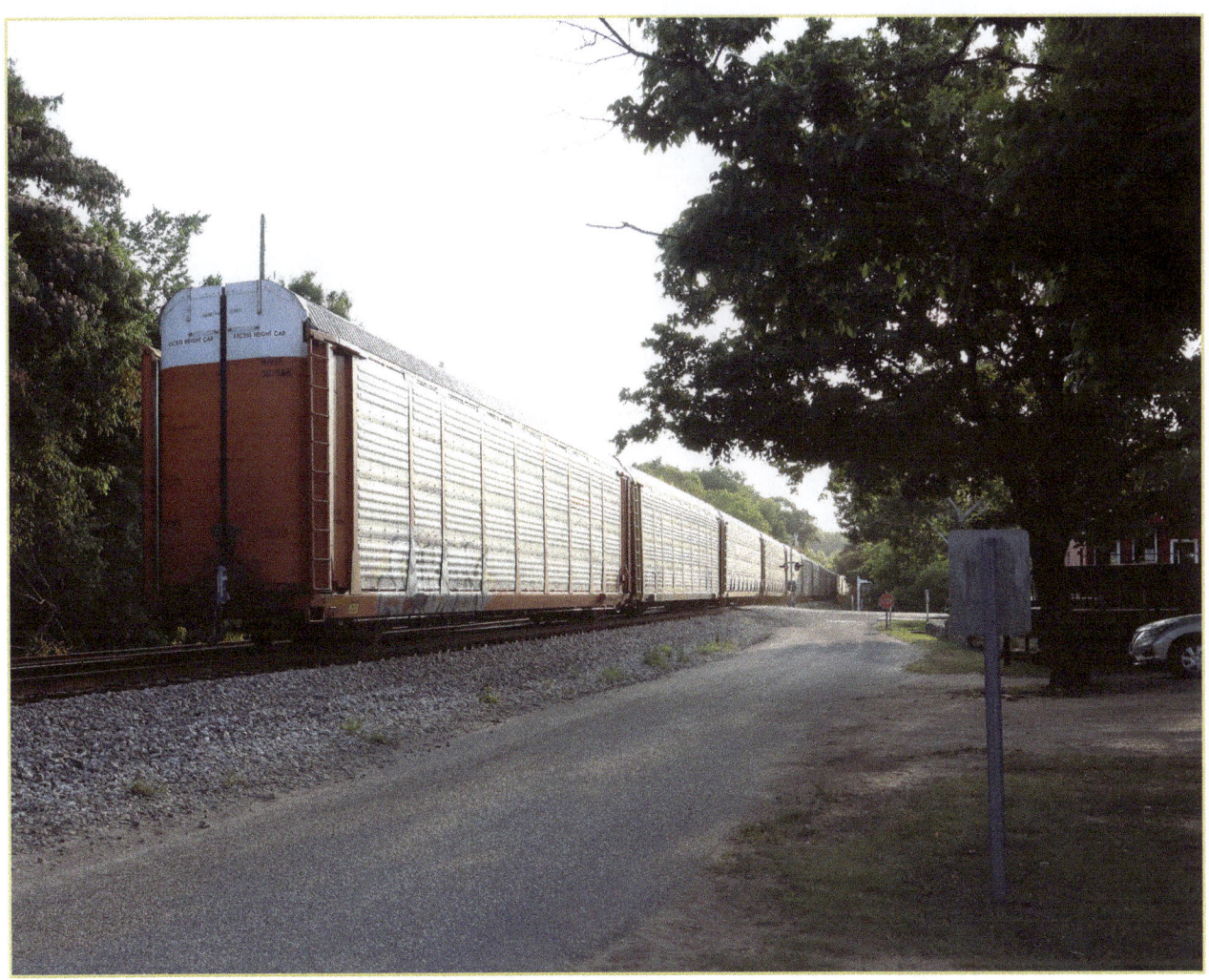

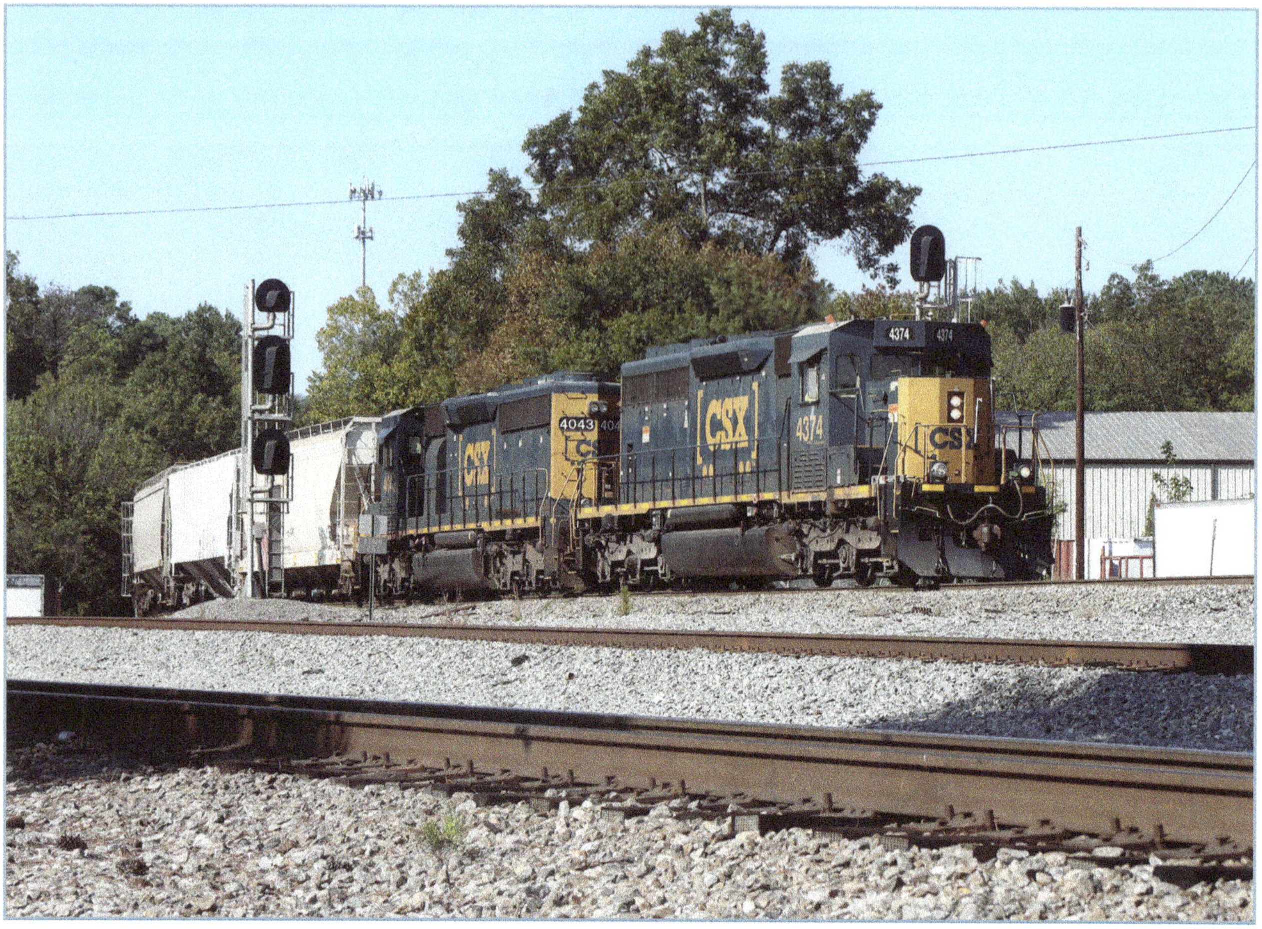

Two CSX SD40-3 Locomotives pull the local train from Boyles Yard into Norris Yard.

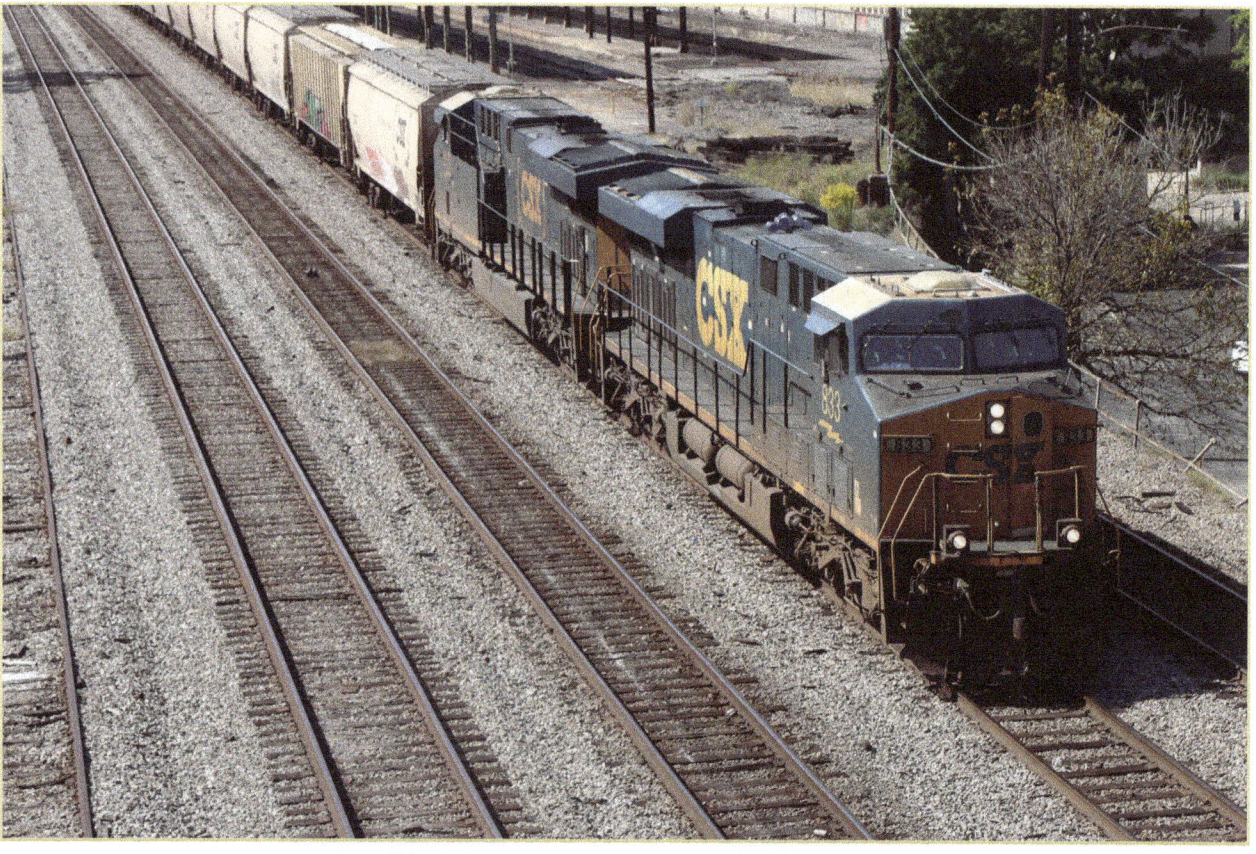

A CSX grain train arrives in Birmingham on a sunny morning.

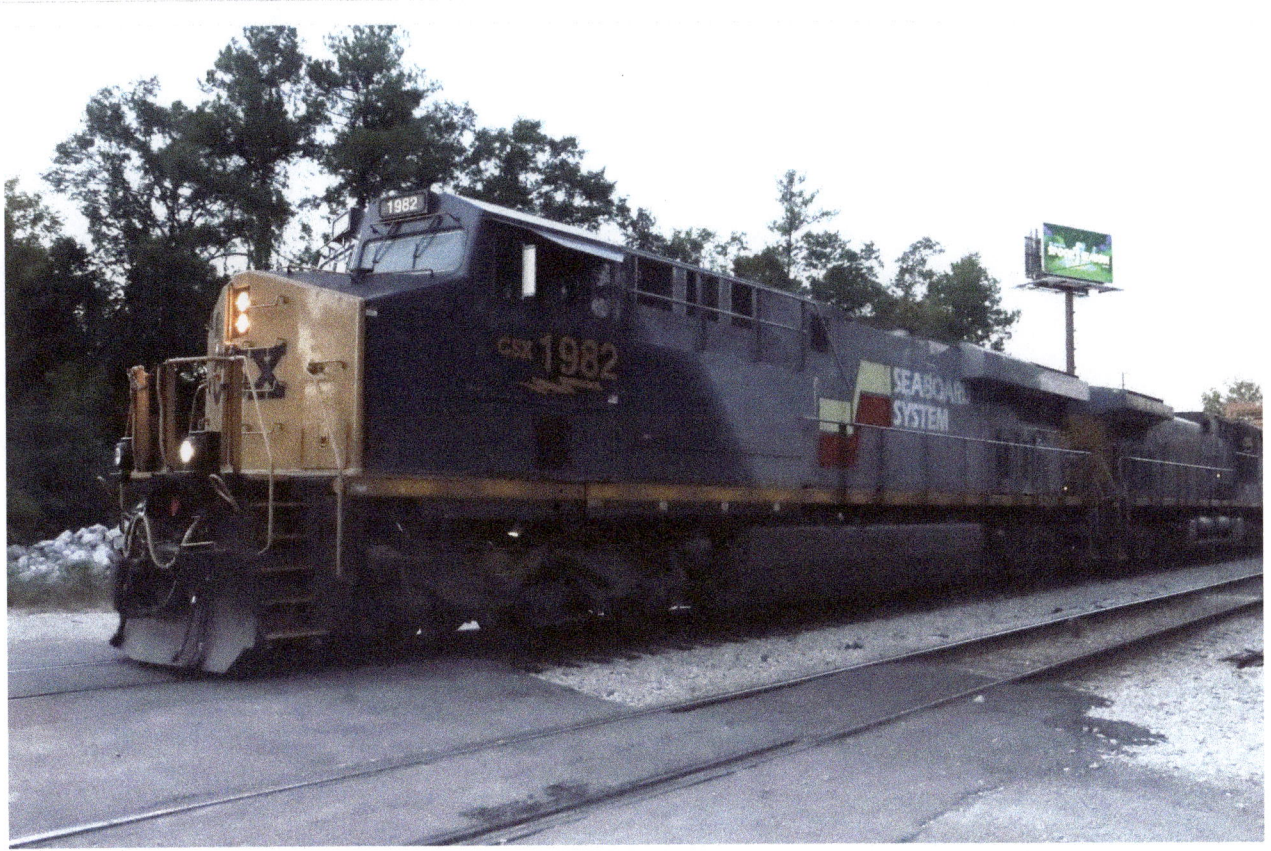
CSX 1982, the Seaboard System heritage unit pulls an eastbound intermodal train toward Georgia.

THE HUNTSVILLE AND MADISON COUNTY RAILROAD AUTHORITY

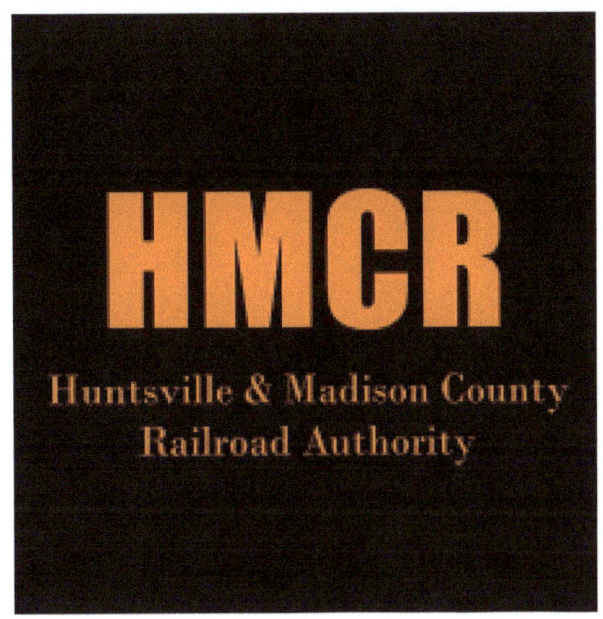

The Huntsville and Madison County Railroad Authority is a shortline railroad created to operate on around 13 miles of track that was abandoned by the Louisville and Nashville railroad. The line it operates on was originally built by the NC&StL Railroad, but was abandoned by the L&N due to it being unprofitable for the larger railroad, making it a prime target for shortlines. The Railroad began operation in 1984 with two EMD end-cab switchers. In 2015, HMCR retired the historic EMD switchers and acquired an all-GE locomotive roster, consisting of a former L&N U23-B locomotive, two B23-7, and four B39-8 locomotives. The railroad primarily hauls commodities in covered hopper cars which you can see in their "yard" right next to the offices of the railroad. The line it runs on interchanges with the Norfolk Southern around a quarter of a mile past their offices.

HMCR's 9554: This aging behemoth is a General Electric U23B, built between 1968 and 1977 and pulling with an impressive-for-the-time engine that reached 2,250 horsepower. This particular unit was ordered by the Louisville and Nashville Railroad with 89 other units, and numbered 2800. After the L&N merged with the Seaboard System, 9554 remained in service with the same number until CSXT was created. CSXT renumbered it as 3301 and painted it orange to show that the locomotive had less power than others. It was finally sold to the HMCR and repainted in their orange-and-black livery. It now serves with other aging GE units serving the city of Huntsville diligently until they are finally sold to museums or scrapped.

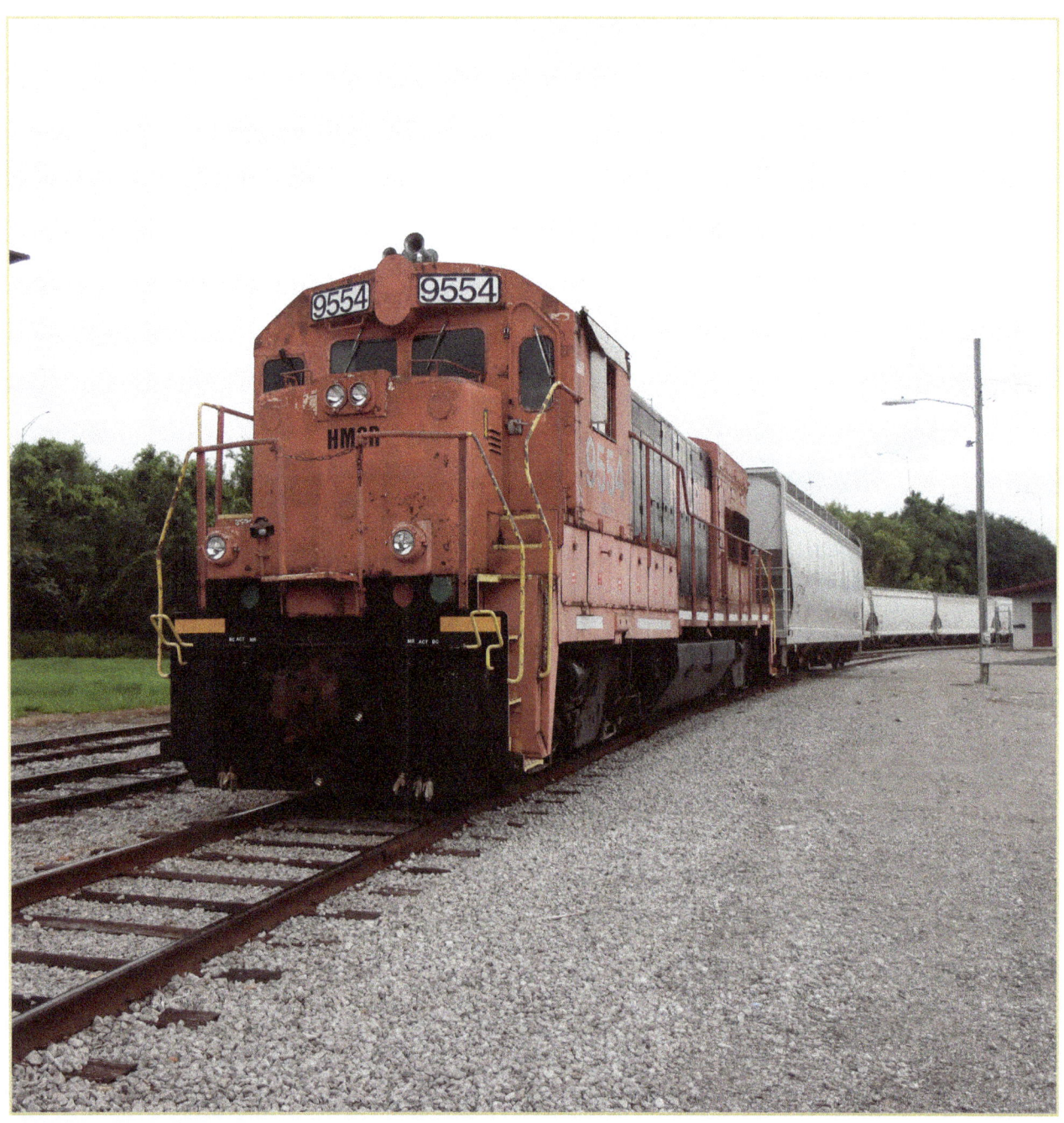

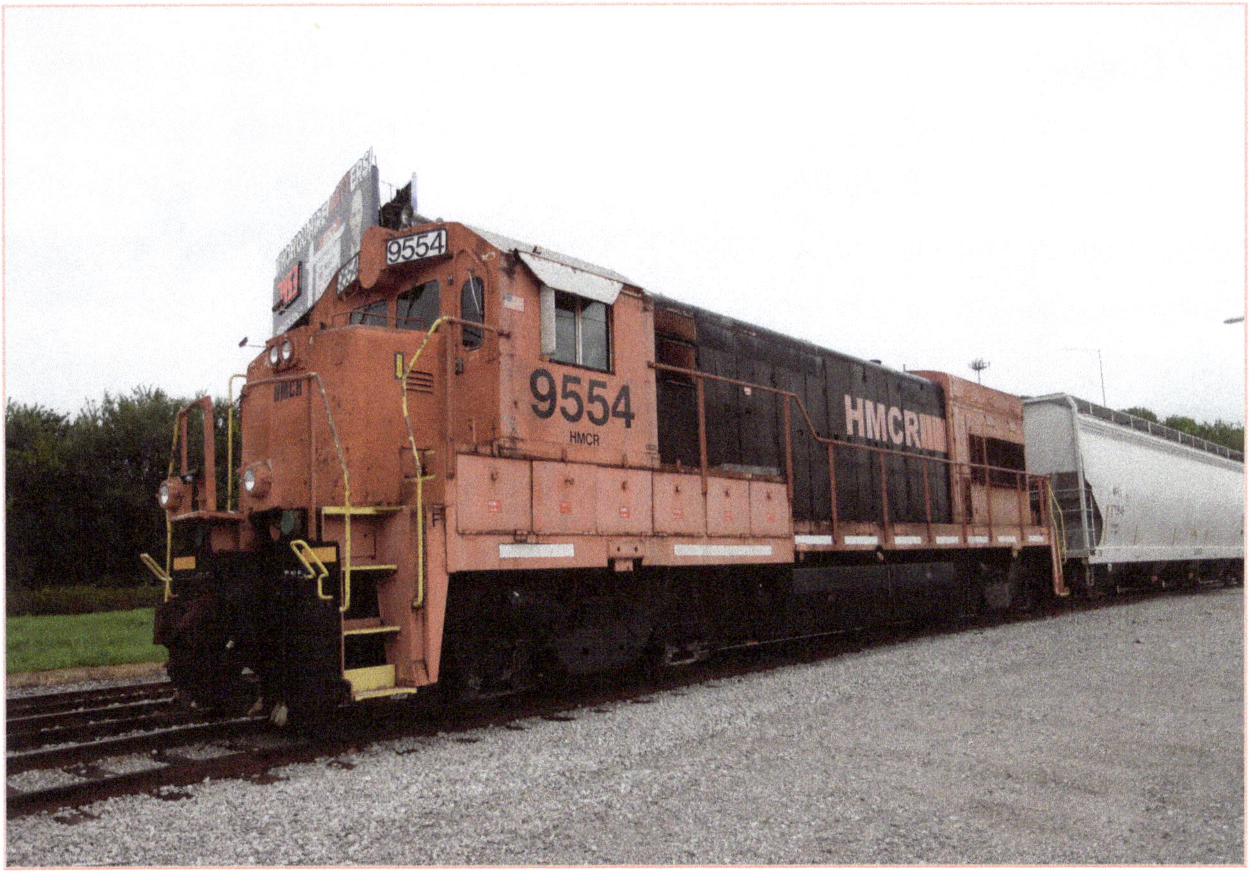

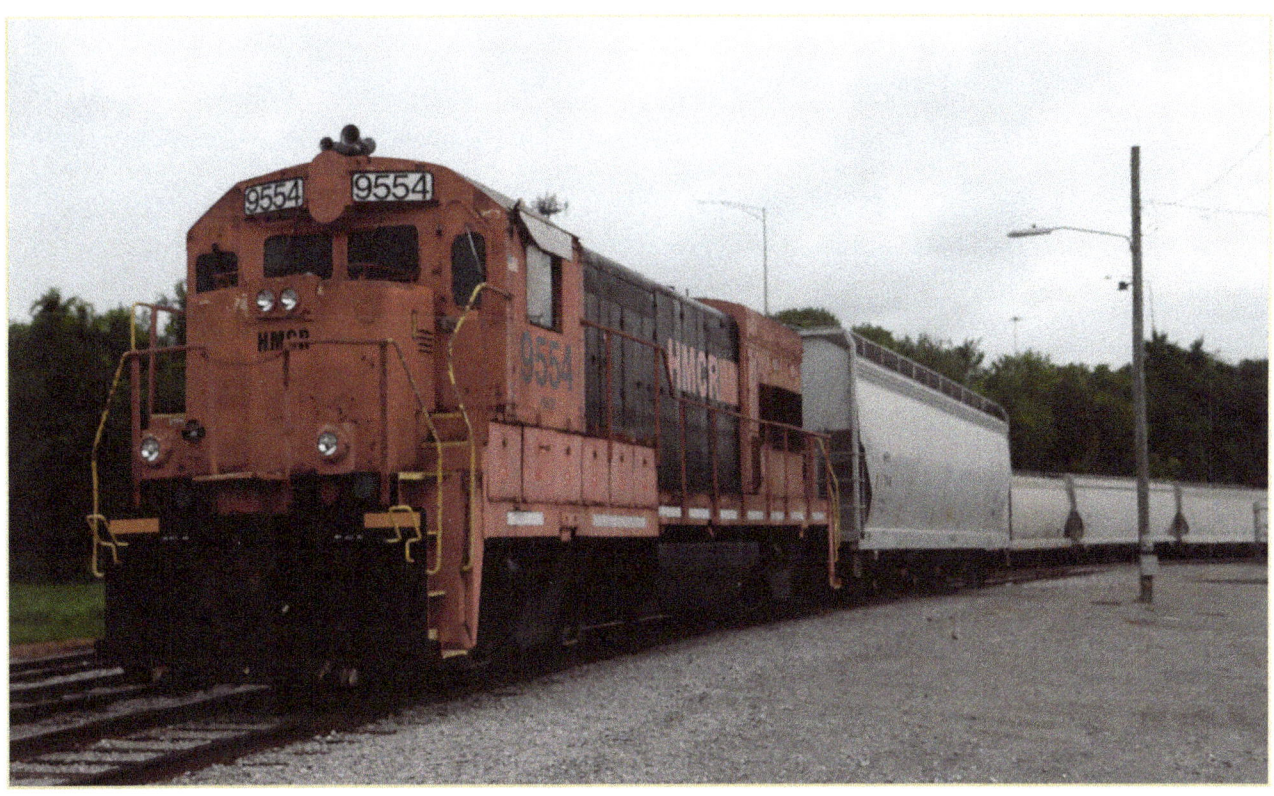

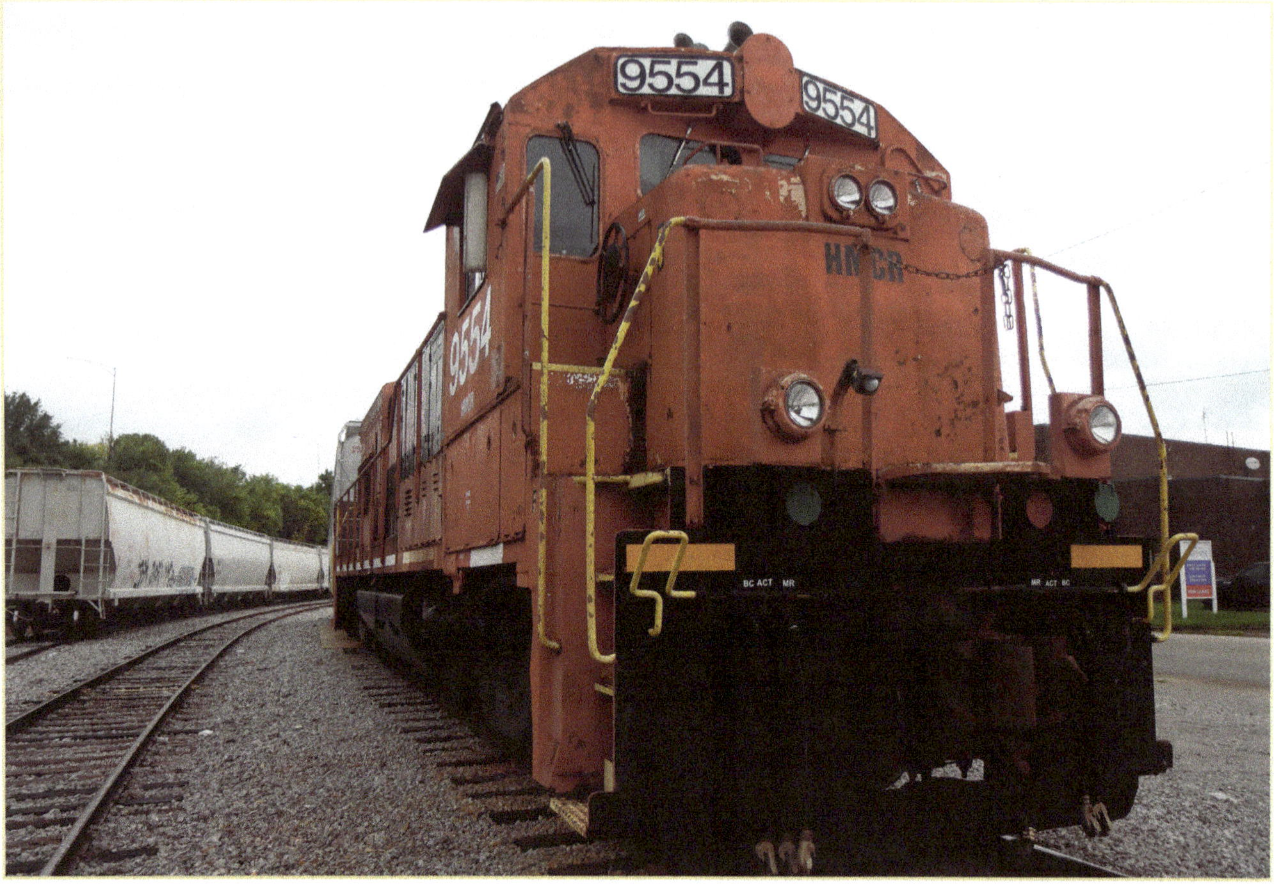

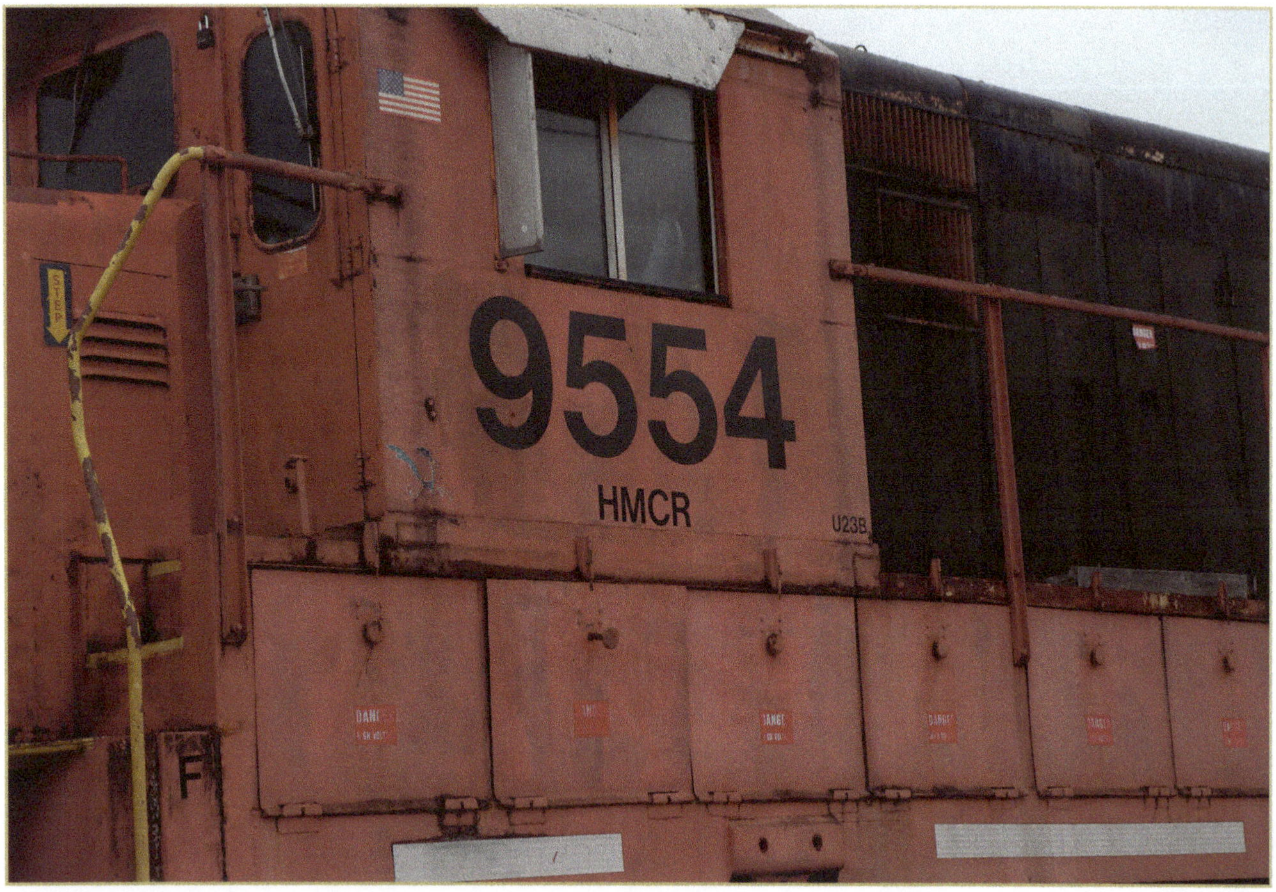

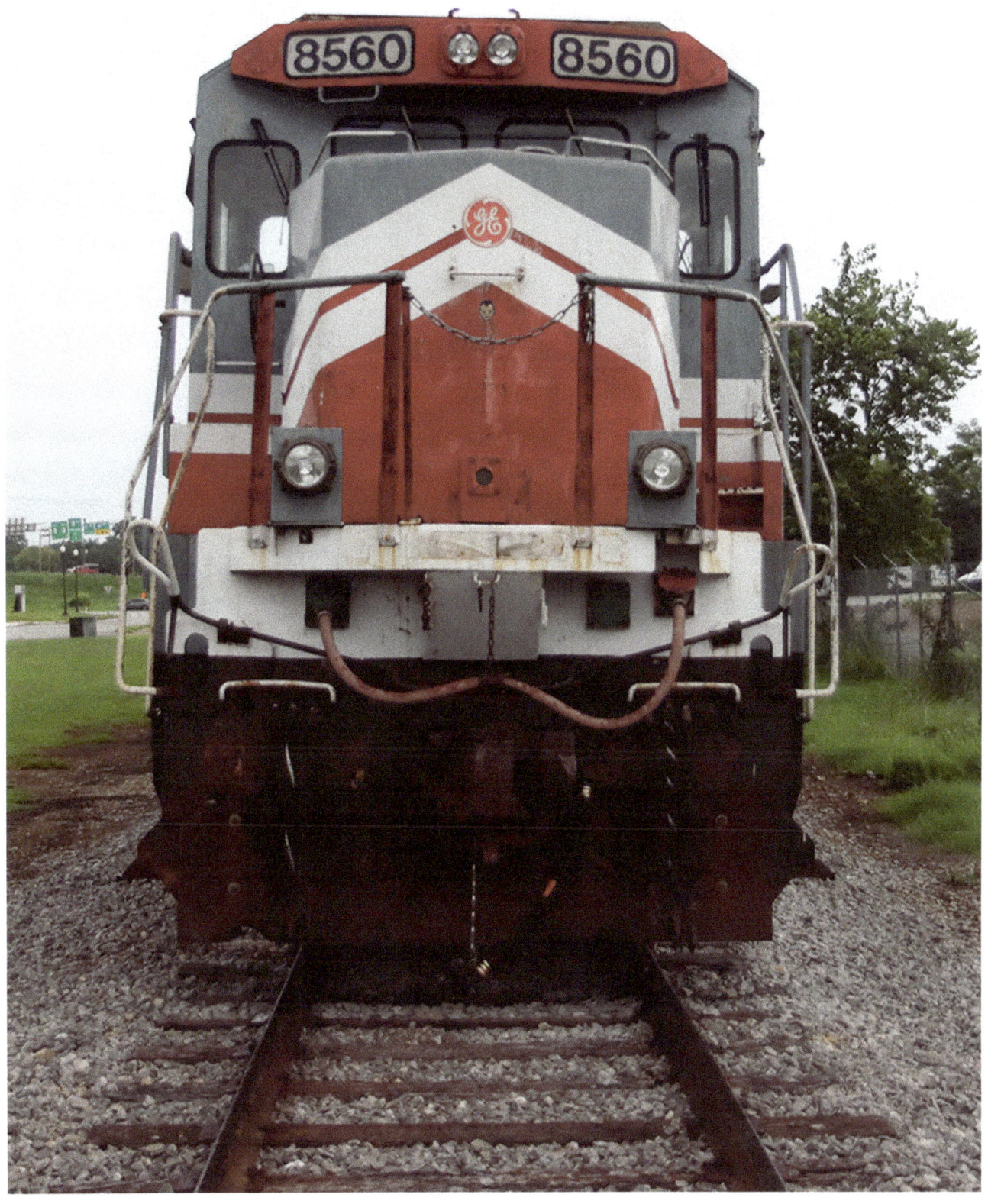

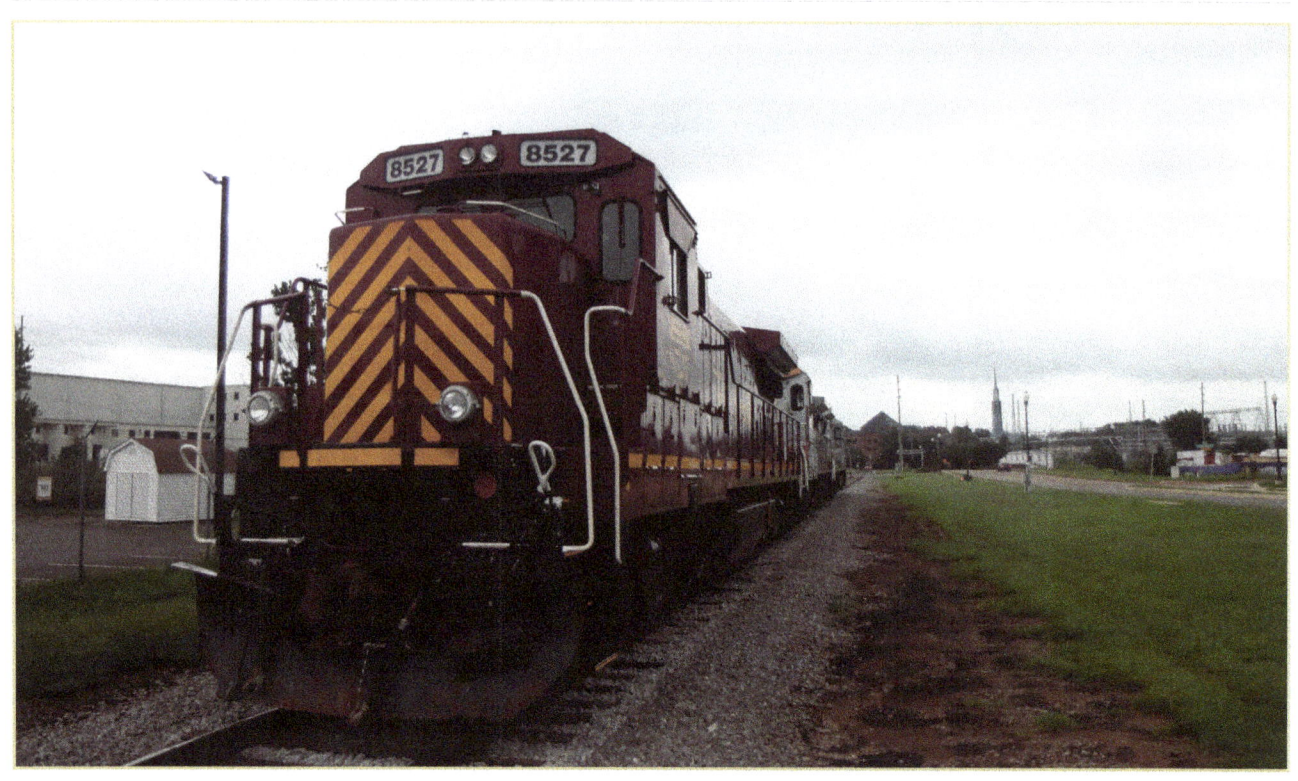

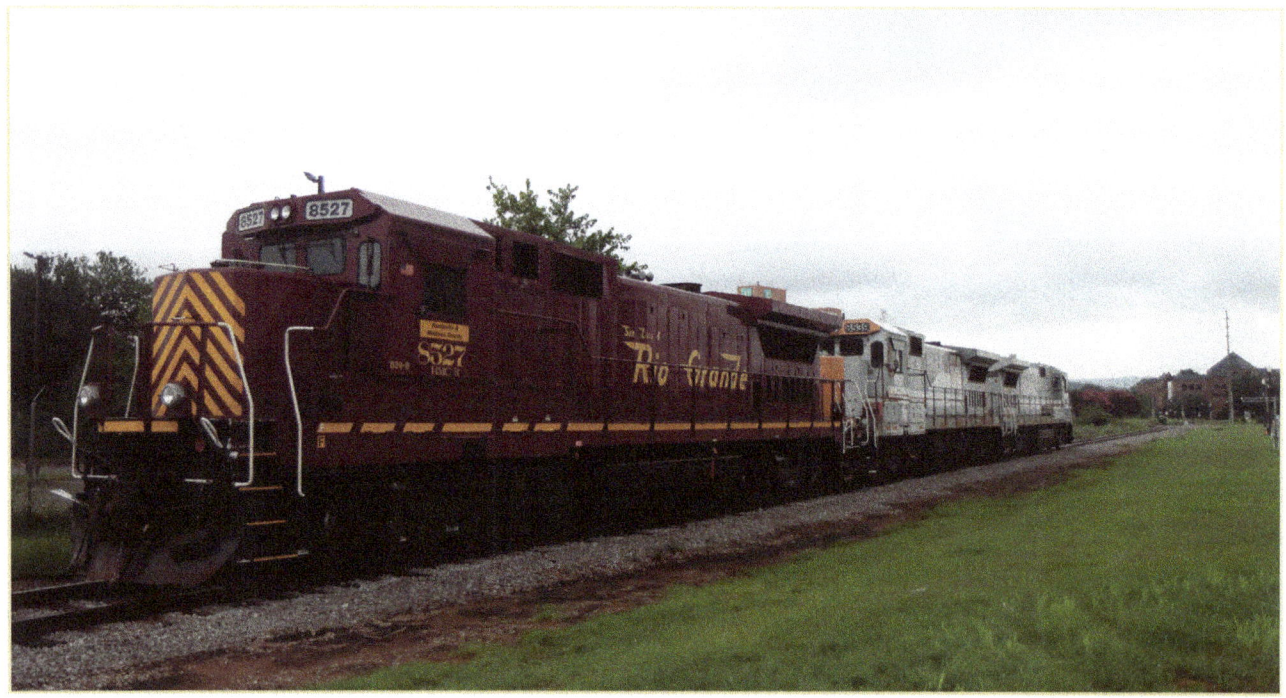

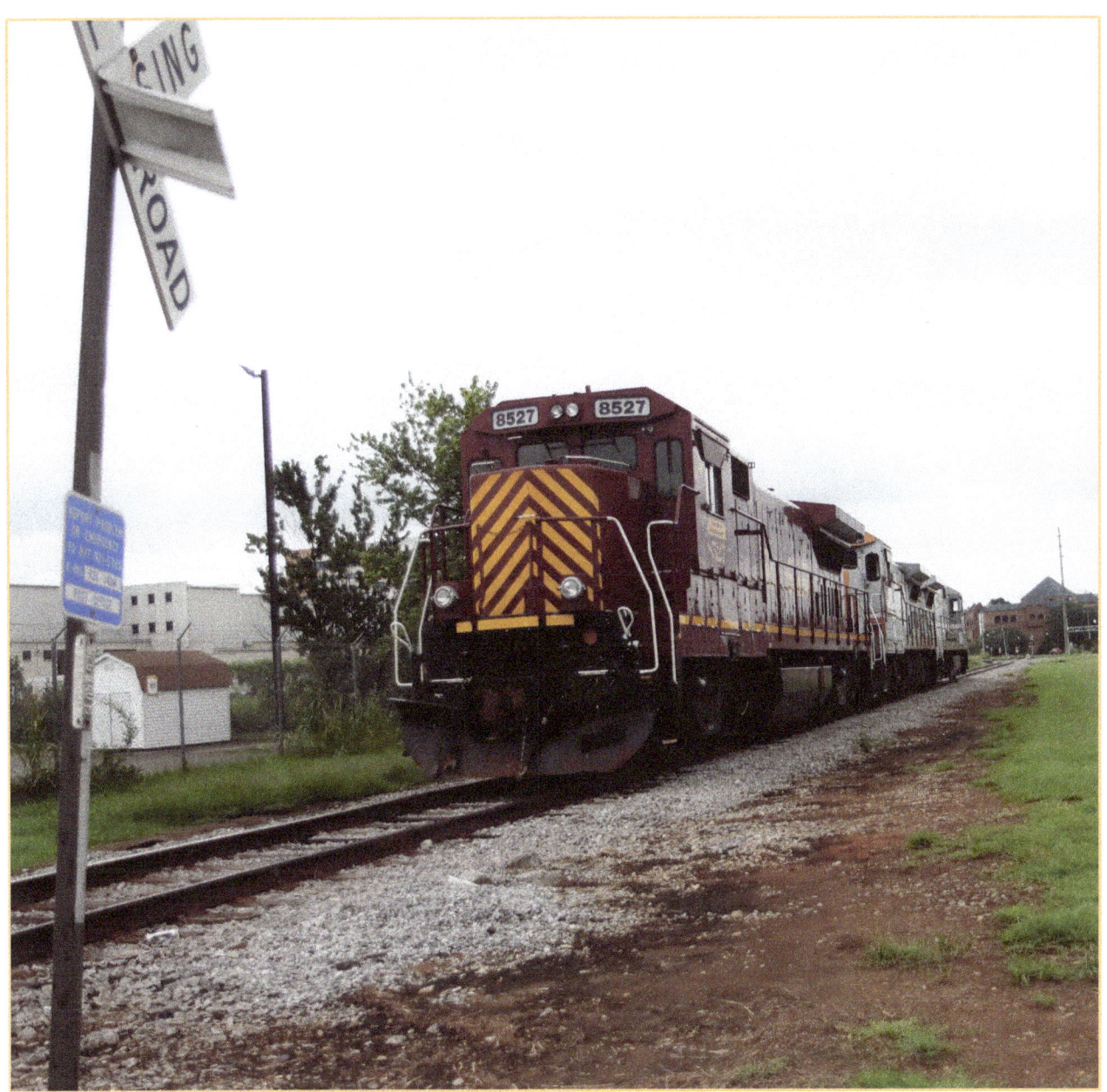

HMCR 8527, a B40-8 originally owned by San Luis & Rio Grande Railroad, sits idle in downtown Huntsville.

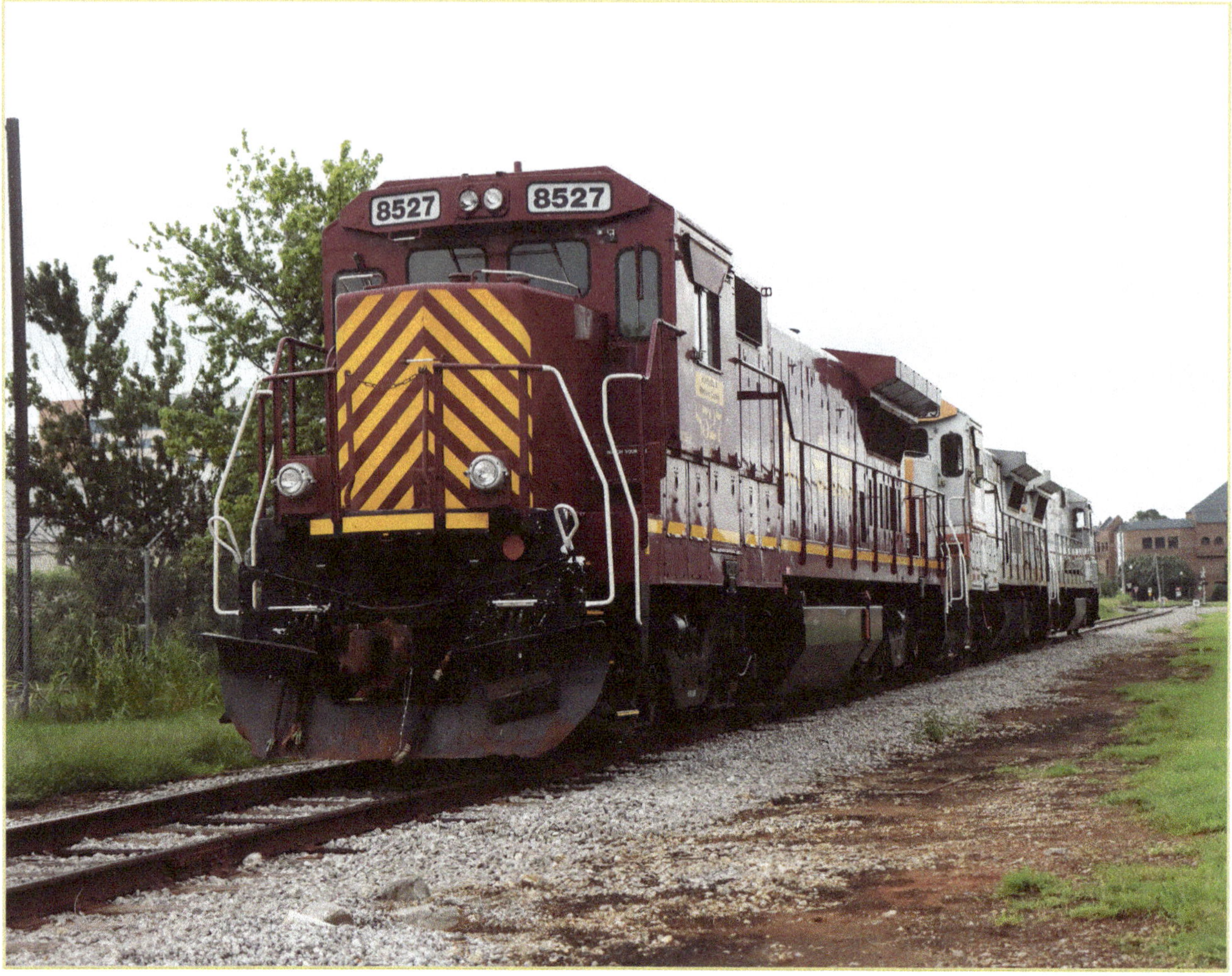

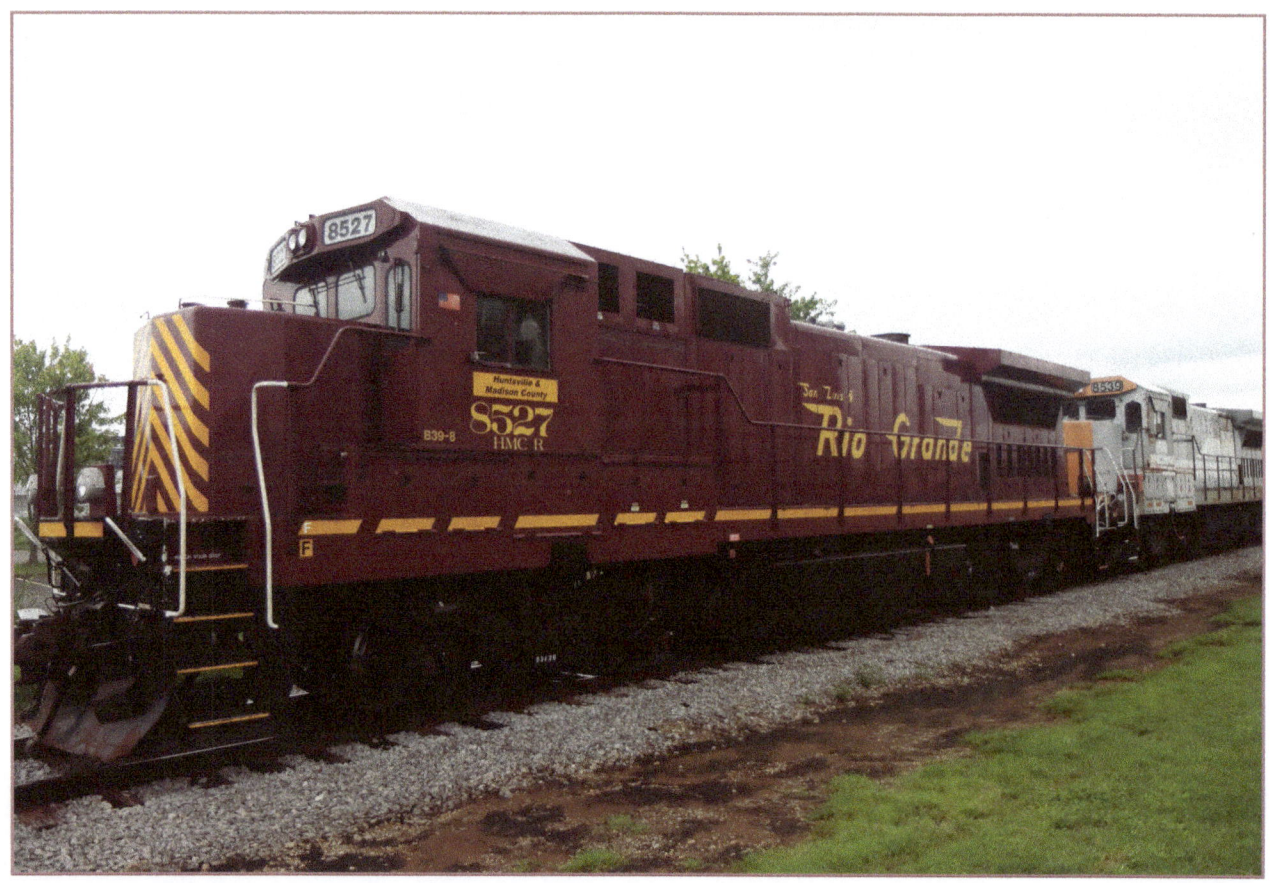

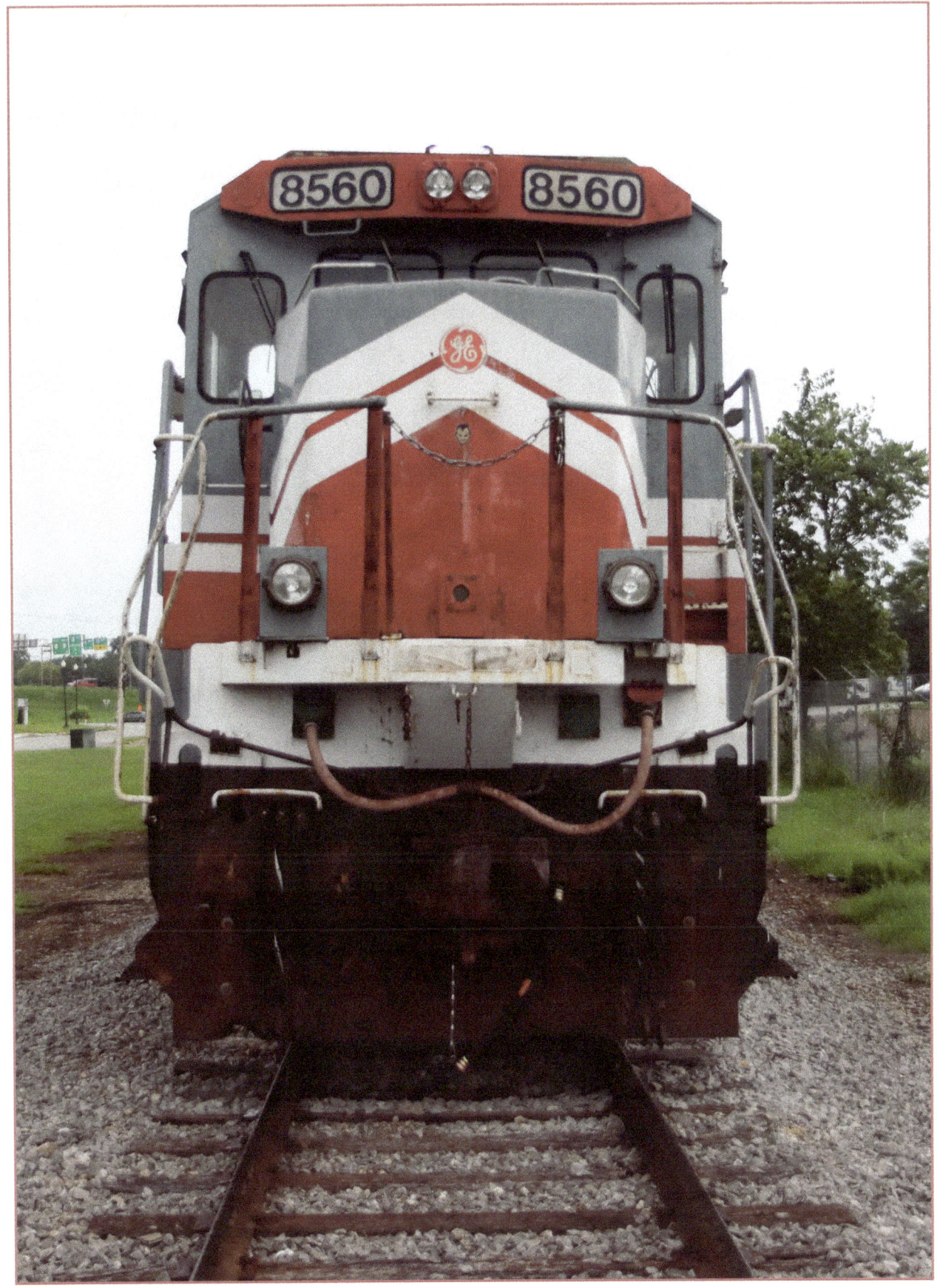

HMCR 8560, still in its GE demonstrator livery, sits in downtown Huntsville with another B40 with the same livery.

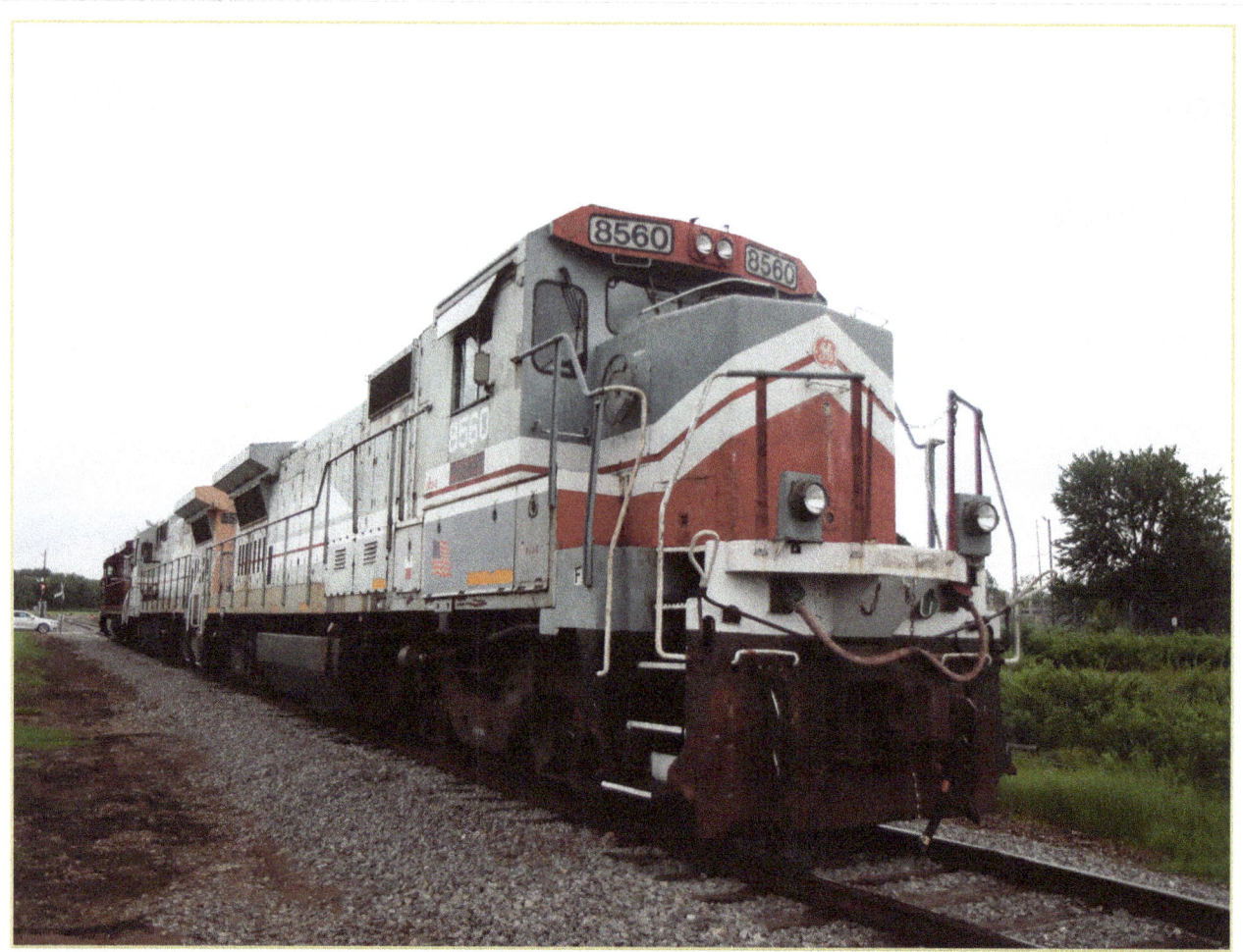

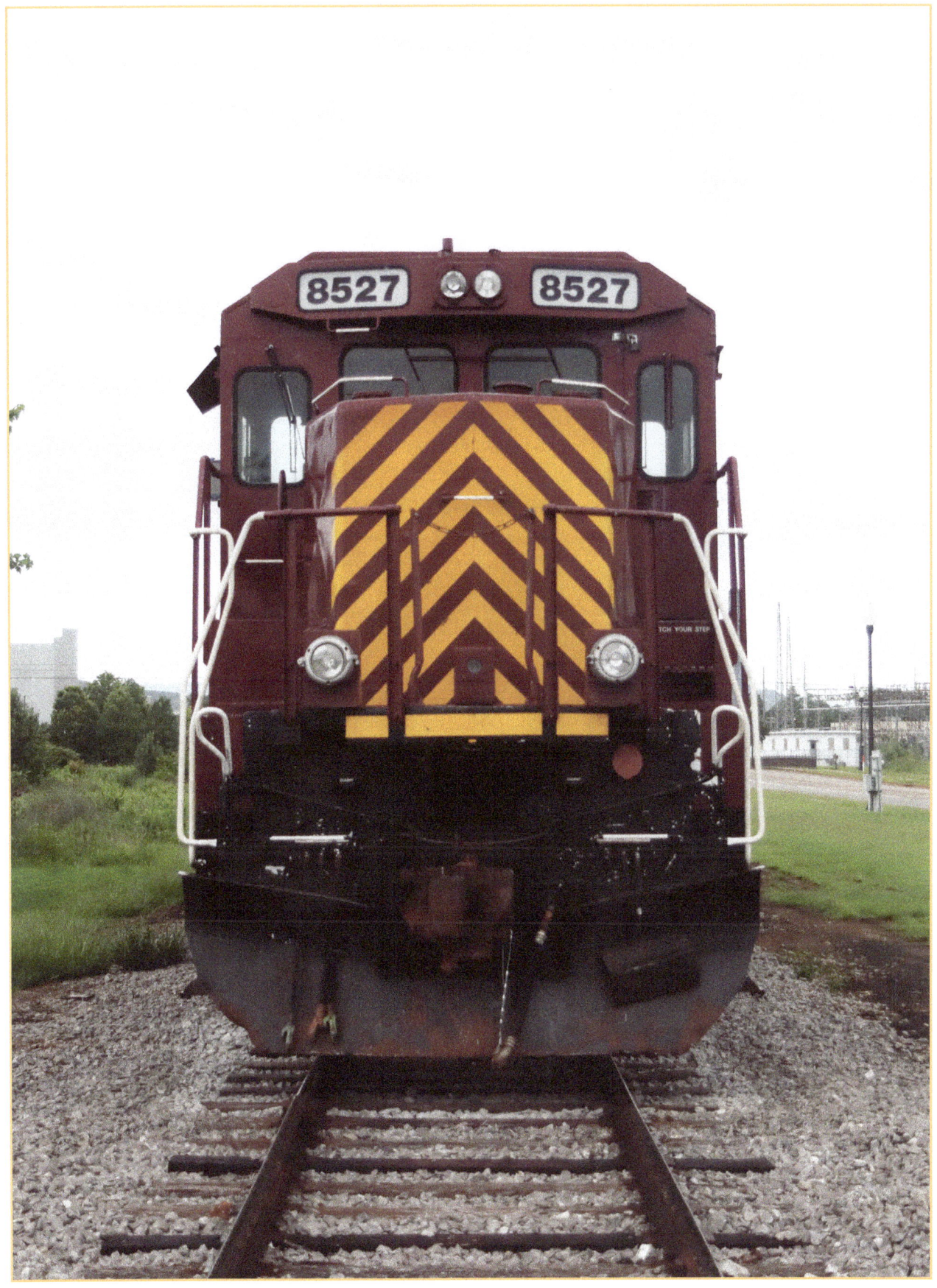

THE ALABAMA AND TENNESSEE RIVER RAILROAD

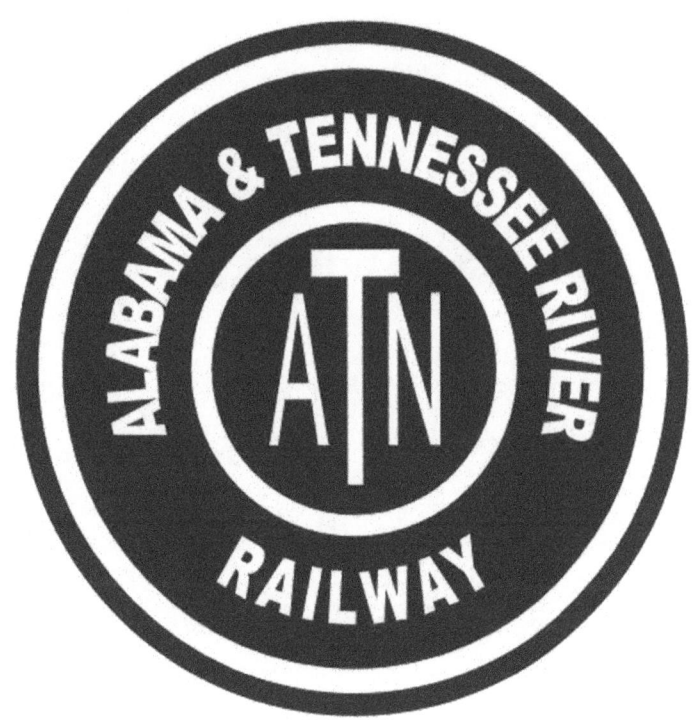

Created in 2004 after a lease of former CSX track, The Alabama and Tennessee River Railroad is a shortline railroad operating mainly between Gadsden and Birmingham, Alabama, but the railroad also leads up to Guntersville, Alabama, and serves the port there. A car ferry used to go across the Tennessee River and provide it access to Huntsville, but has since been abandoned. Headquartered in Gadsden, the railroad is an OmniTrax company. The headquarters in Gadsden are right next to the company's yard and has access to the Norfolk Southern main along with the Gadsden Industrial Park. However, since most of the Industrial Park is now abandoned, the spur is almost never used. The company's locomotive roster consists of all EMD locomotives, notably having five tunnel motor locomotives, along with former Burlington Northern, CSX, Southern Pacific, and Canadian National locomotives. Others have been repainted to the point of not being able to tell what railroad they come from.

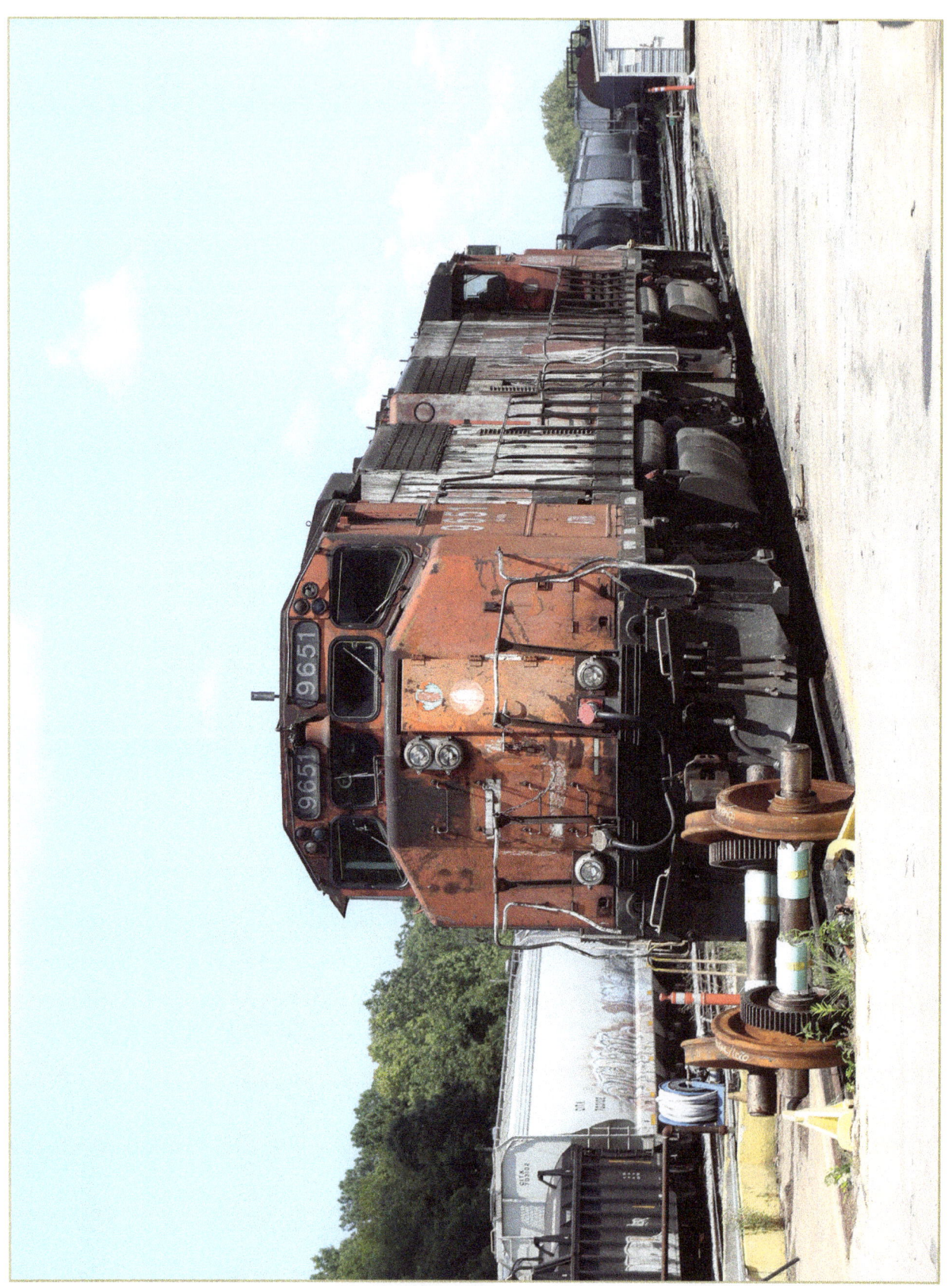

A pair of former Canadian National GP40s sits in the ATN Yard in Gadsden.

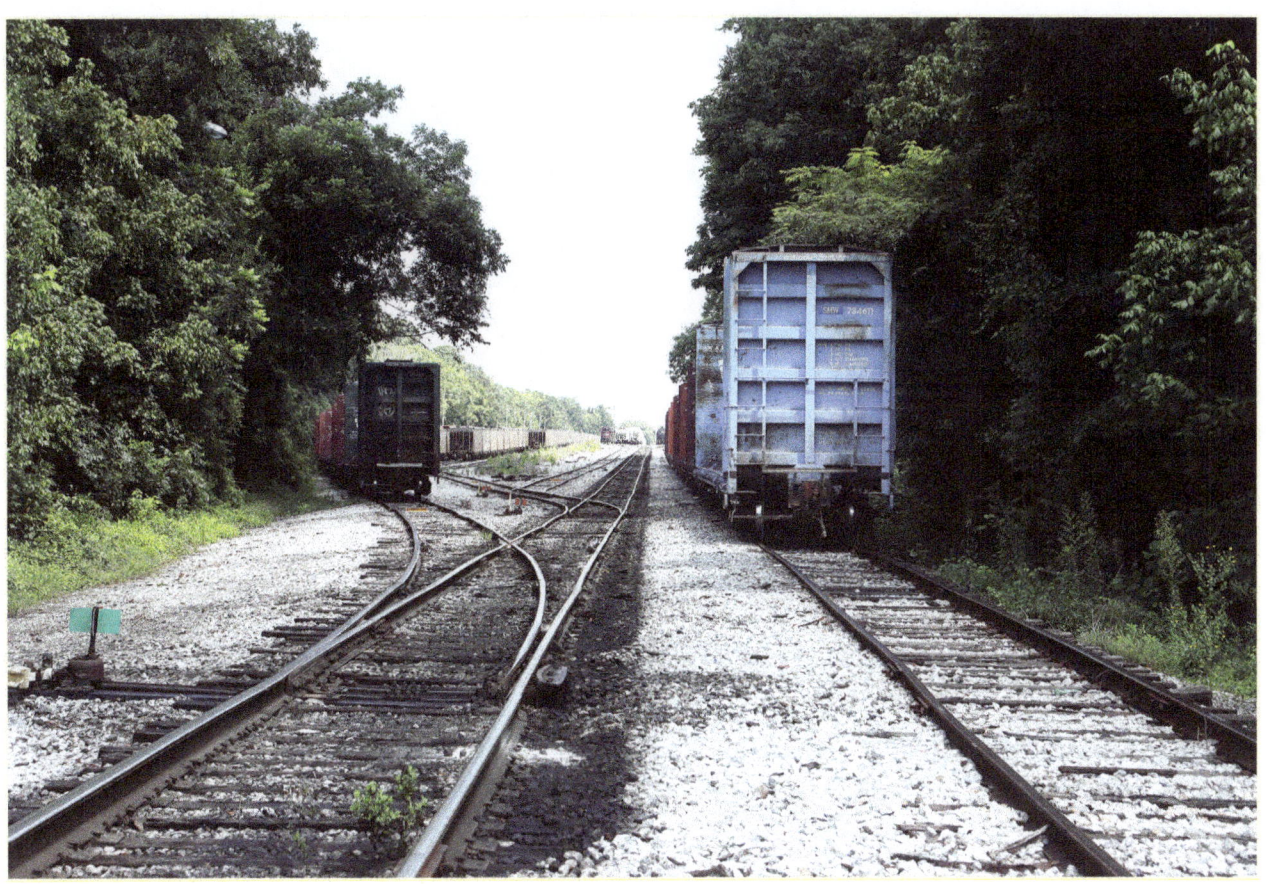

A view from one end of the ATN Yard in Gadsden.

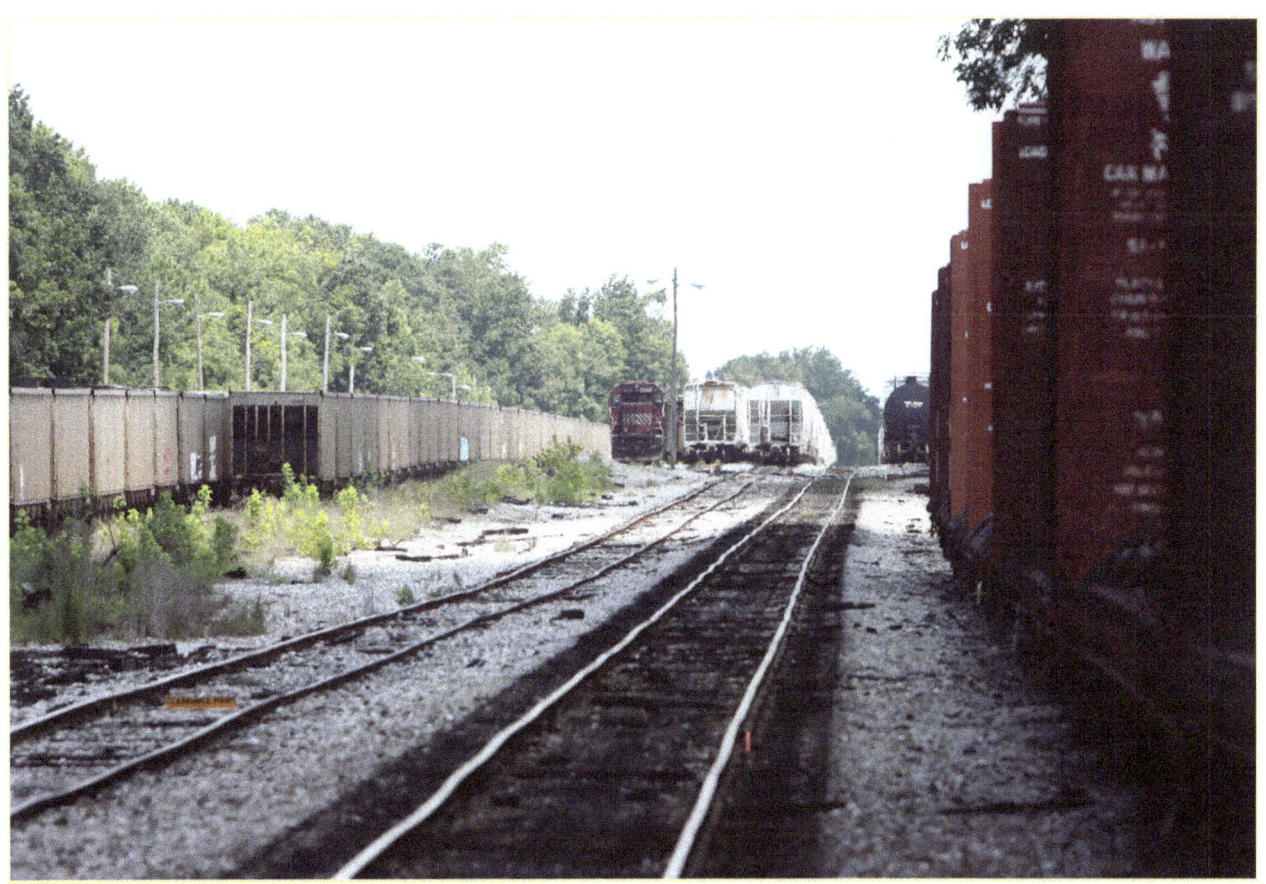

One of the ATN's EMD locomotives in the far end of the yard.

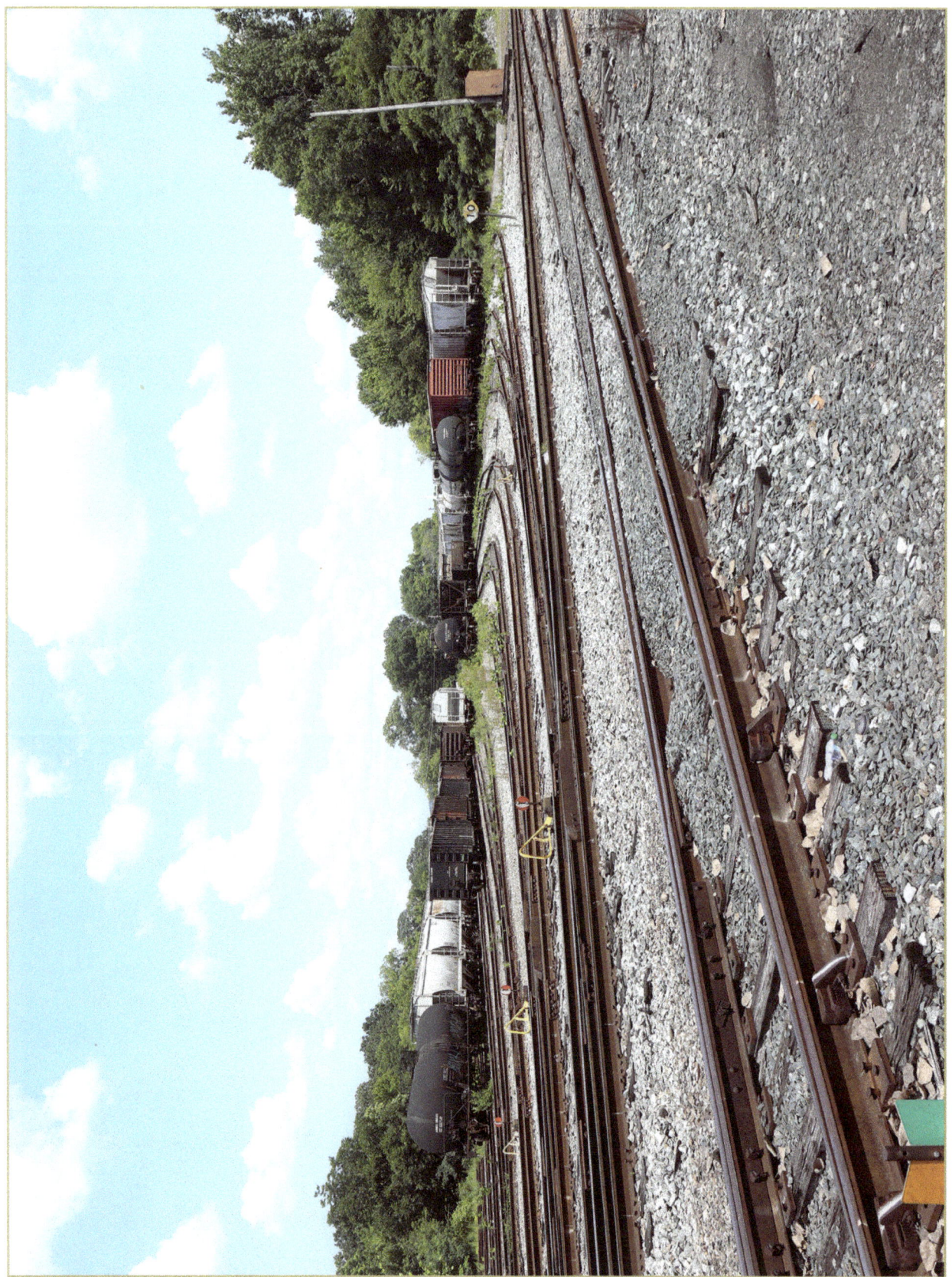

Storage tracks at the end of the ATN yard.

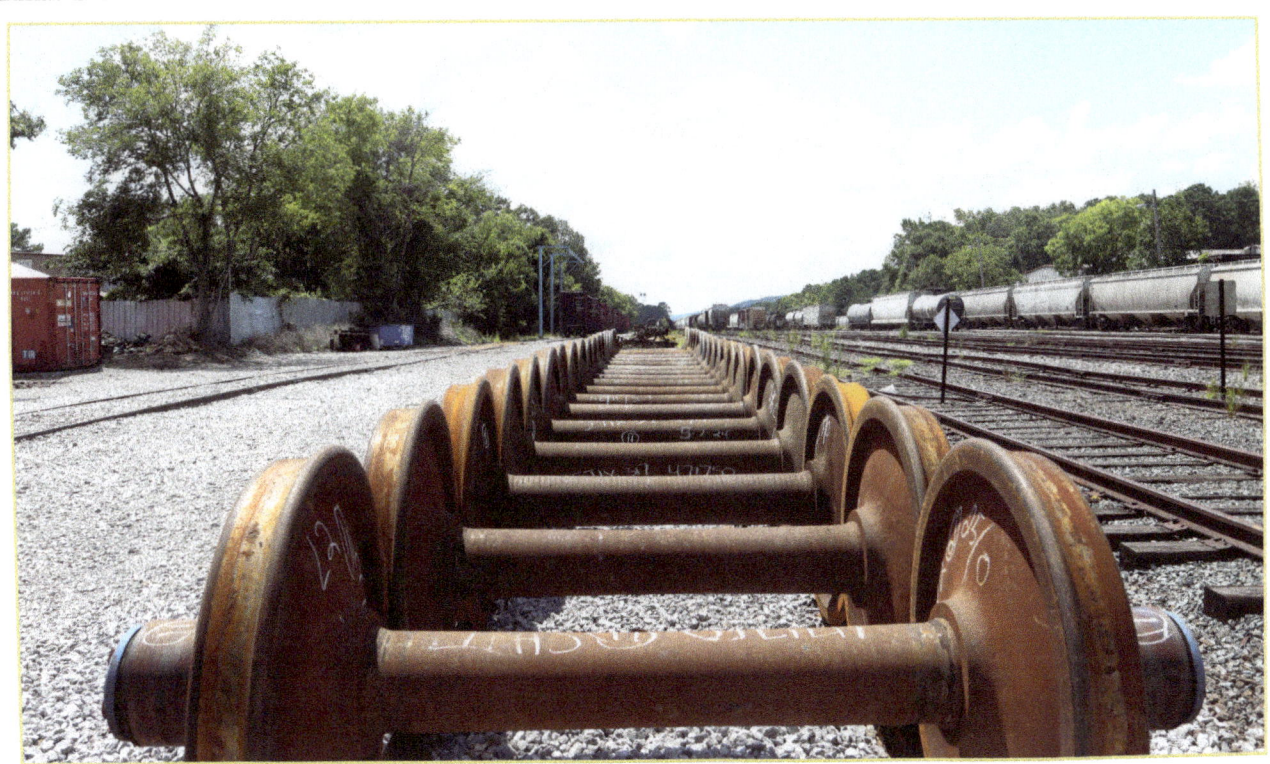

Spare wheels.

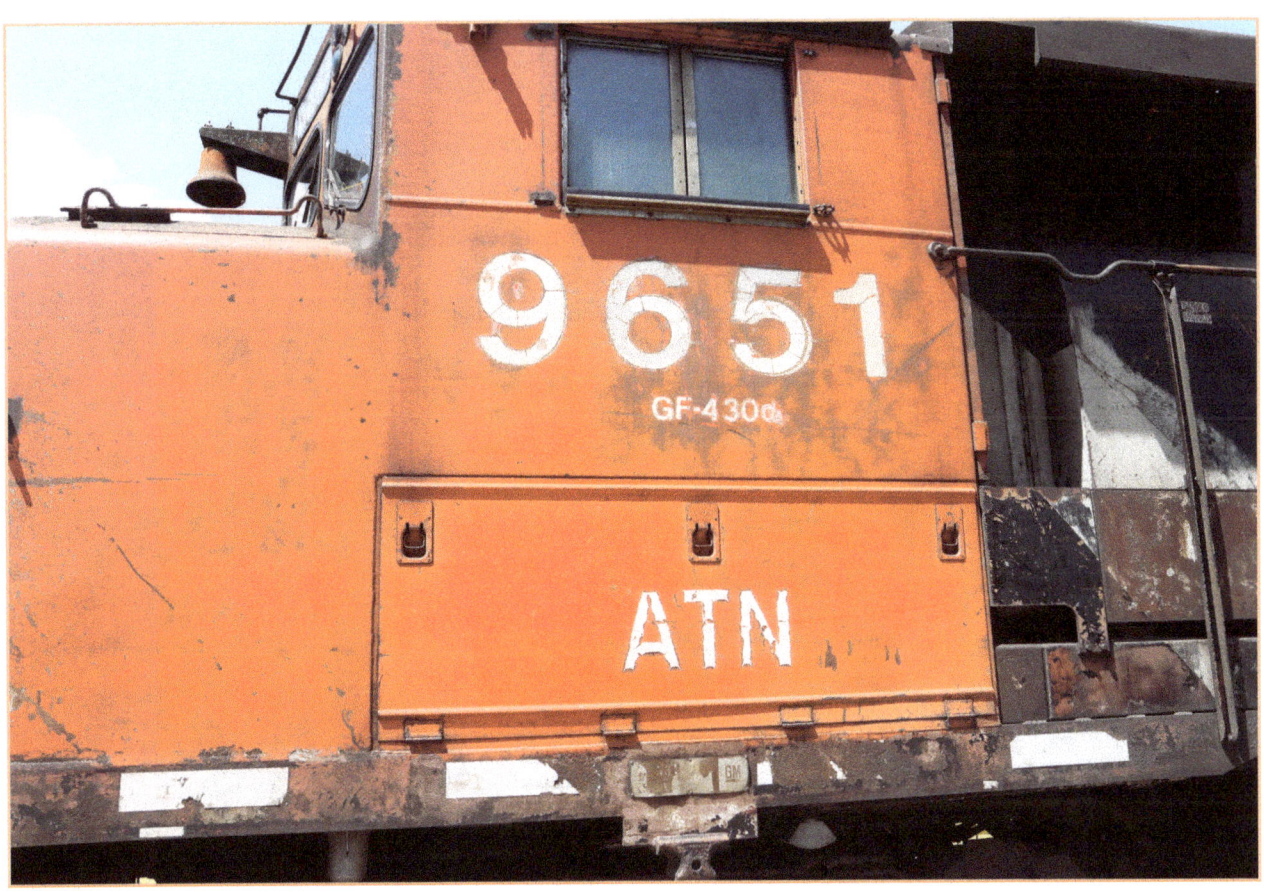

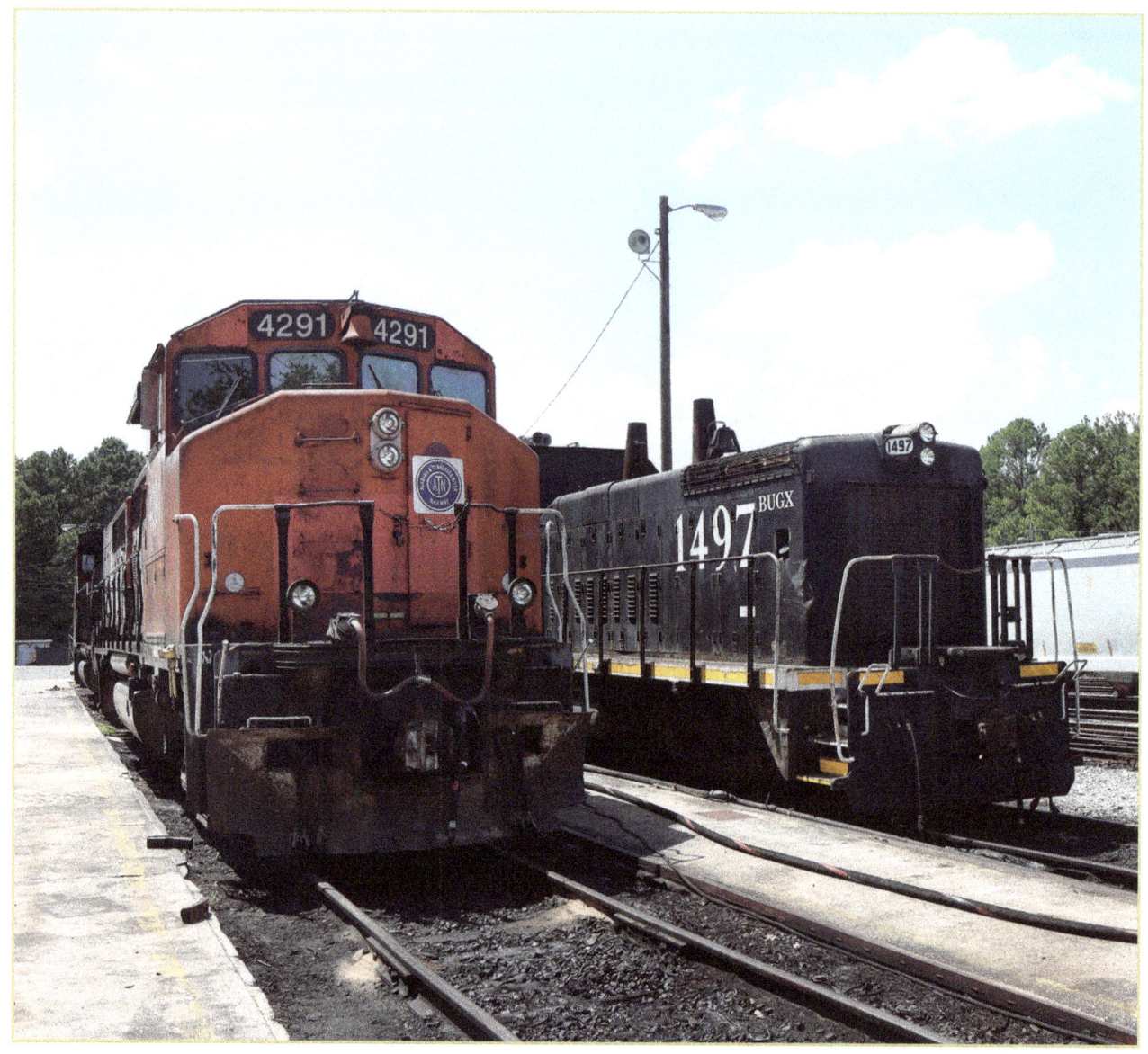

ATN SW14 1497 sits next to the two GP40s.

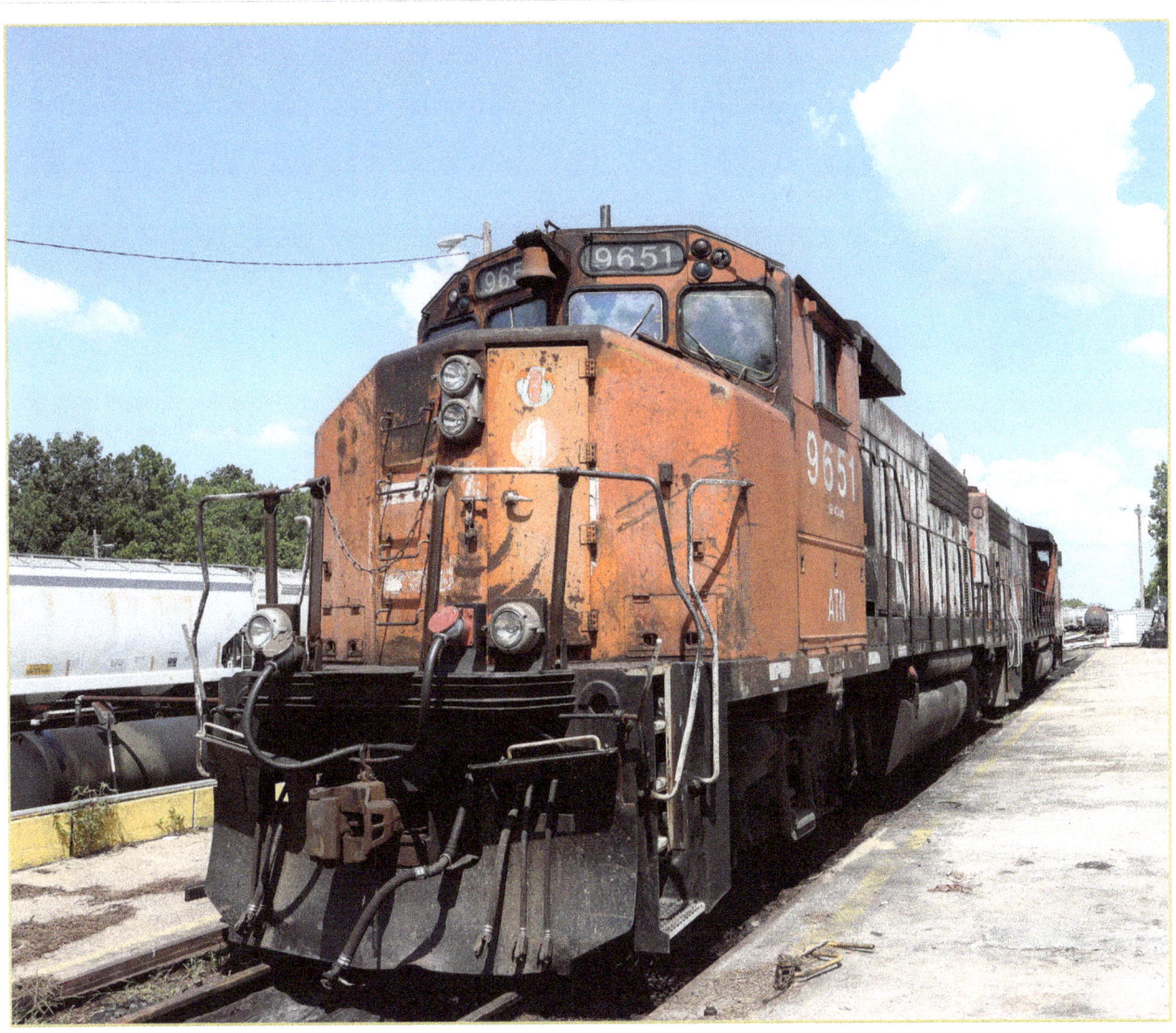

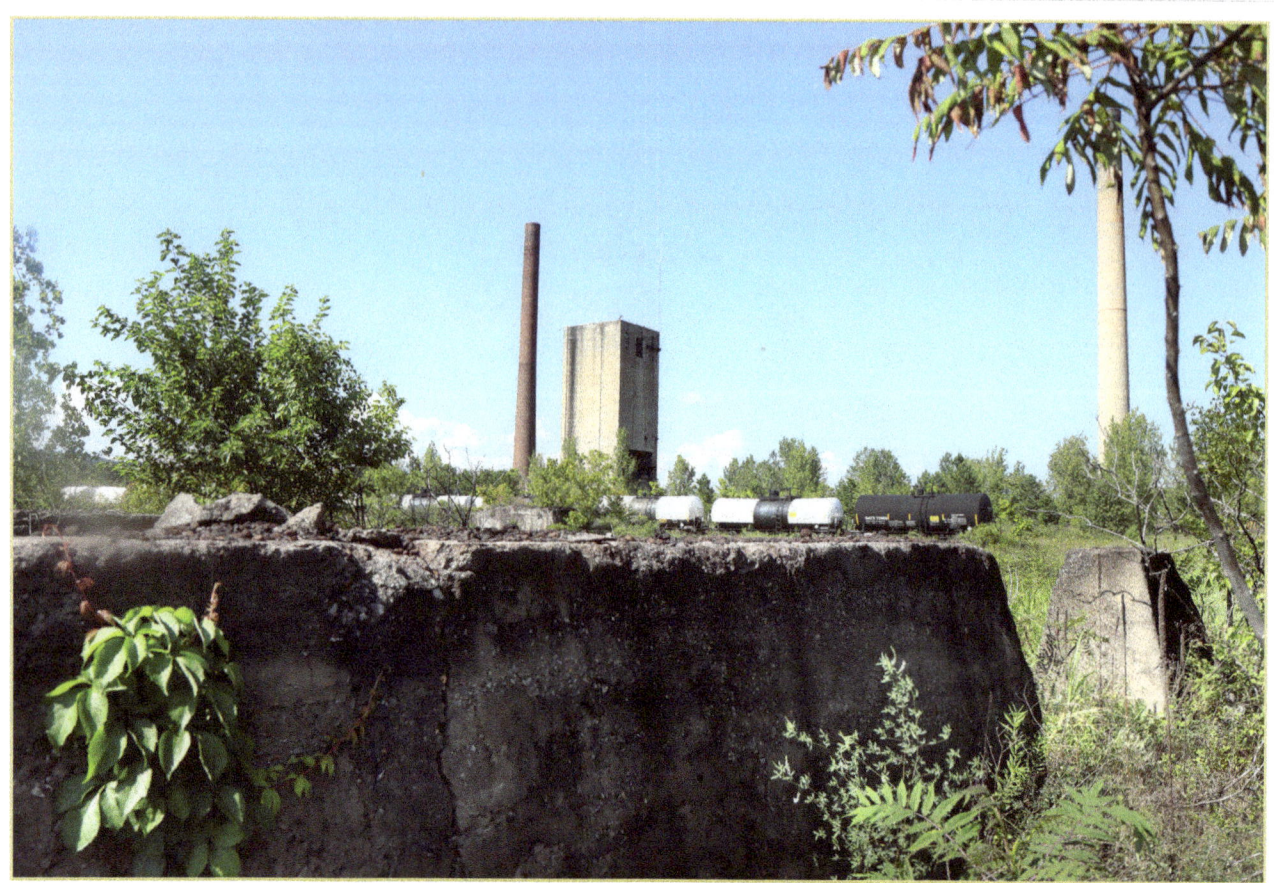
The view from inside the overgrown Gadsden Industrial Park. There used to be many industries inside that the ATN would serve, but most are abandoned now.

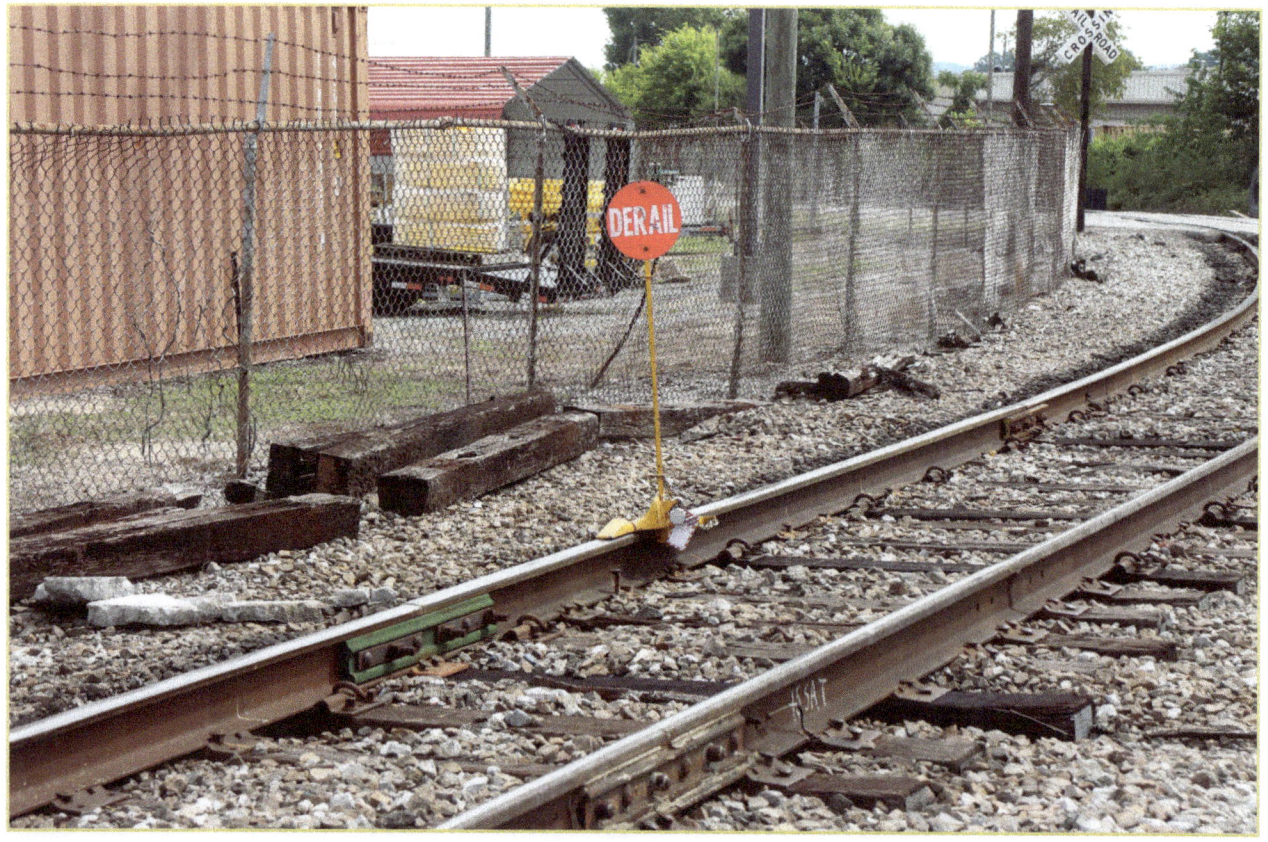
A derail set up by a track maintenance crew on the ATN's line.

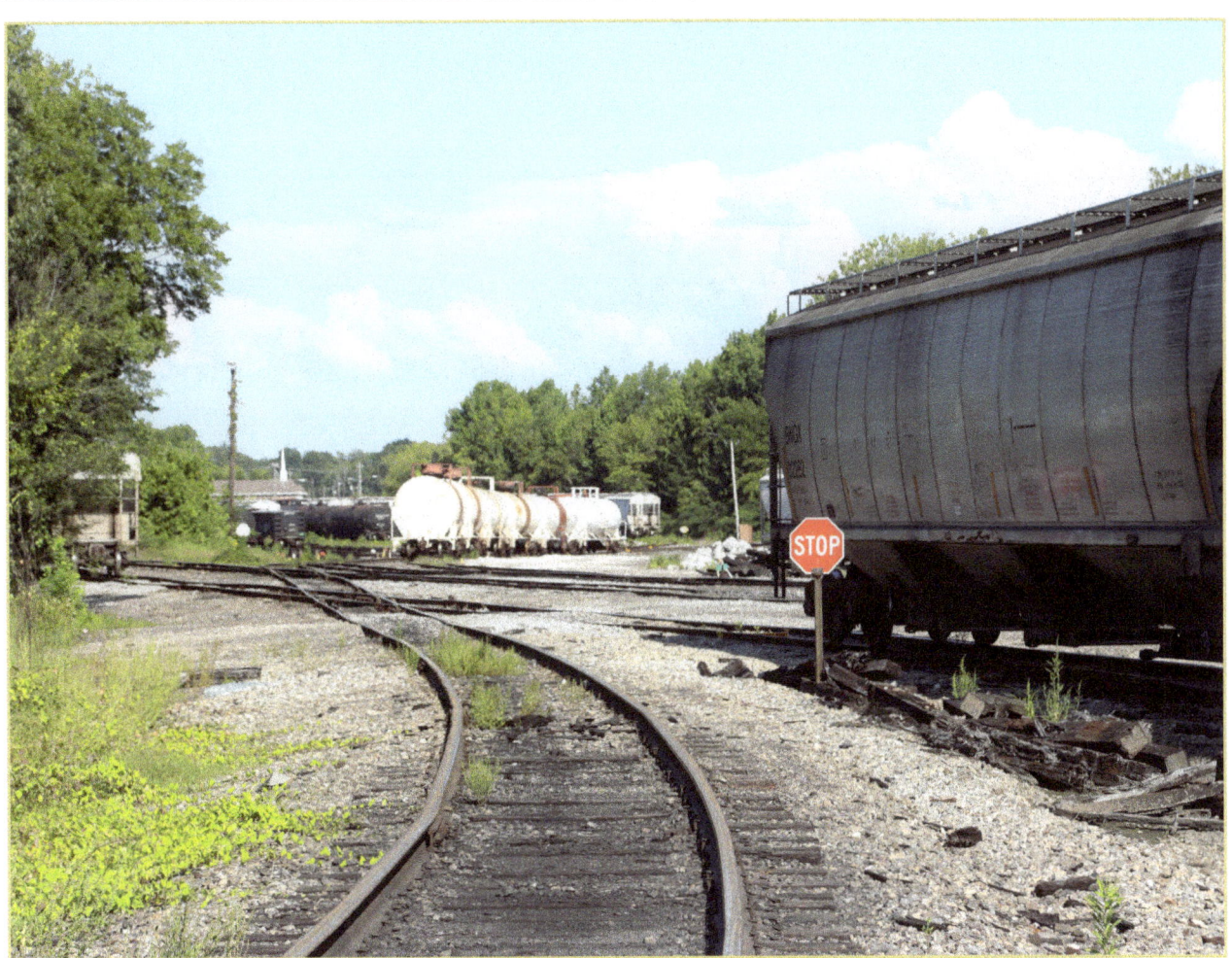
A spur track that leads into the ATN Yard.

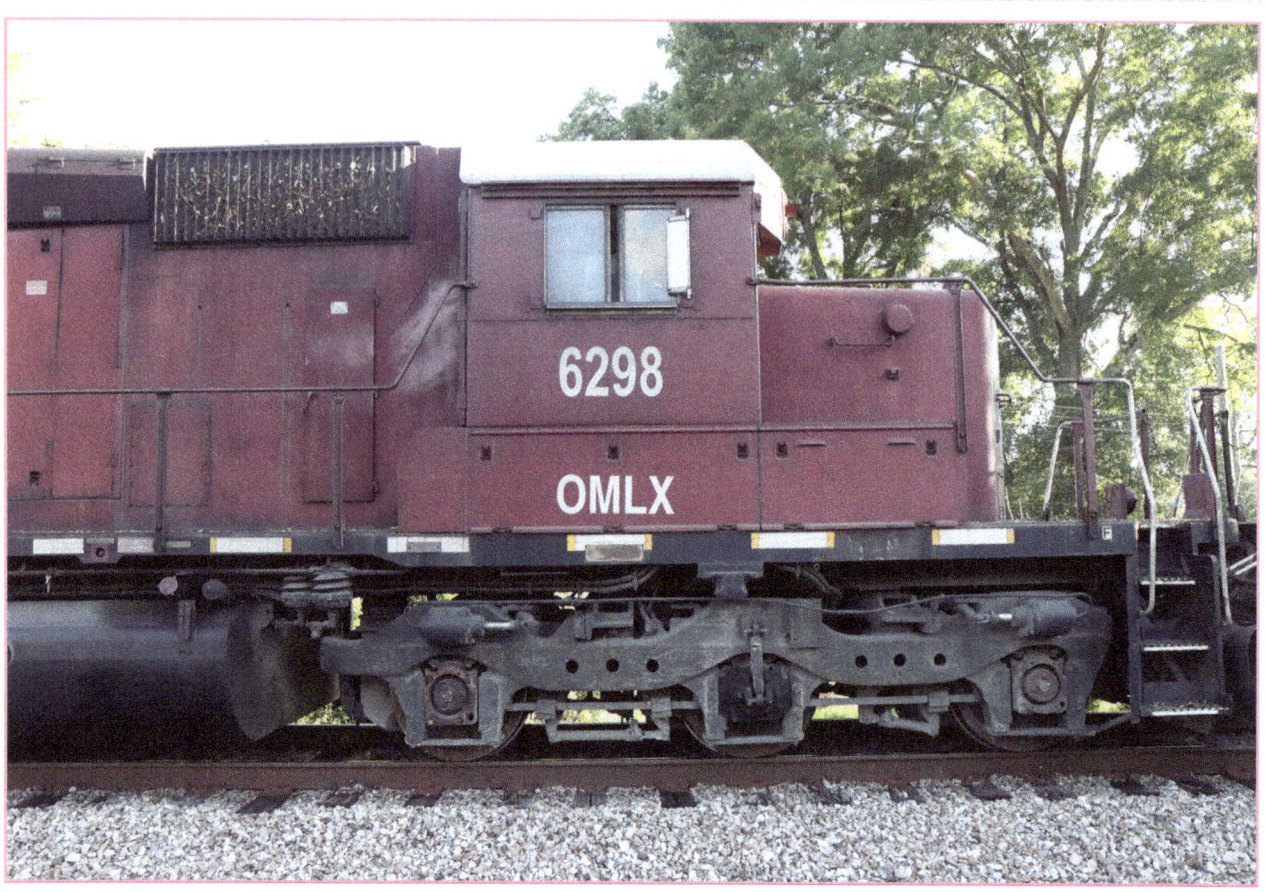

A GP20, painted in red, at the rear of the ATN train.

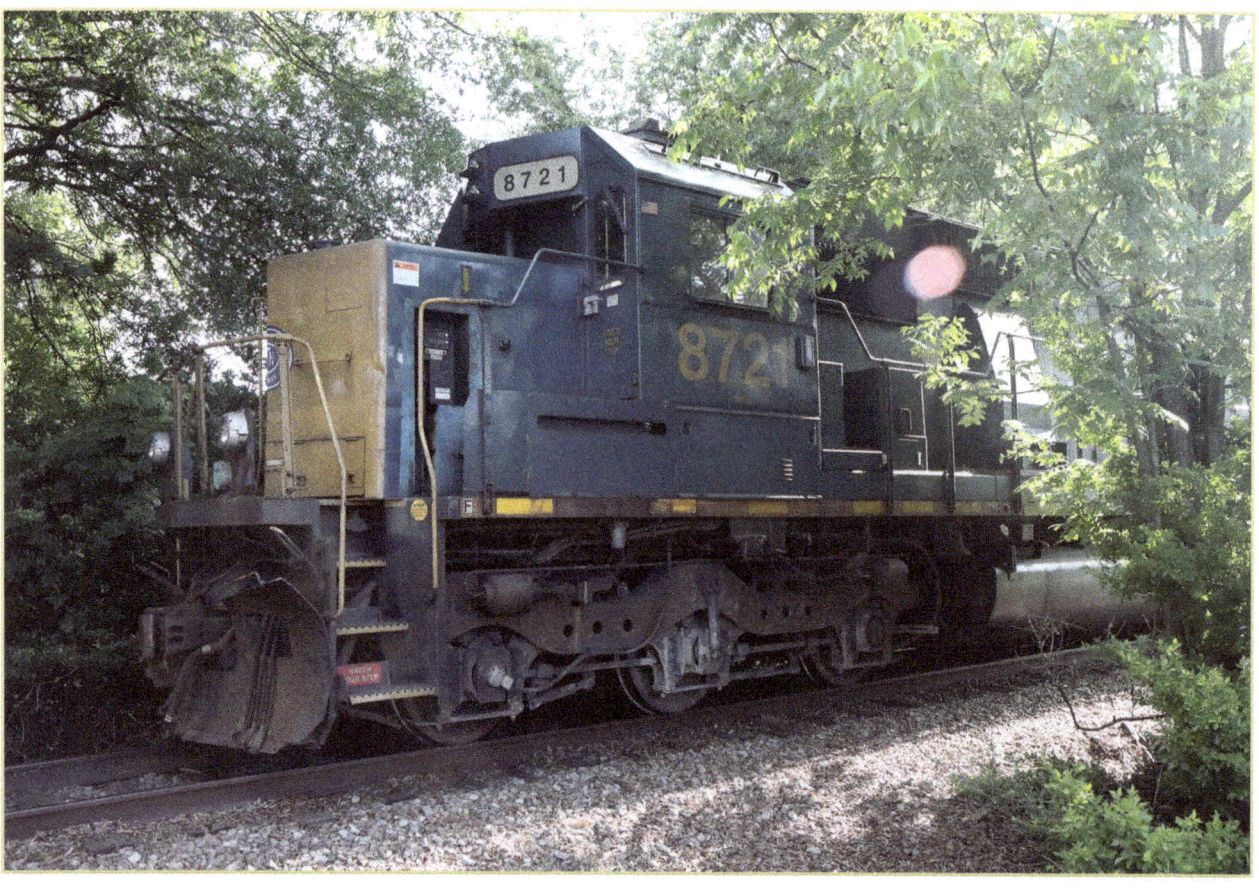

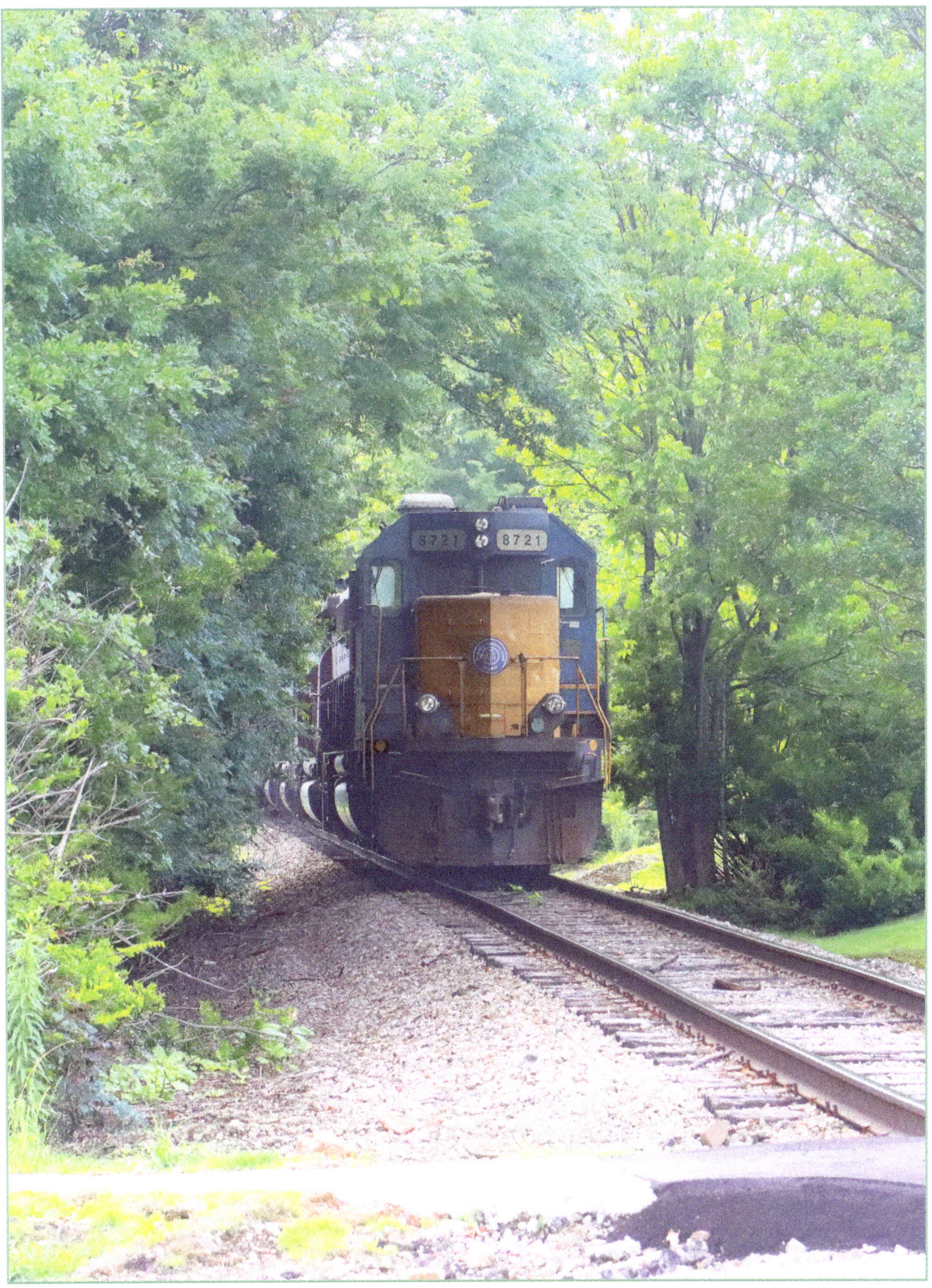

ATN 8721, a former CSX SD60, idles in Irondale.

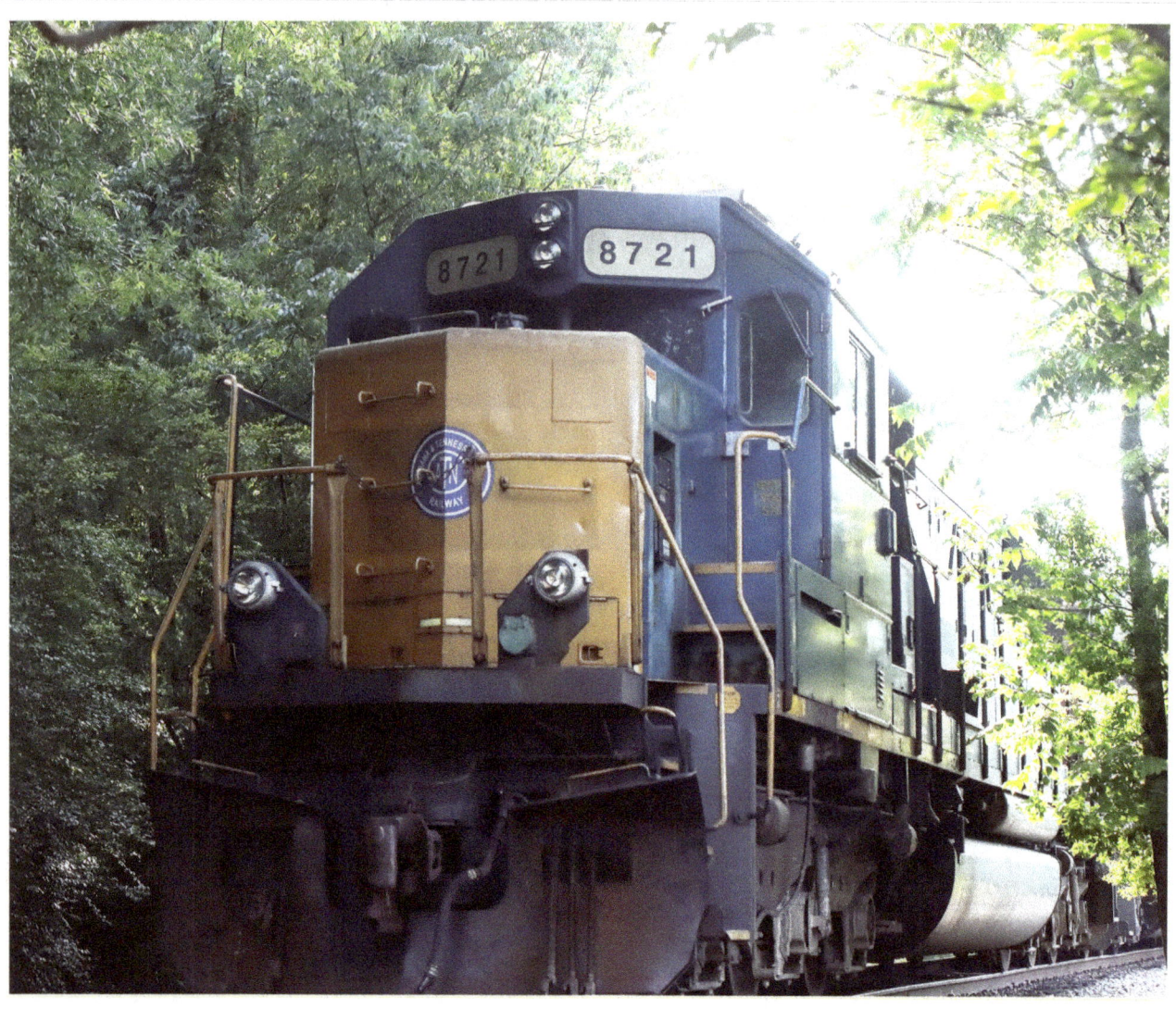

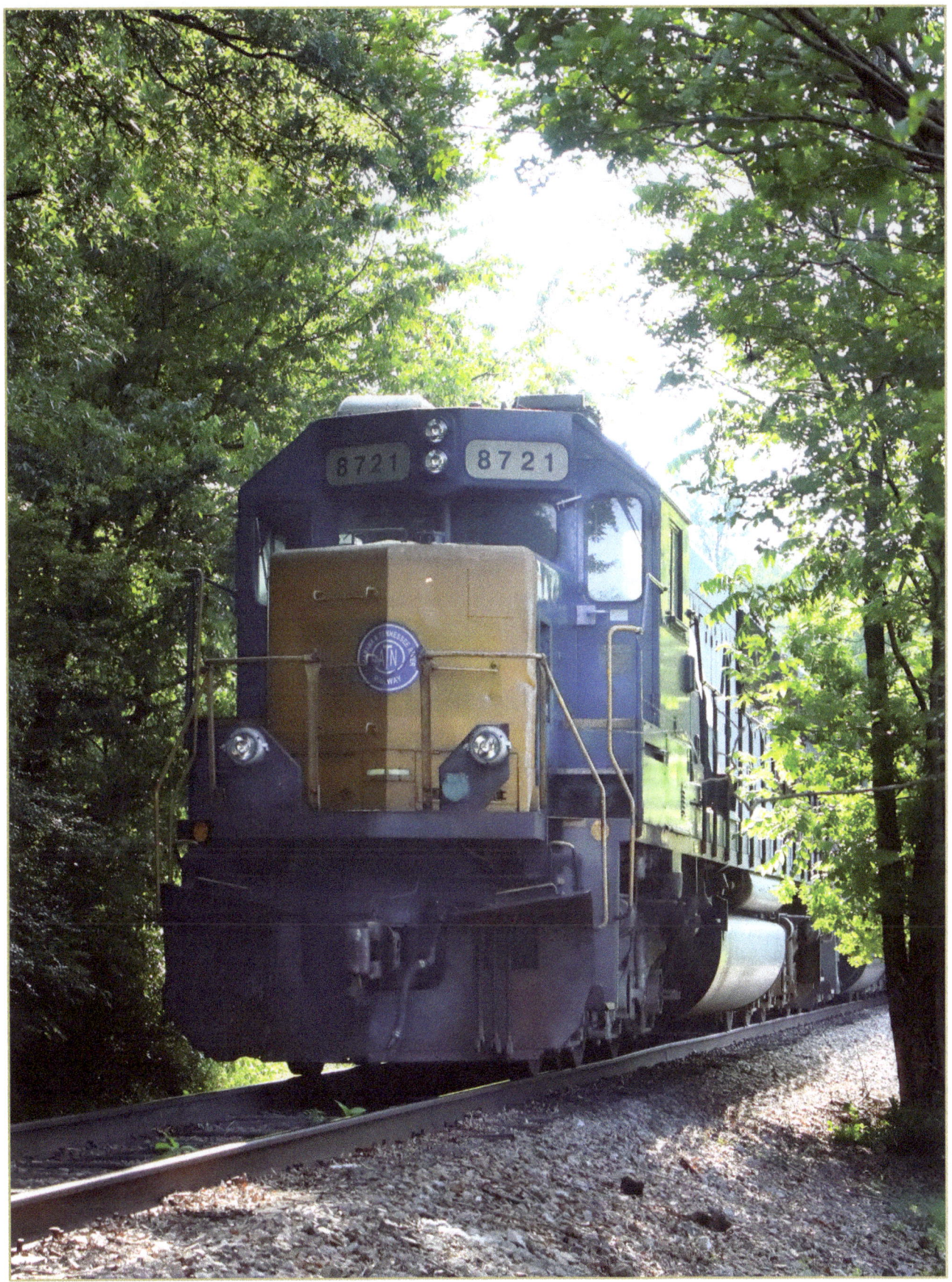

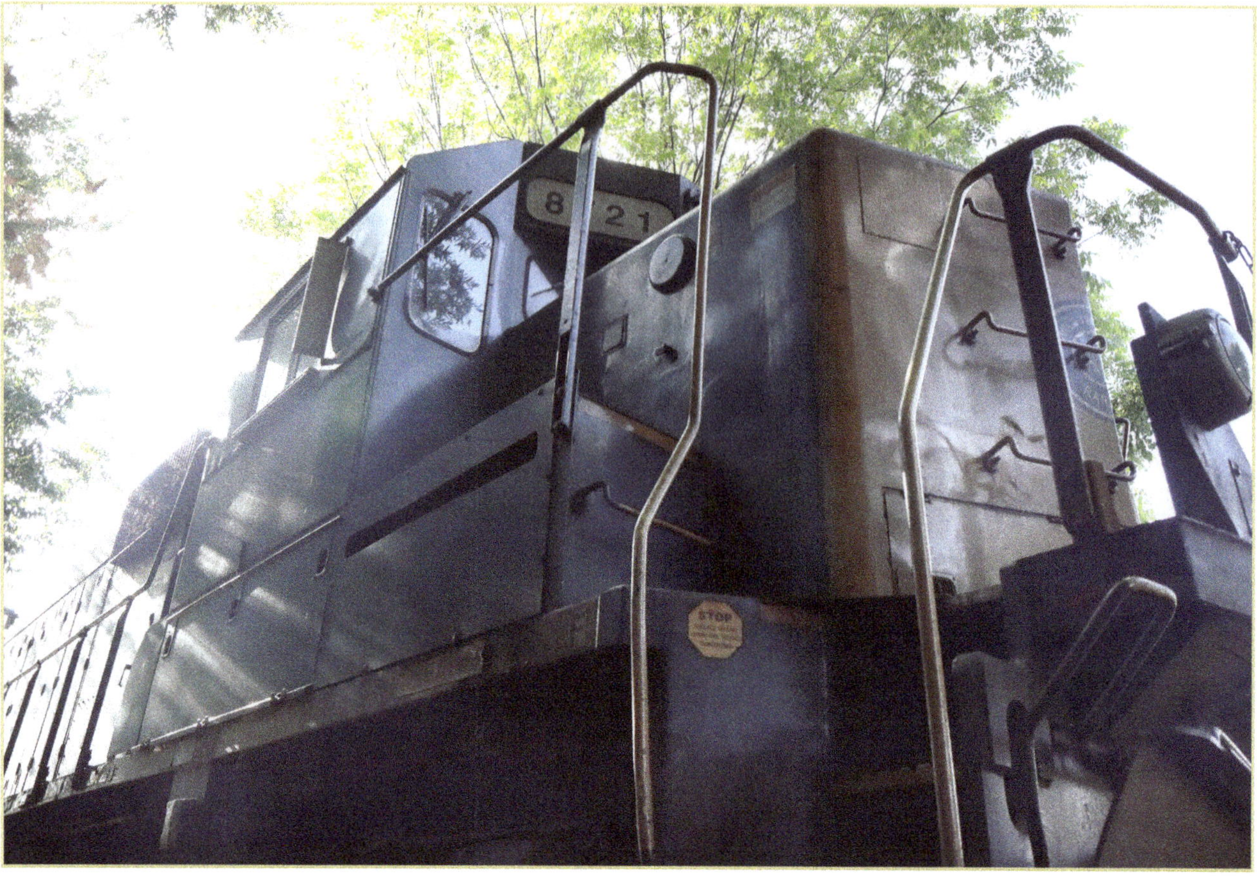

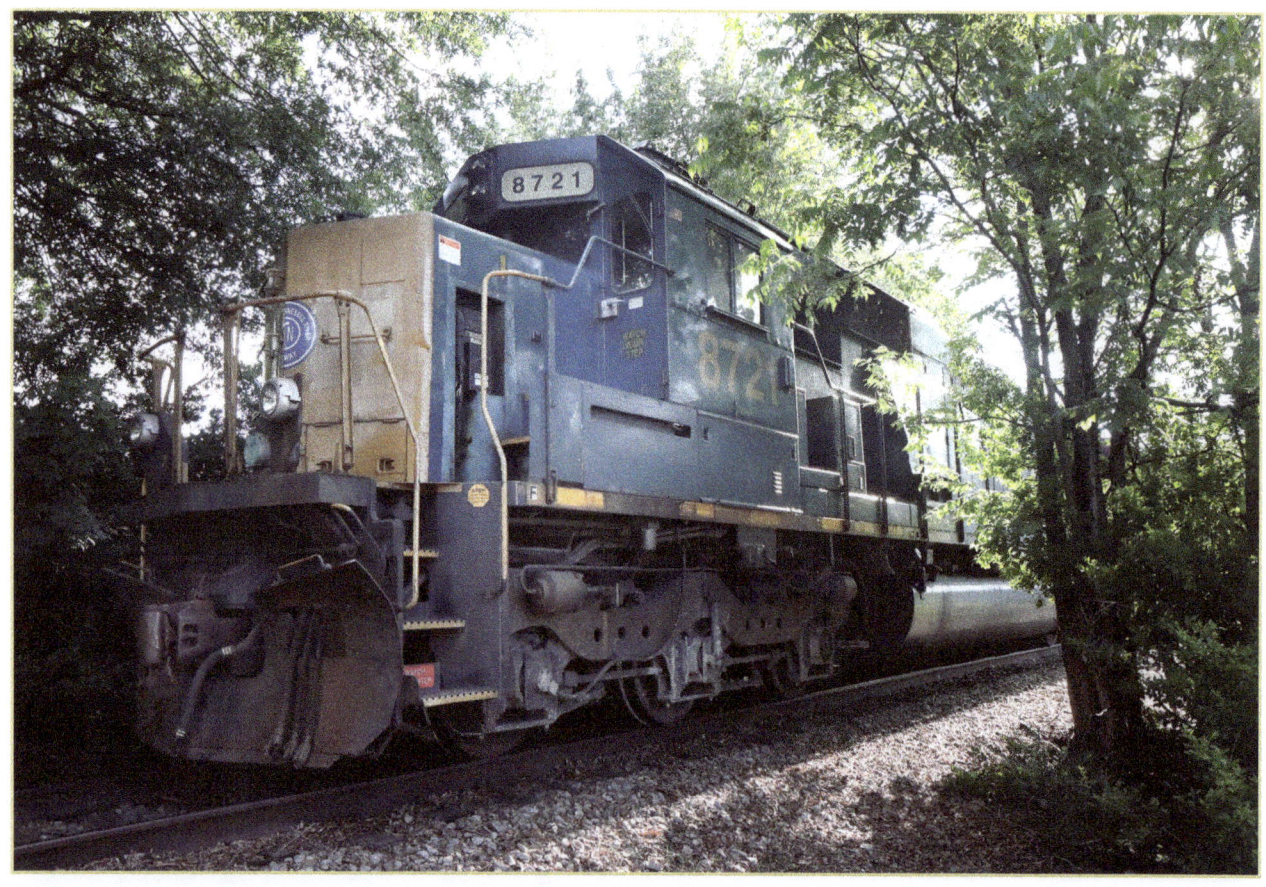

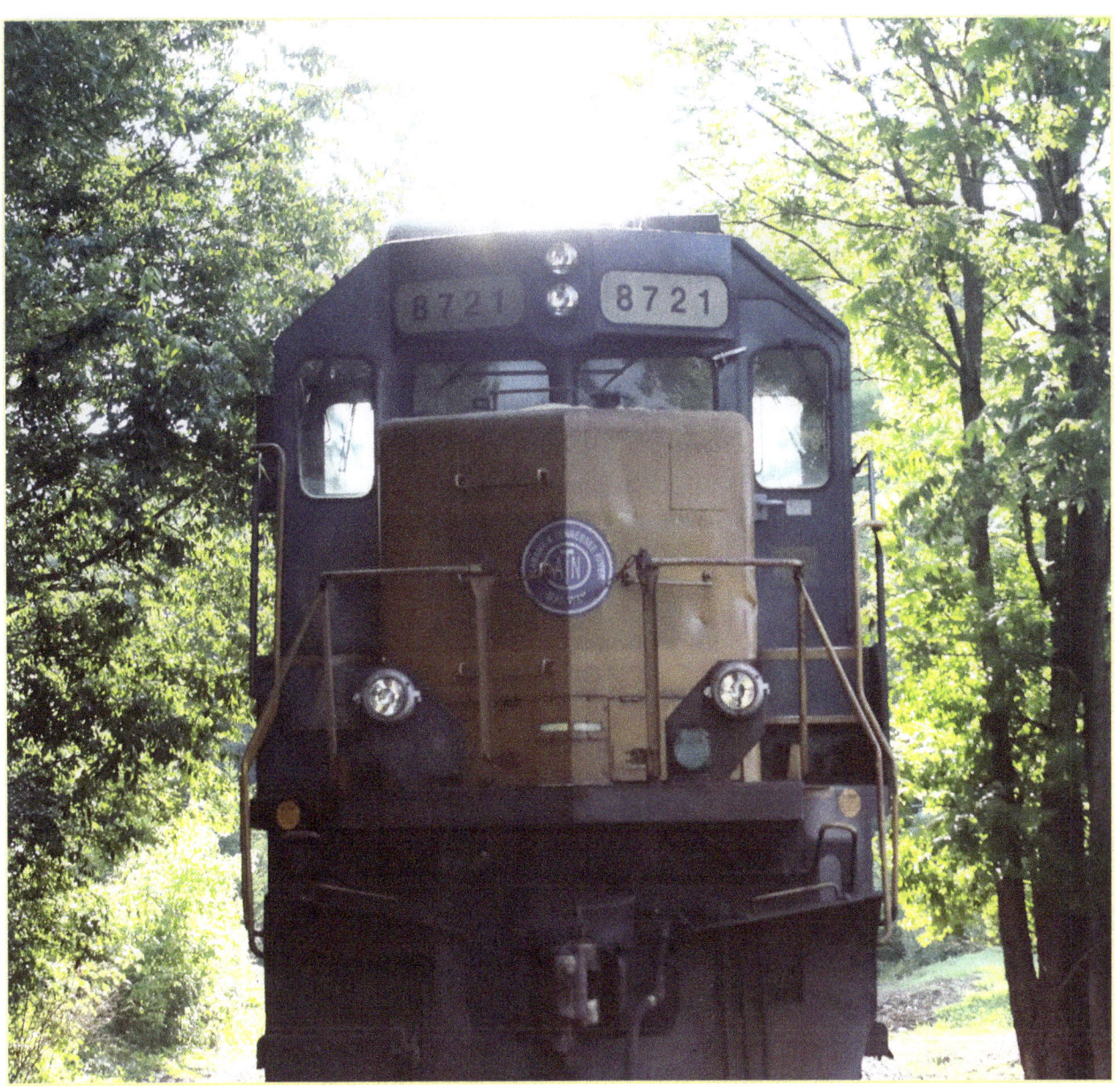

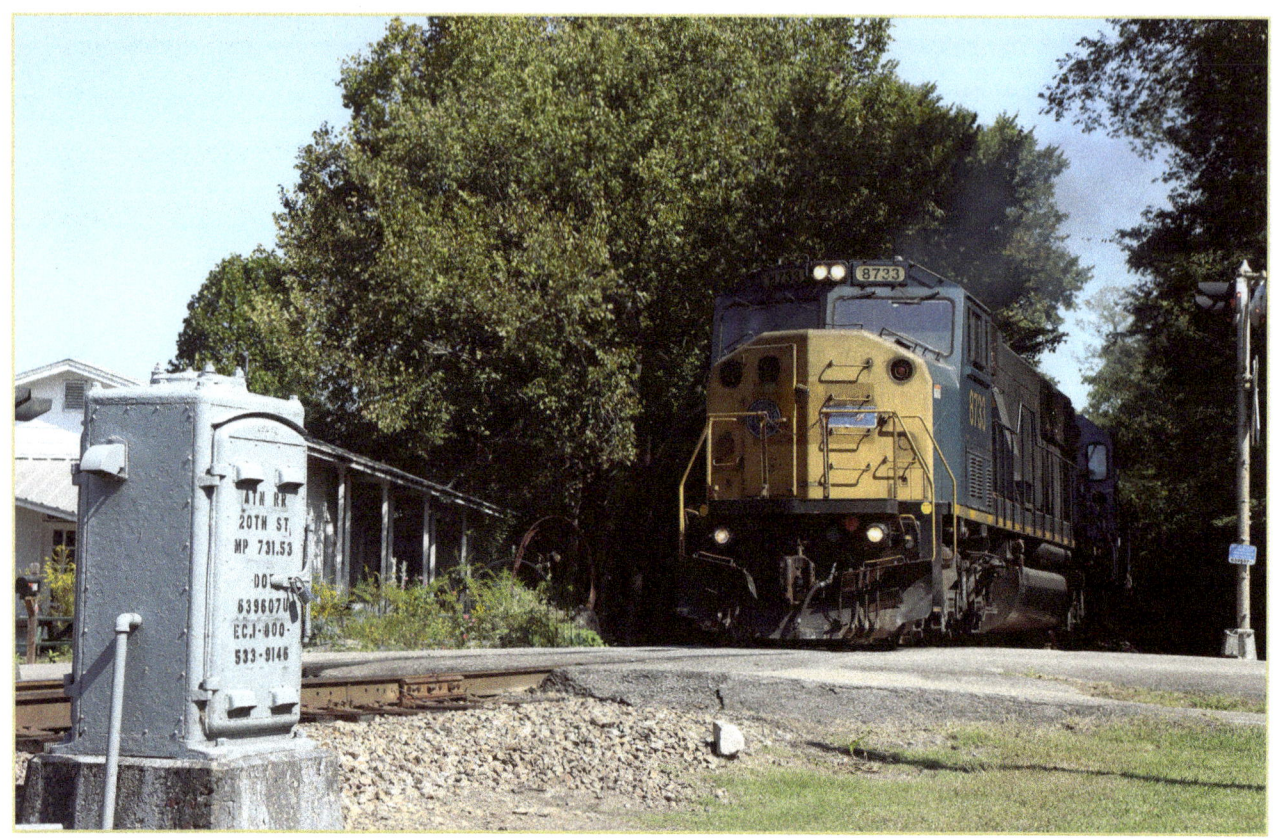

A former Conrail and CSX SD60I pulls an ATN train through Irondale on its way to Birmingham.

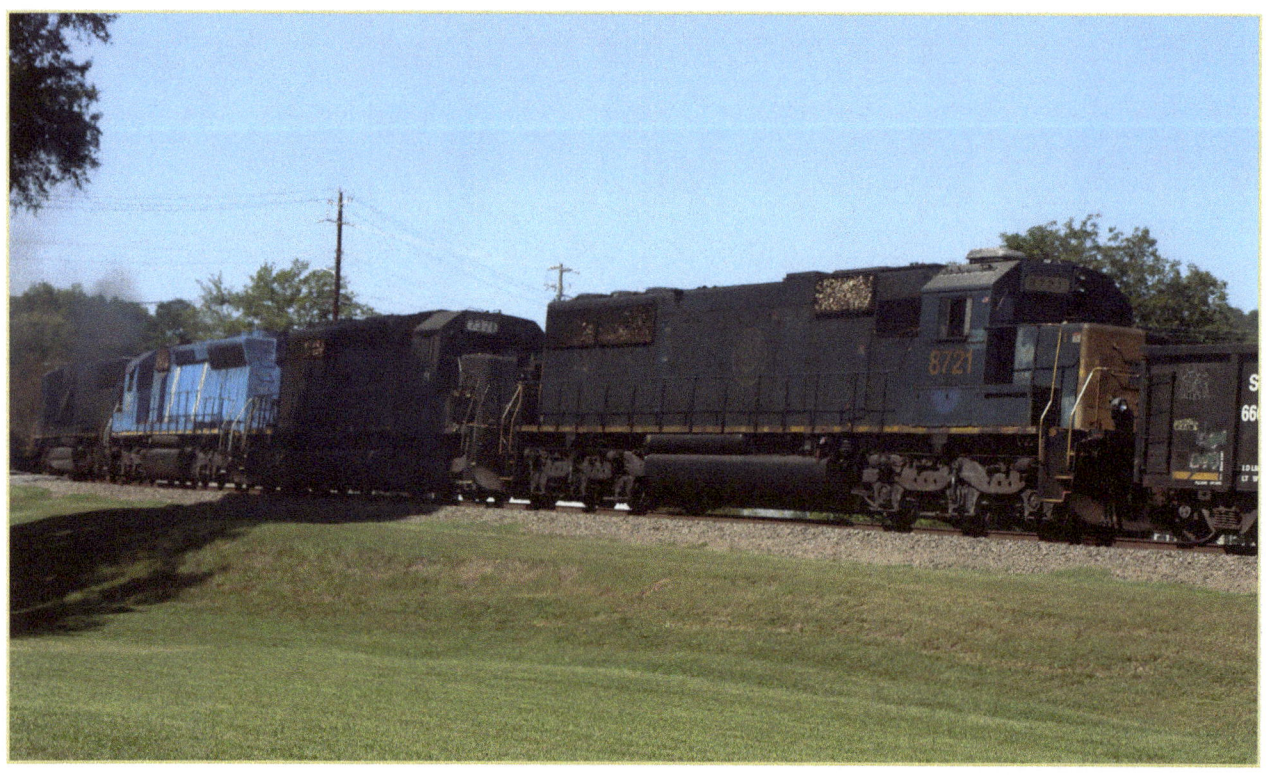

A bright blue SD40-3, a very dirty SD40-2, and a former CSX SD60 trail on an ATN train bound for Birmingham.

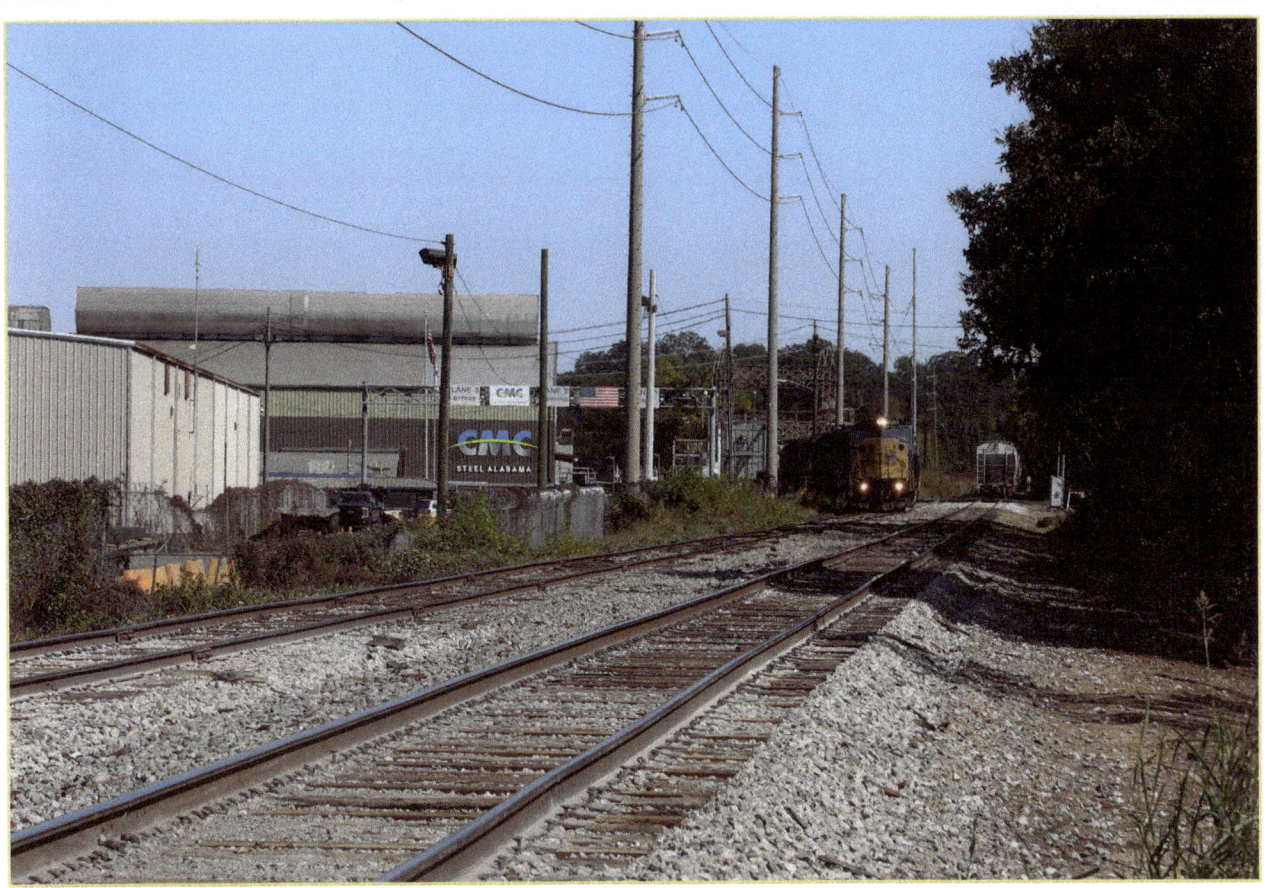

The ATN serves this steel plant in downtown Birmingham, regularly dropping off gondolas to be filled with scrap and other metal goods.

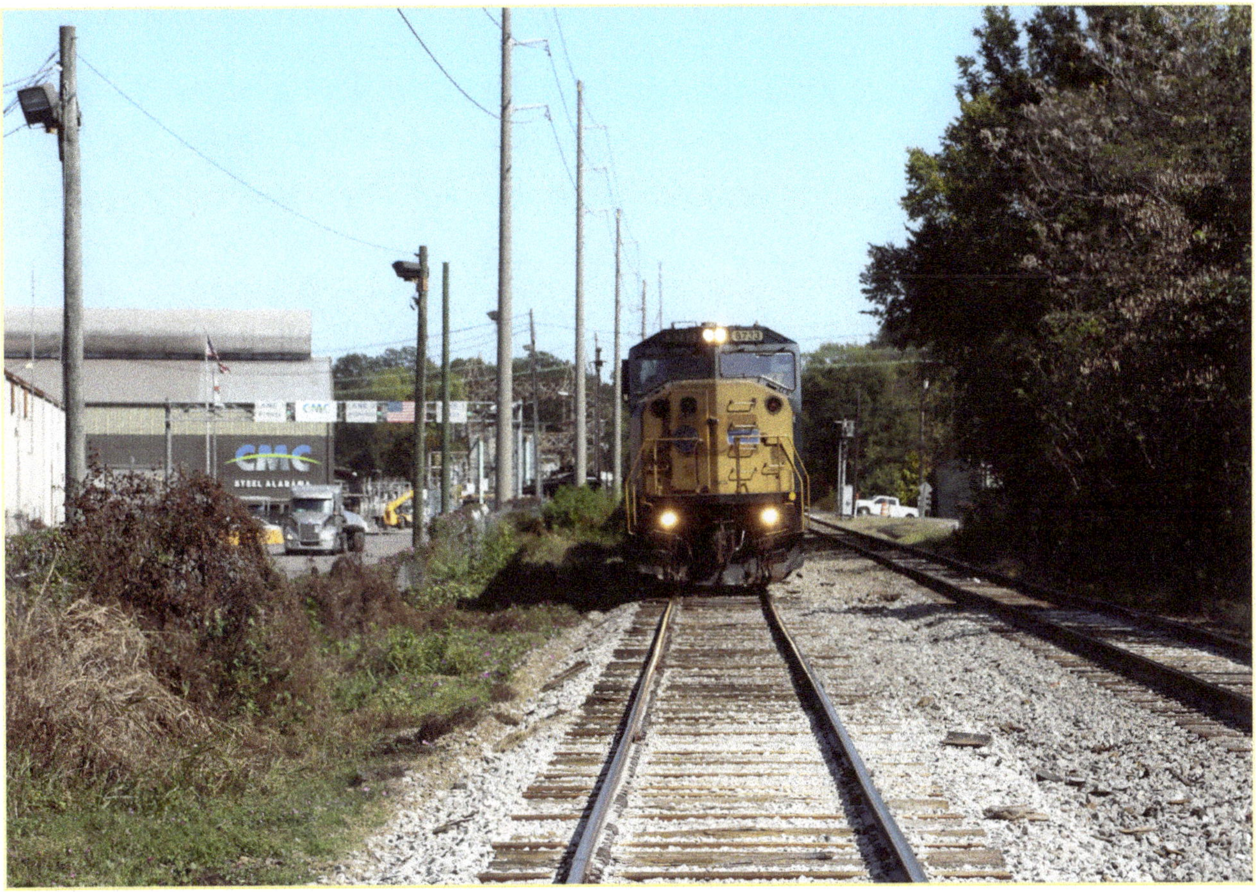

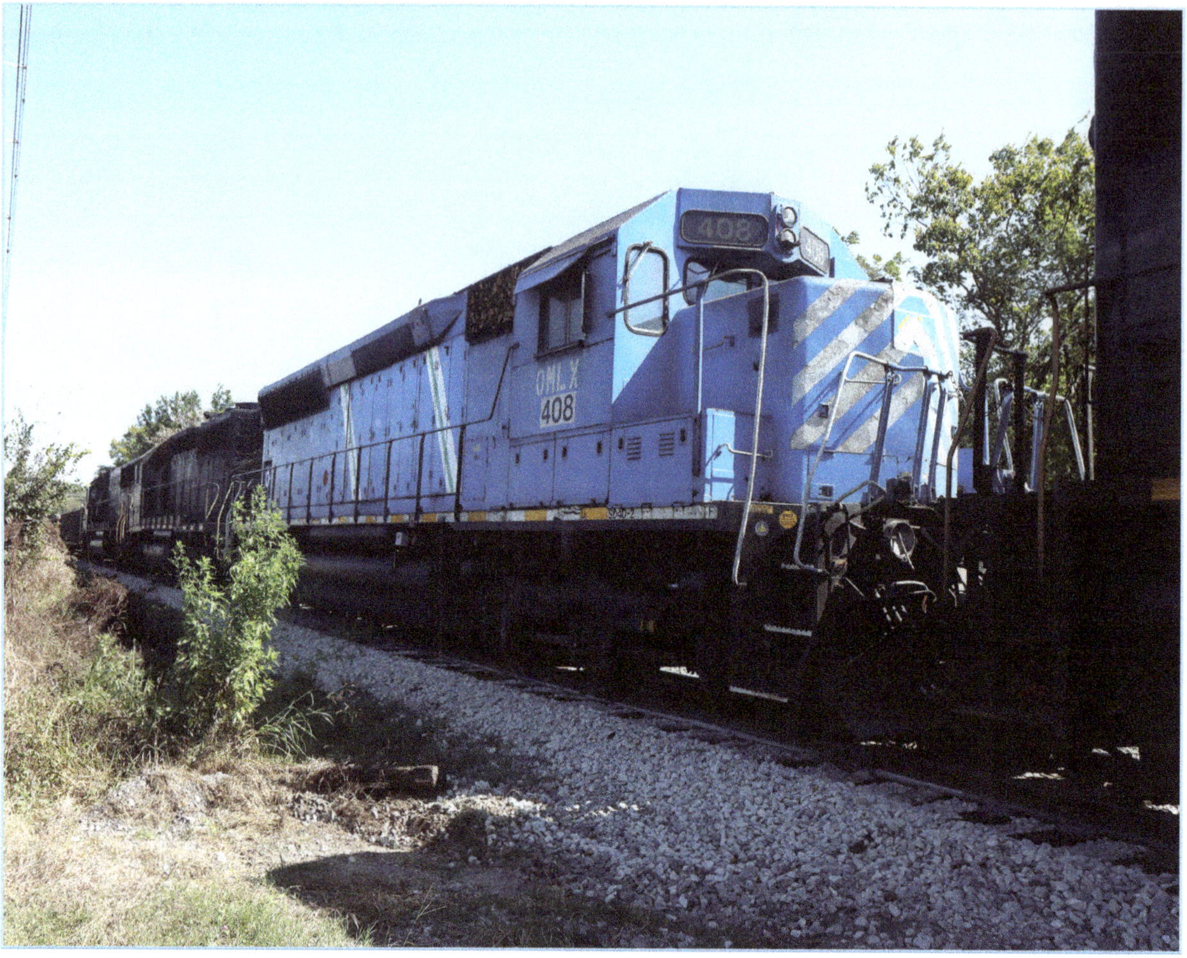

An OmniTRAX painted SD40-3 without cab modifications trails on the ATN's road train in Birmingham.

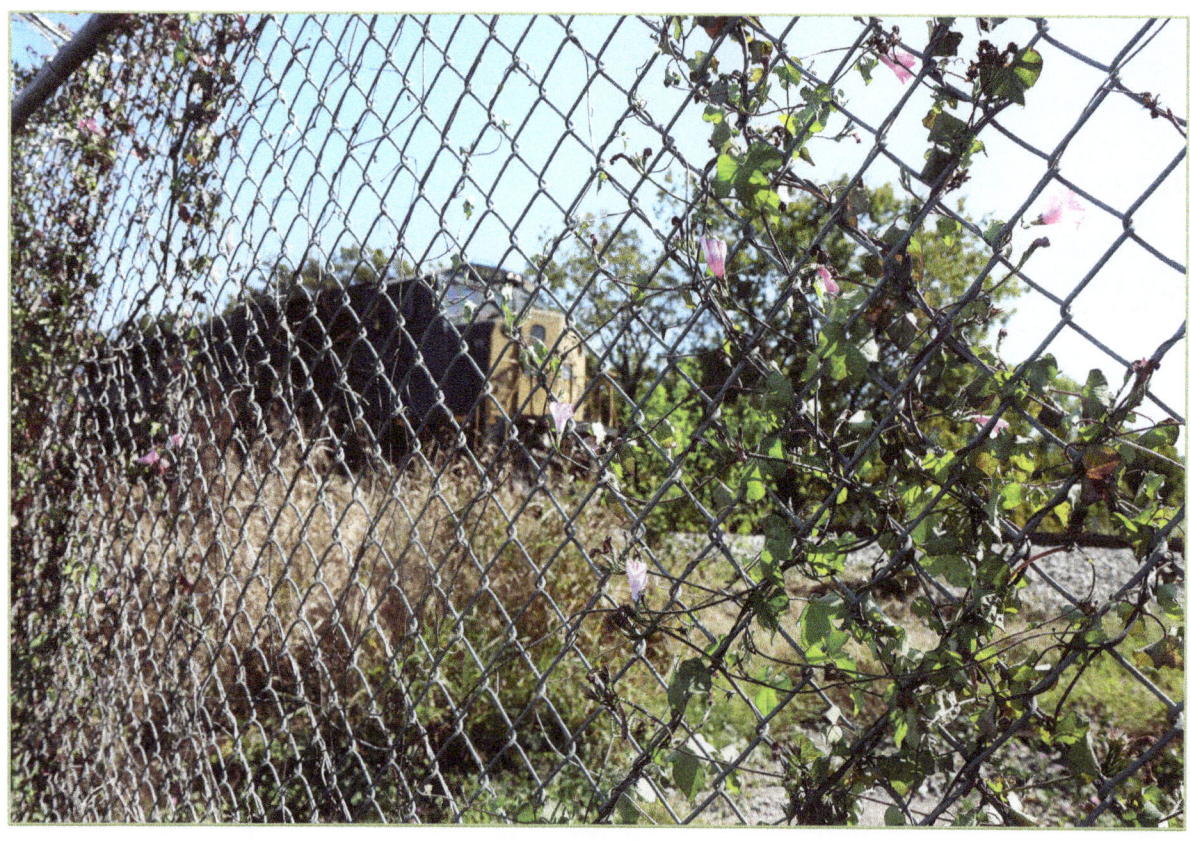

AMTRAK

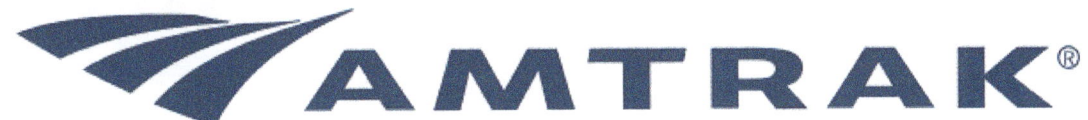

Amtrak is the government-funded rail transport company of America. Founded in 1971, they run numerous trains throughout the country, with two coming through Alabama, the westbound and eastbound Crescent, numbered 19 and 20. The Crescent was originally run by the Southern Railroad using multiple railroads' track. Today it is run solely on Norfolk Southern track by Amtrak alone. Running every day, the train itself normally consists of two Amtrak locomotives and around ten cars.

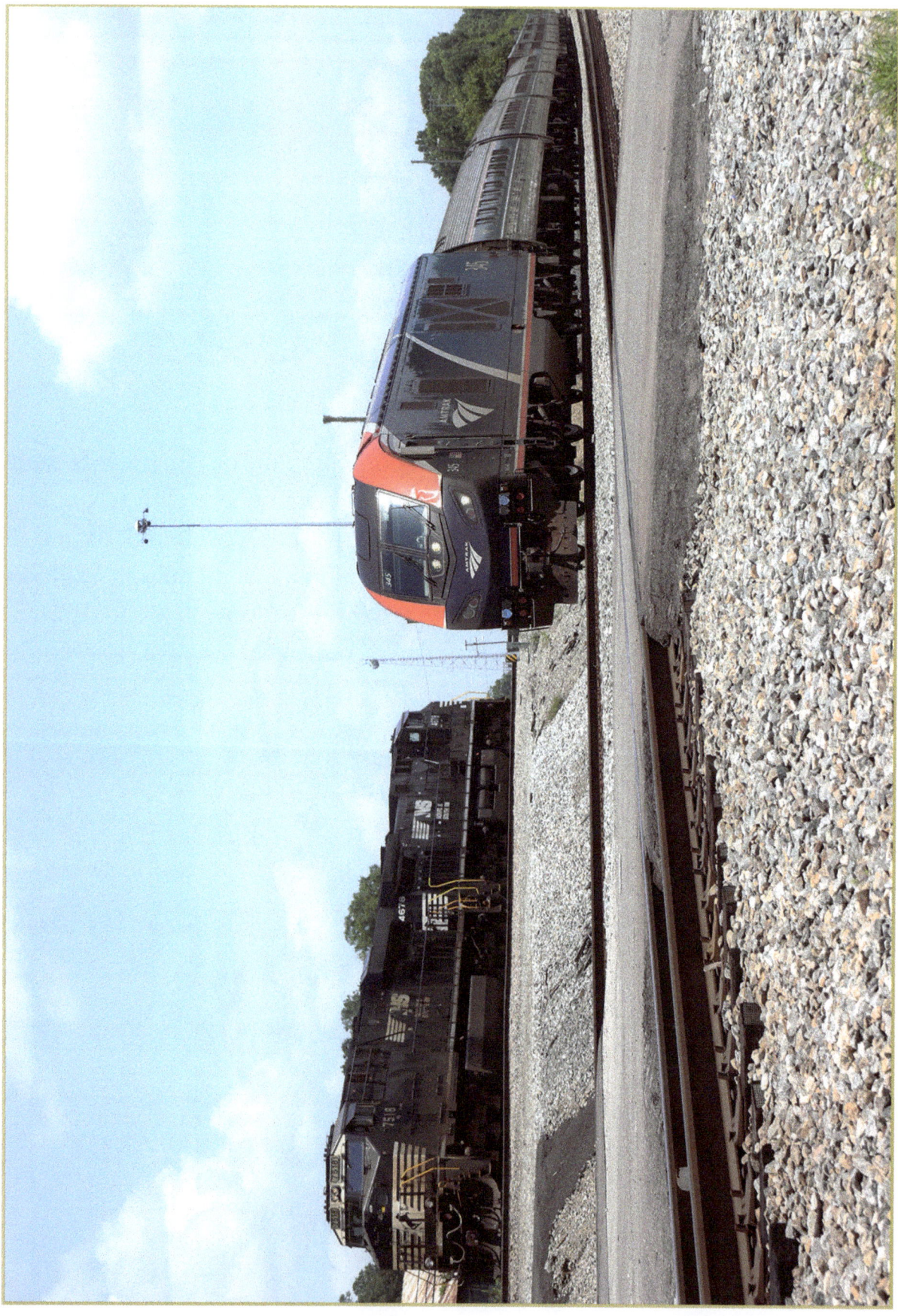

The Crescent passes two parked locomotives at Norris Yard.

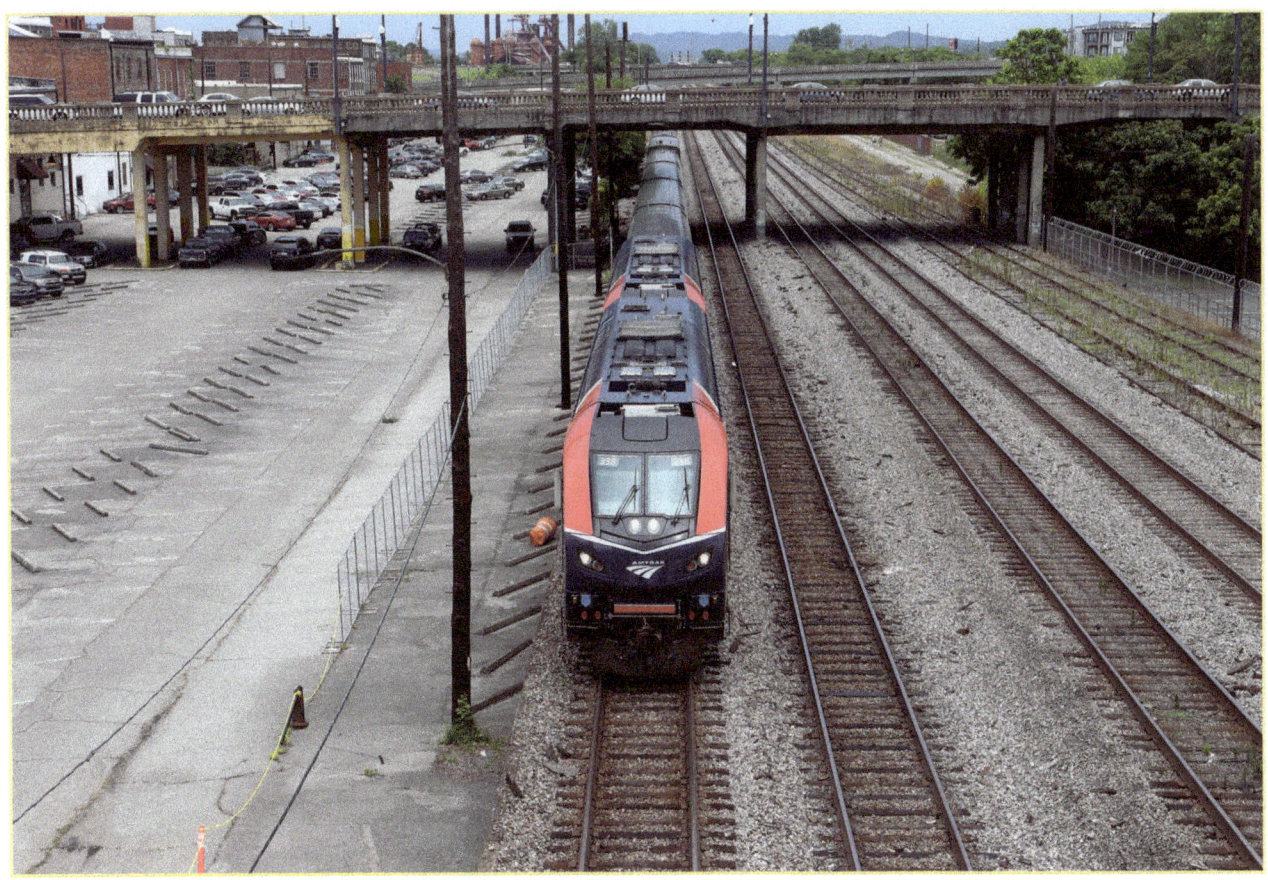

Two new ALC-42 locomotives lead the westbound Crescent through Birmingham.

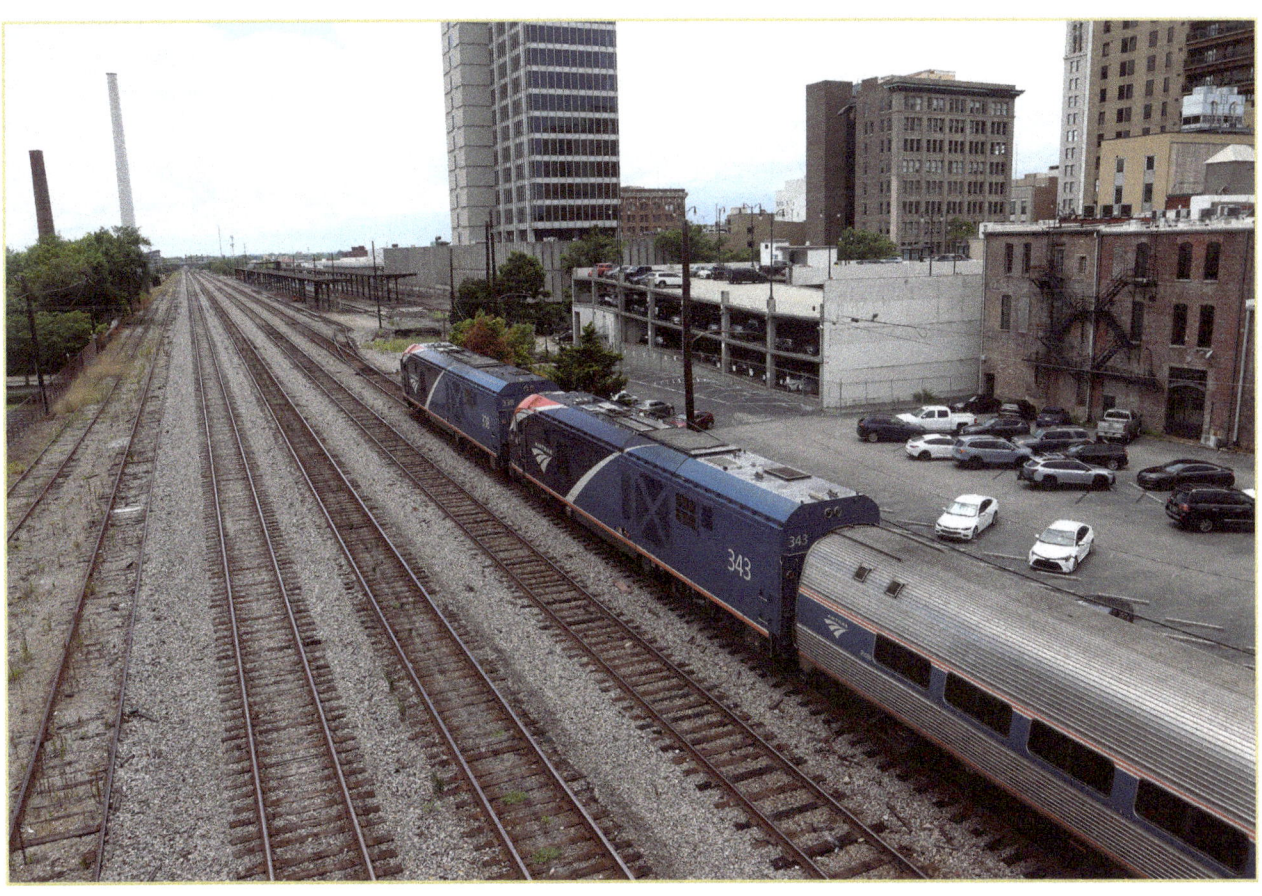

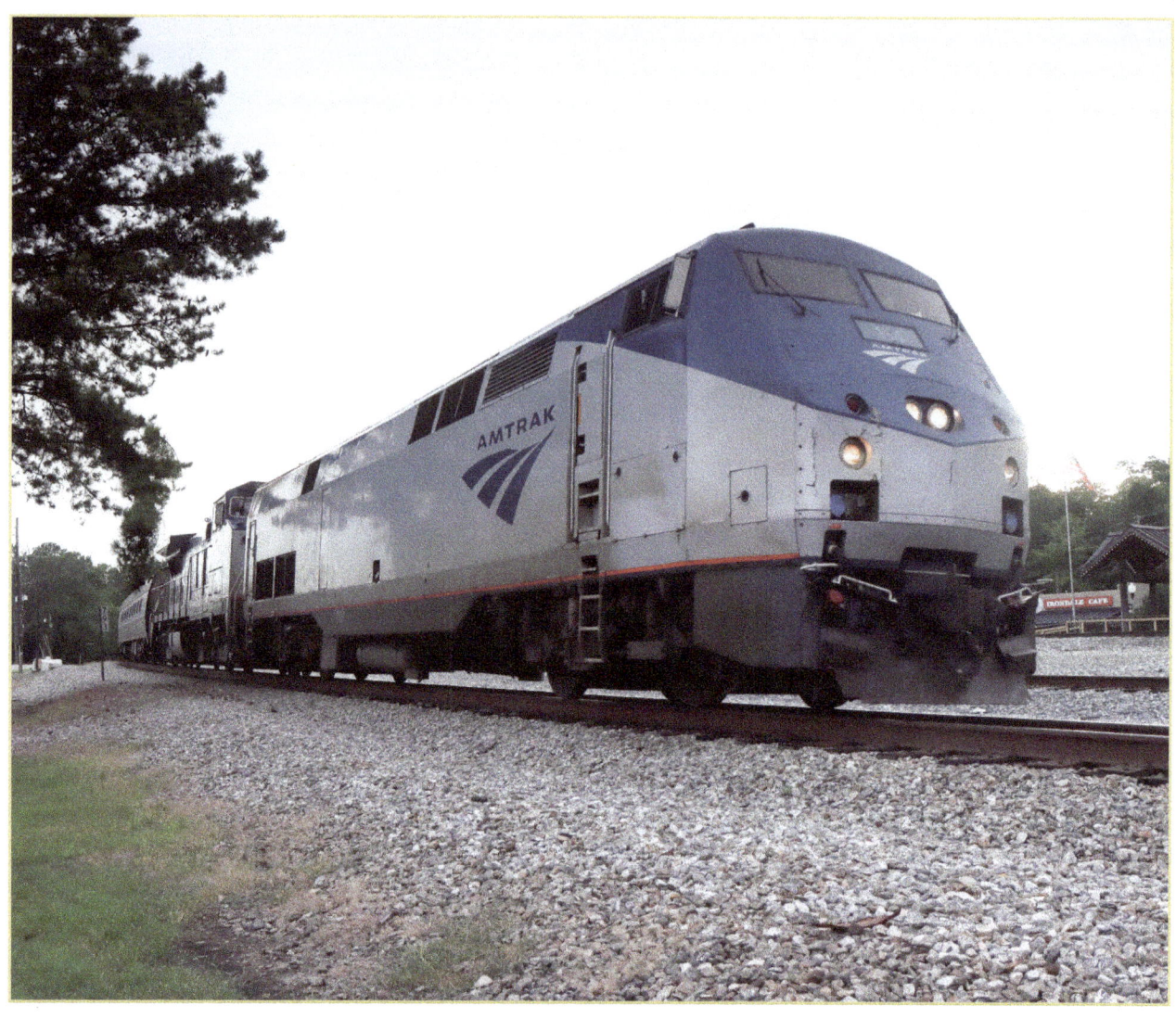

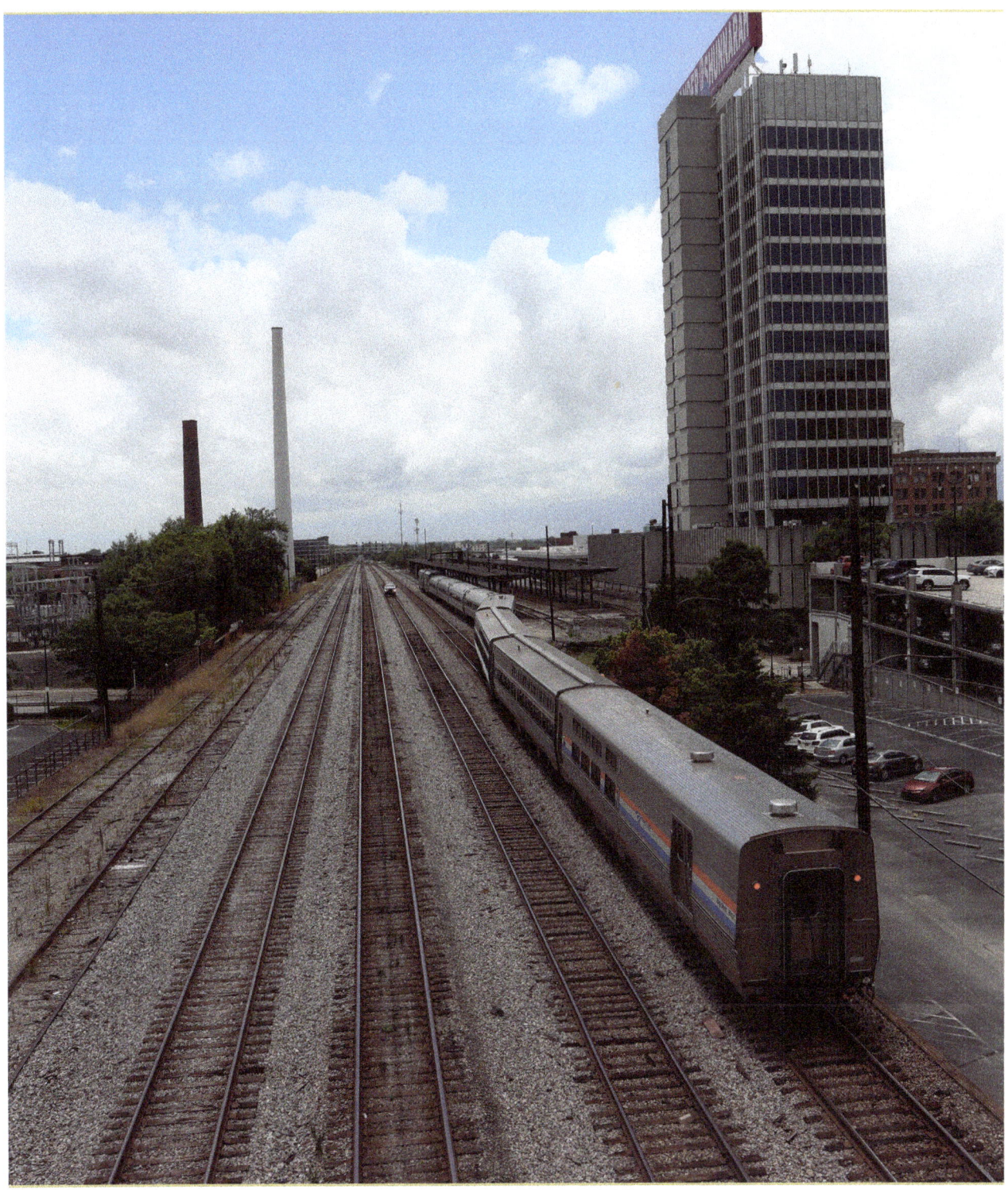

The Crescent pulls into the old L&N Station in Birmingham.

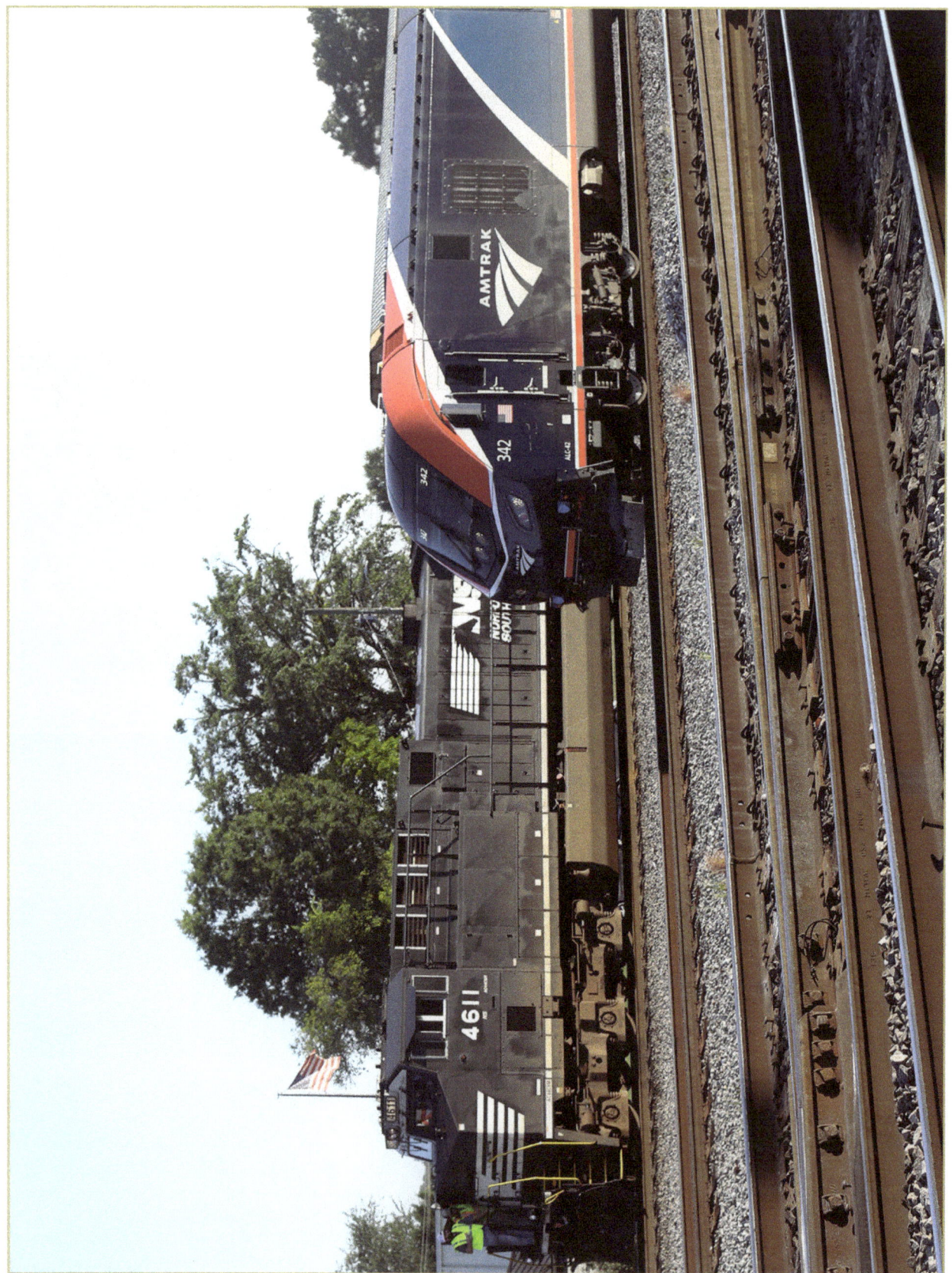

Two Norfolk Southern employees watch the eastbound Crescent pass through Irondale.

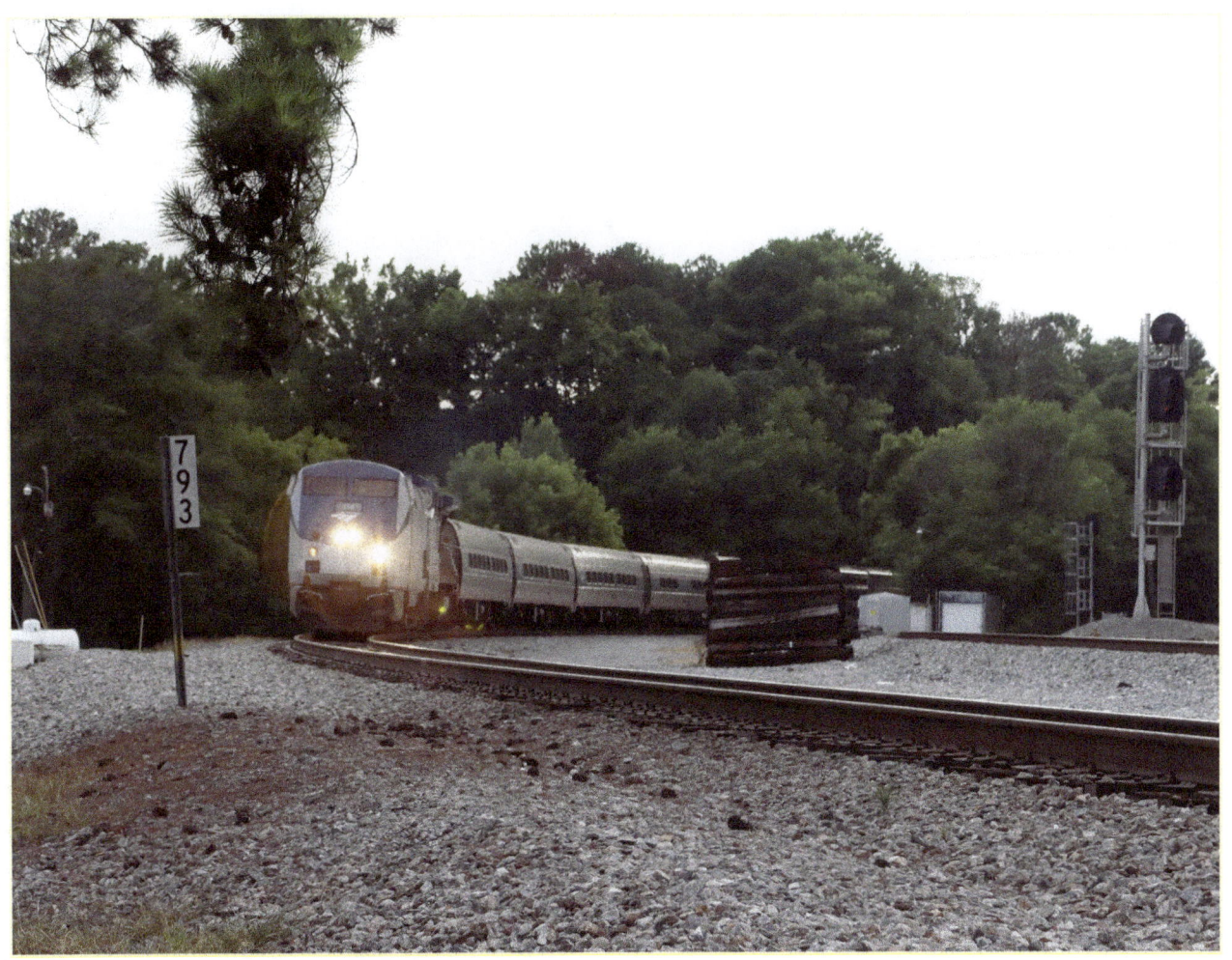
The eastbound Crescent rolls through Irondale.

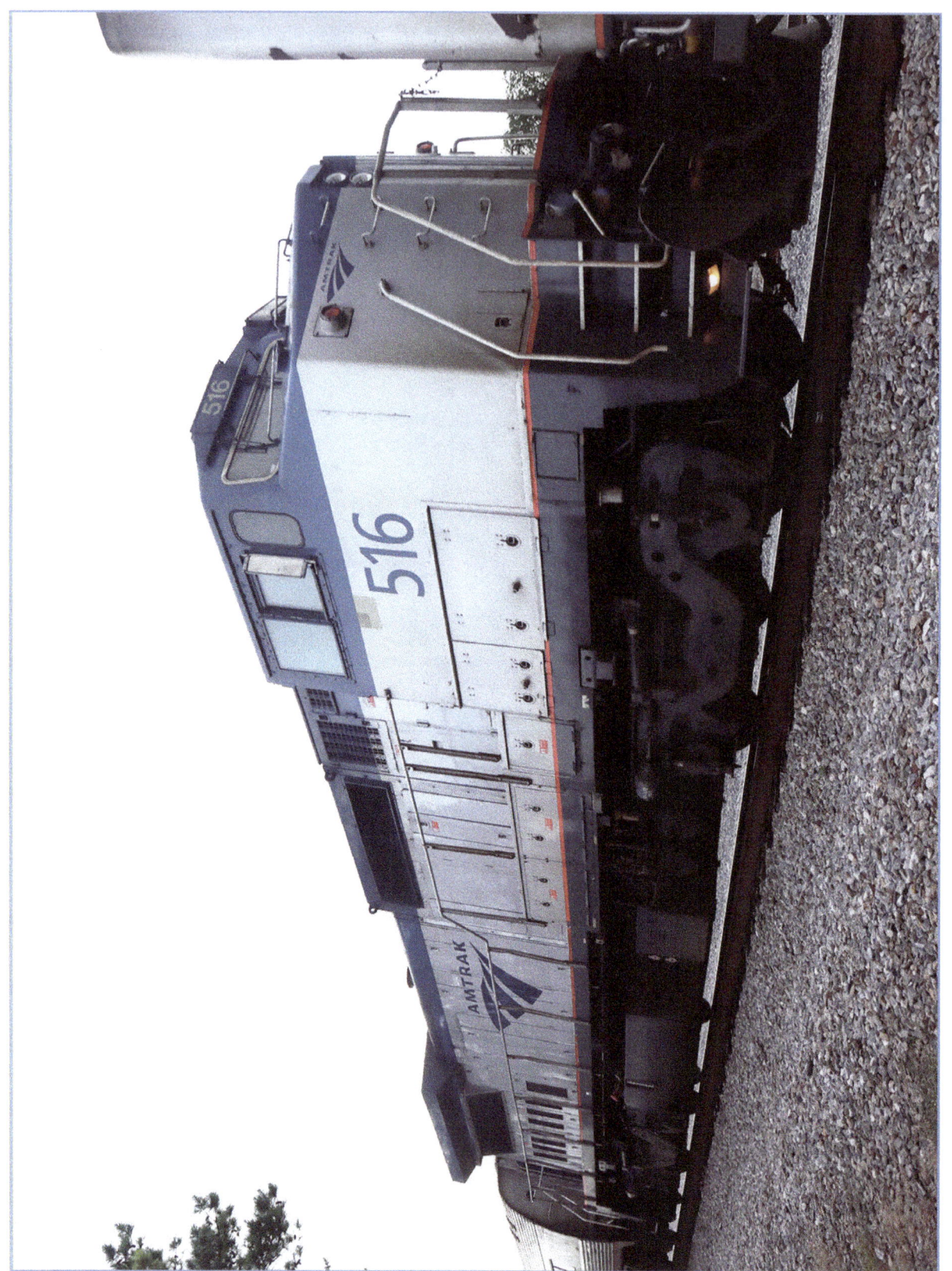

Amtrak 516 is a GE Dash 8 ordered by Amtrak with nineteen others in 1991 to replace Amtrak's aging fleet of F40PHs. Four locomotives are no longer used, and the remining sixteen are normally assigned to yard service and only used when there is no power available.

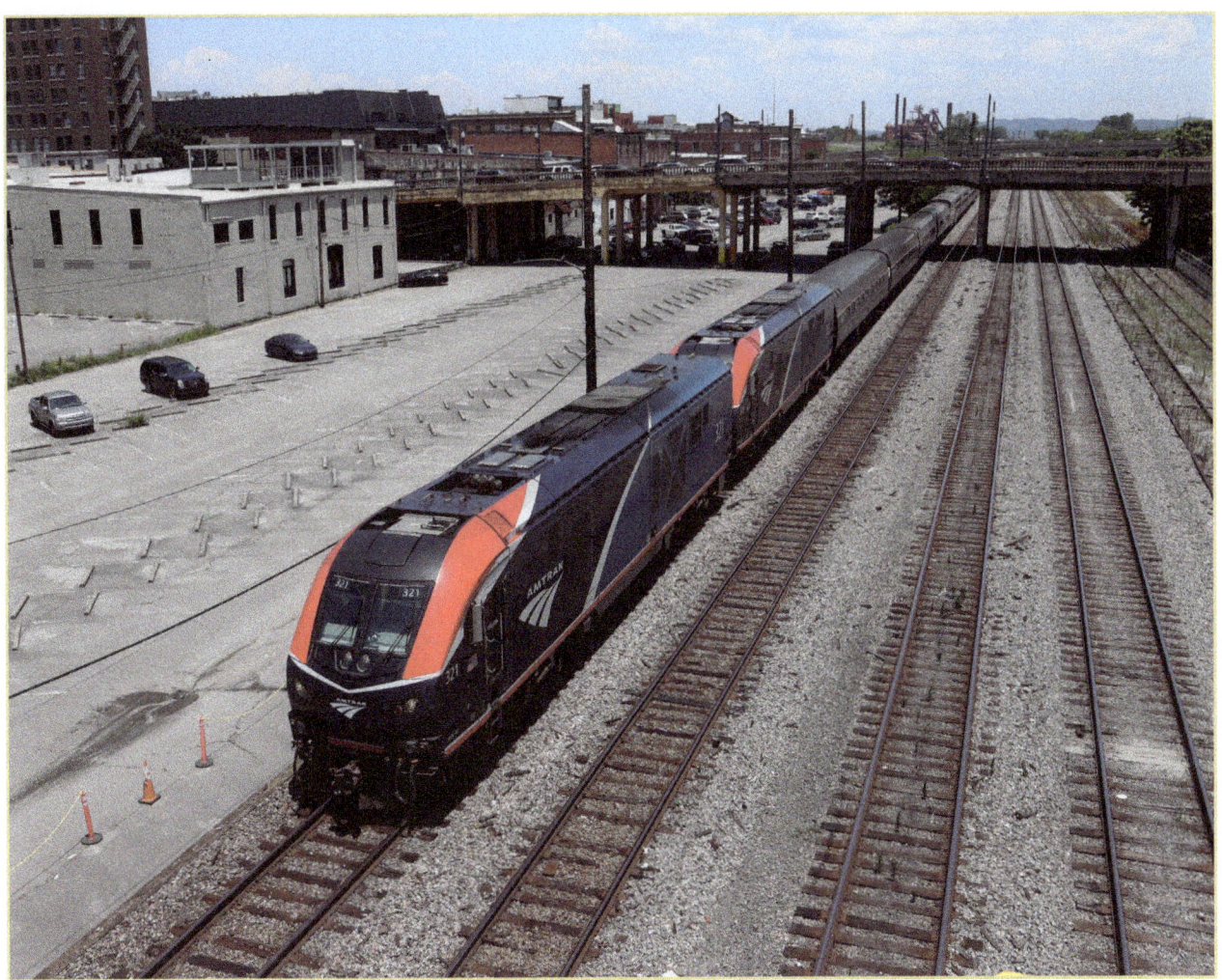

Two new ALC-42s lead a shortened Crescent toward Bessemer and everywhere else the train stops.

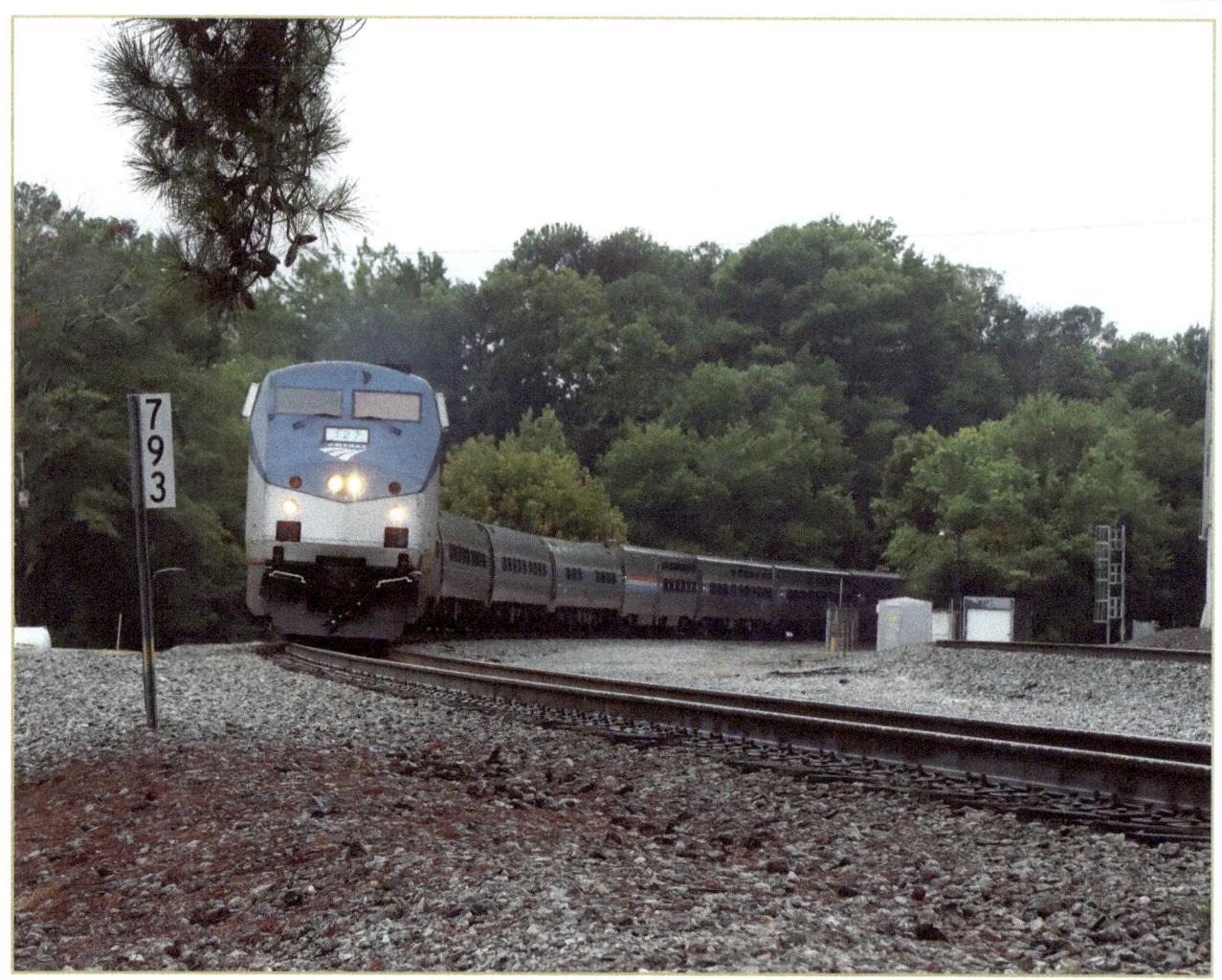
Two aging P42s lead a very long Crescent eastward toward Anniston and eventually New York.

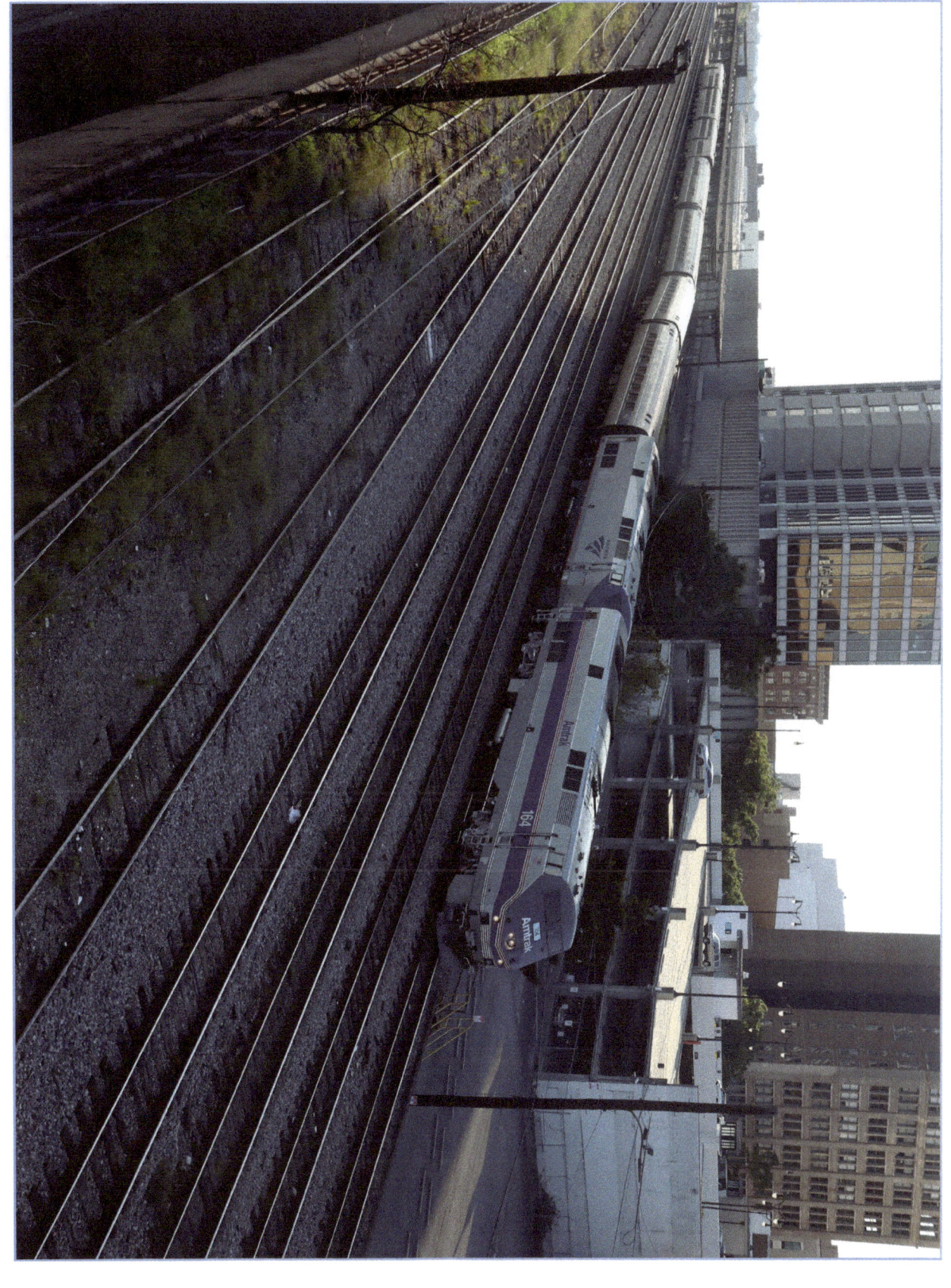

The Amtrak Phase IV Heritage Unit pulls the Crescent out of the Birmingham Amtrak station.

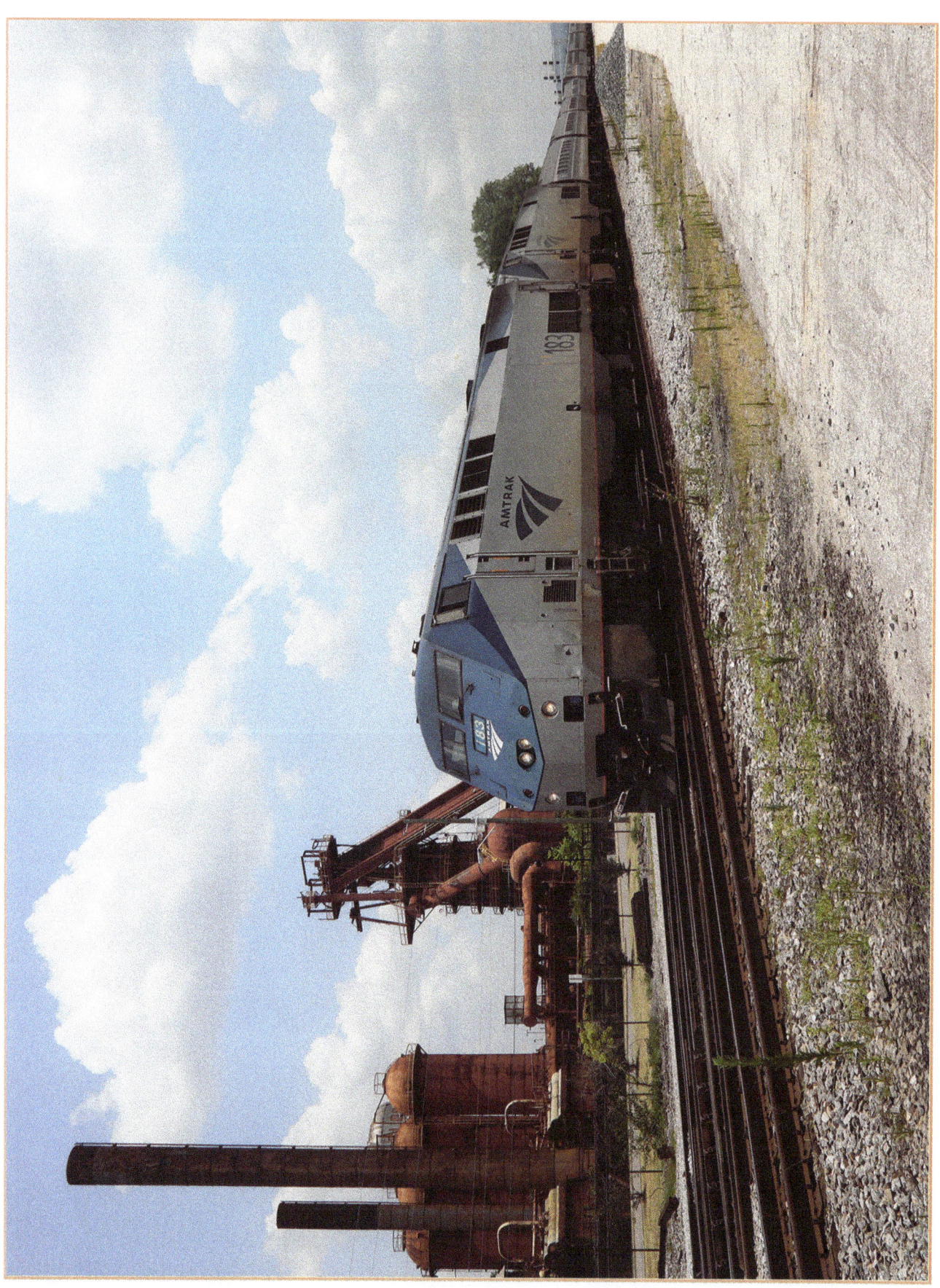

ABOUT BRAYDEN DEXTER GREENE

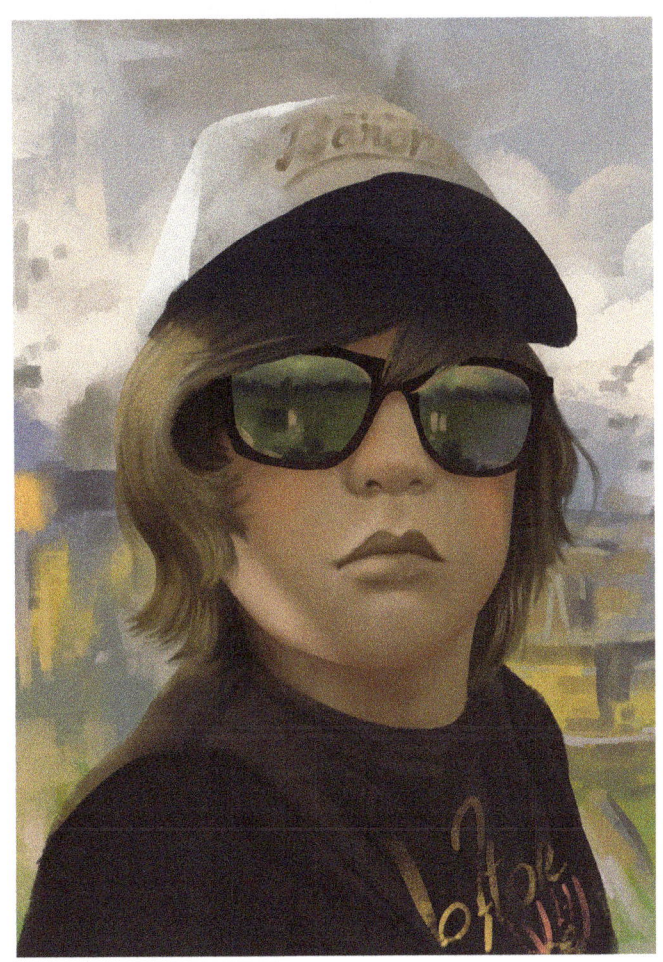

Brayden is a teenager from the suburbs of Birmingham, Alabama. His hobbies include photography, model railroading, video games, bass guitar, and studying nature. His career interests right now lean toward ornithology and photography. His summer project before starting high school, *Trains of Alabama* is Brayden's first book. Find him at BraydenDexterGreene.com.

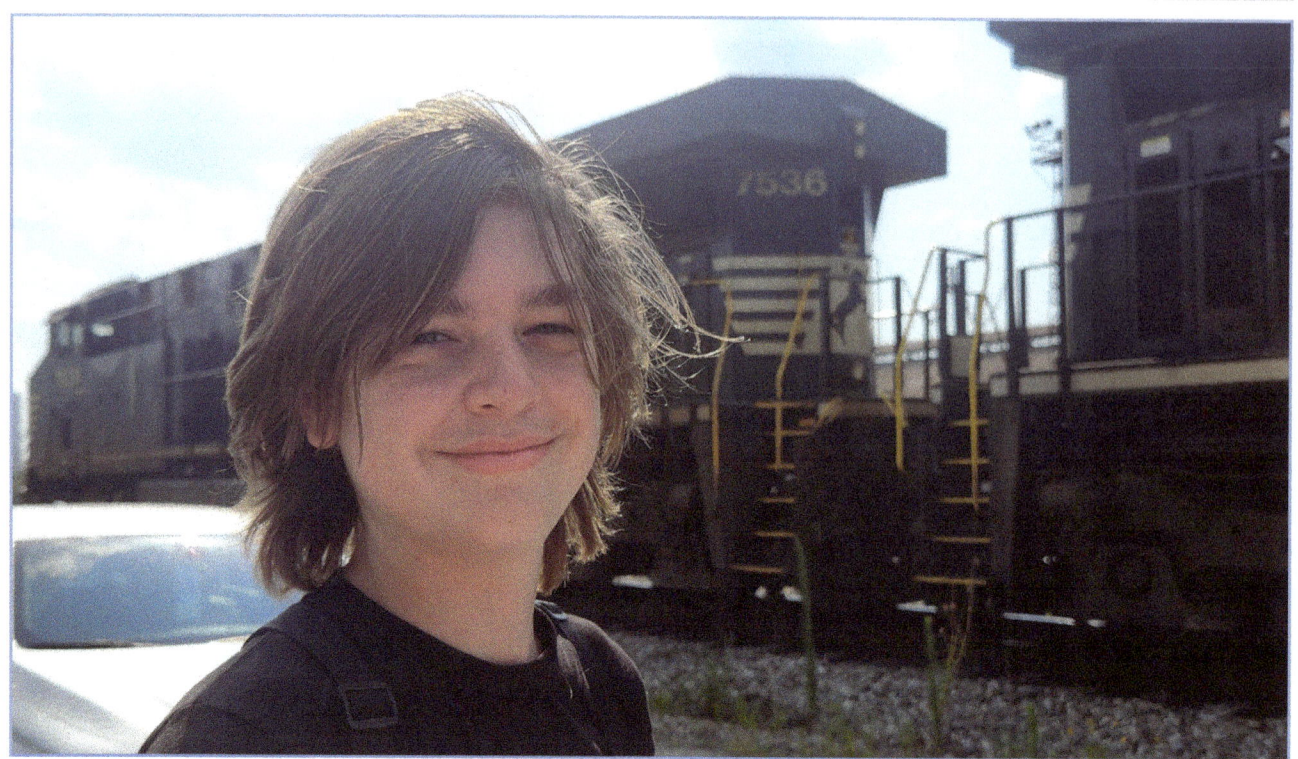

Fresh Ink Group
Independent Multi-media Publisher

Fresh Ink Group / Push Pull Press
Voice of Indie / GeezWriter

༄

Hardcovers
Softcovers
All Ebook Platforms
Audiobooks
Worldwide Distribution

༄

Indie Author Services
Book Development, Editing, Proofing
Graphic/Cover Design
Video/Trailer Production
Website Creation
Social Media Management
Writing Contests
Writers' Blogs
Podcasts

༄

Authors
Editors
Artists
Experts
Professionals

༄

FreshInkGroup.com
info@FreshInkGroup.com
X: @FreshInkGroup
Facebook.com/FreshInkGroup
LinkedIn: Fresh Ink Group
Instagram: @FreshInkGroup and @FIGPublishing

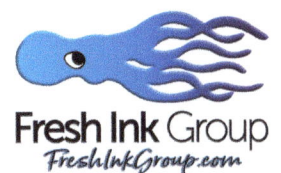

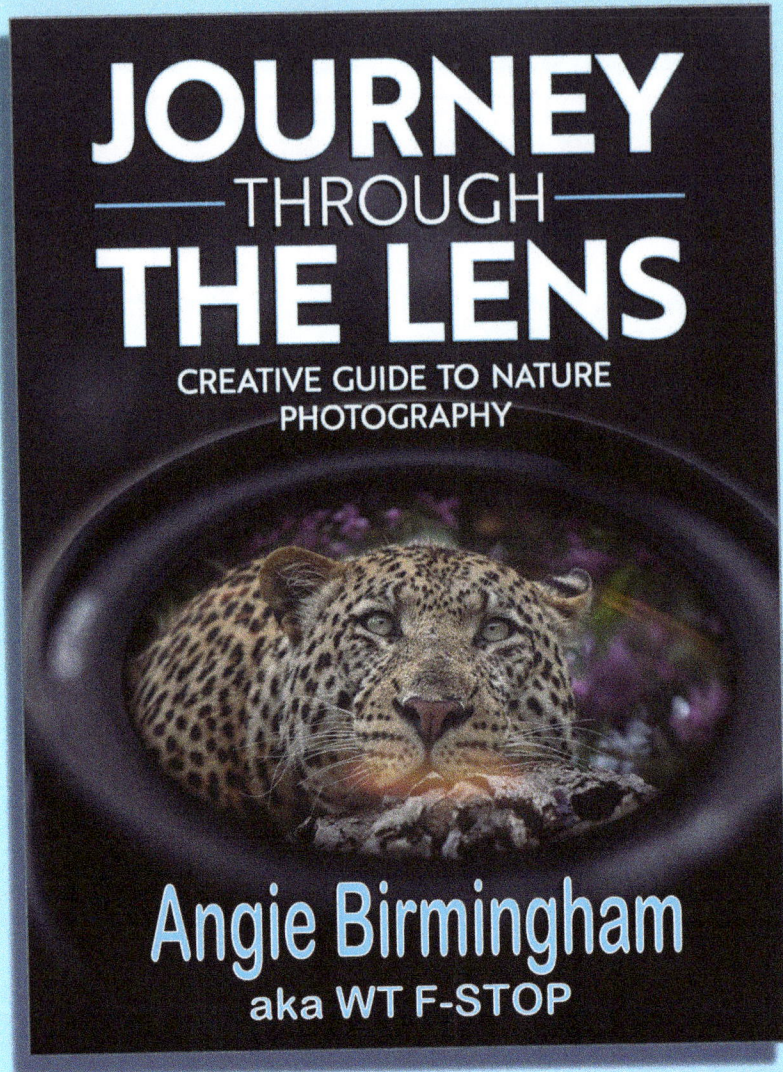

JOURNEY THROUGH THE LENS
CREATIVE GUIDE TO NATURE PHOTOGRAPHY

Angie Birmingham
aka WT F-STOP

Celebrated wildlife photographer Angie Birmingham ("WT F-STOP") introduces burgeoning photo-takers to their photo equipment and helps them develop the techniques for stunning outdoor photography. From mastering exposure to optimizing focus and lighting, Angie shows how to find the right styles to tell visual stories and present compelling images. Learn landscape composition along with the best ways to shoot animals, birds, and flowers; and find out how skilled photographers capture all the details while manipulating backgrounds and mood. From newcomers to professionals, everybody who loves taking wildlife pictures will thrill at how easy Angie makes it for you to continue your own *Journey Through the Lens*.

Hardcover
Softcover
All Ebook Formats

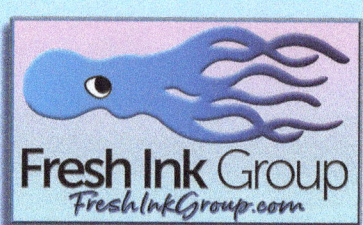

Fresh Ink Group
FreshInkGroup.com

What drives a man to spend 26 years performing night after night? To persevere through a stifling tour bus, bad food, strange women, flared tempers, a plane nearly blown from the sky? Just how did that troubled military brat with a dream claw his way from dirt-floor dive-bar shows to the world's biggest stages? Aviator, author, and Country Music Hall of Fame drummer Mark Herndon lived that dream with one of the most popular and celebrated bands of all time. He learned some hard lessons about people and life, the music industry, the accolades and awards, how easy it is to lose it all . . . and how hard it is to survive, to embrace sobriety, to live even one more day. Herndon's poignant memoir offers a tale at once cautionary and inspirational, delightful and heartbreaking, funny yet deeply personal. From innocence to rebellion to acceptance, can a man still flourish when the spotlight dims? Are true forgiveness, redemption, and serenity even possible when the powerful say everything you achieved somehow doesn't even count? That you're not who you and everyone who matters thought you were? Mark Herndon refuses to slow down. So look back, look ahead, and join him on the trip. He's taking *The High Road*.

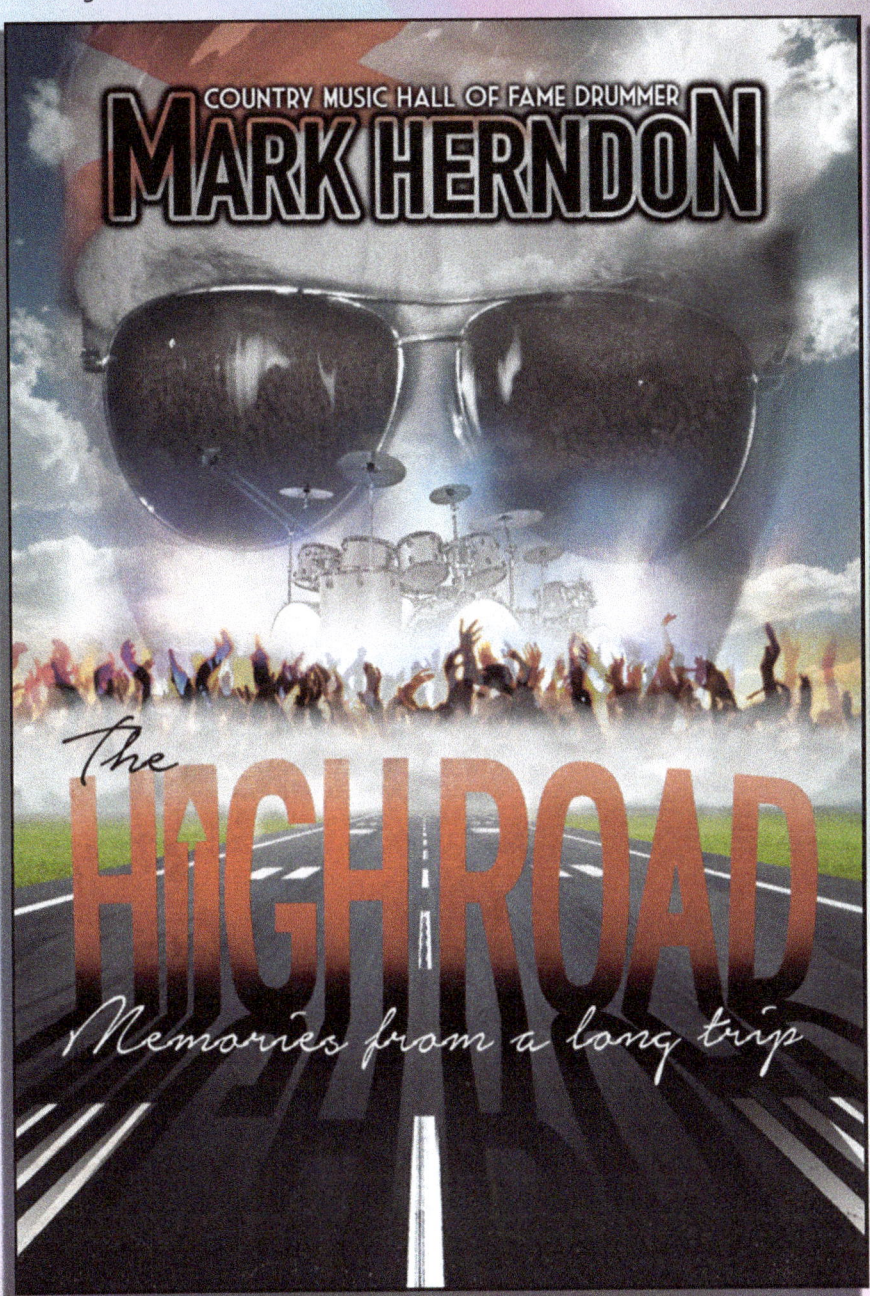

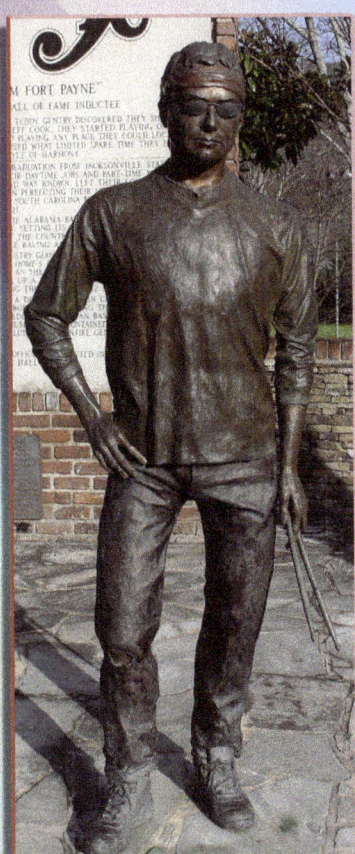

Jacketed Hardcover

Softcover

All Ebook Formats

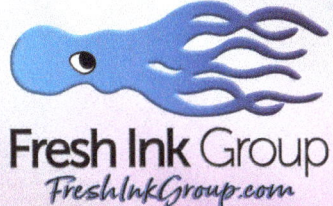

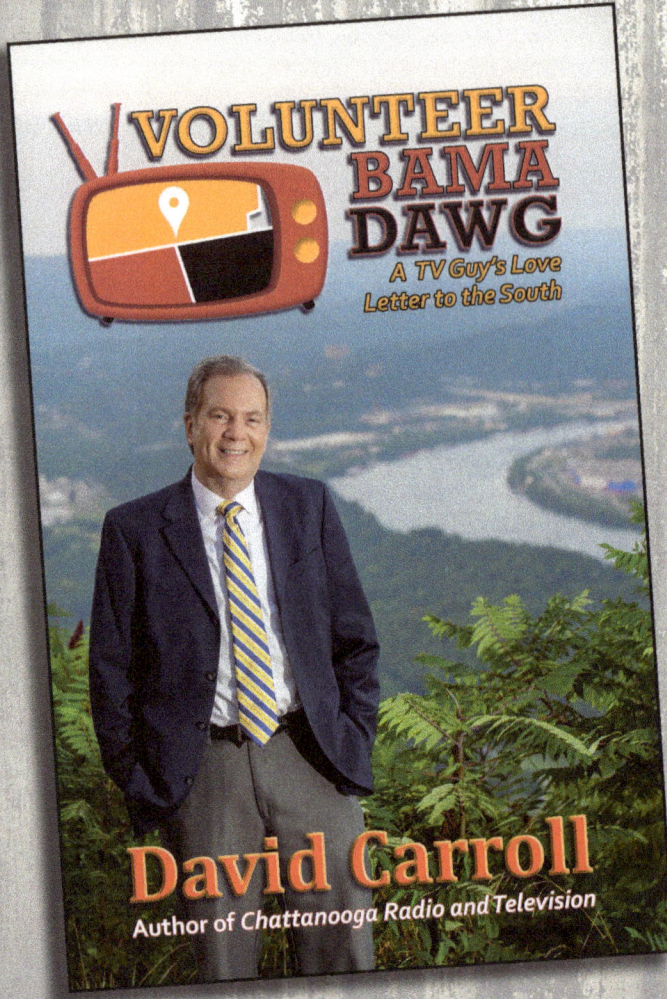

Volunteer Bama Dawg: a TV Guy's Love Letter to the South collects more than sixty of Chattanooga broadcaster David Carroll's most popular essays, combining humor, history, and tributes to some unforgettable characters.

A native of Bryant, Alabama, David Carroll has been a radio and TV personality in Chattanooga, Tennessee, for more than thirty years. He started his radio career in South Pittsburg, Tennessee, before becoming the first voice on Chattanooga's KZ-106 at the age of 21. Since then, he has reported on education issues and has anchored the evening news for almost thirty years.

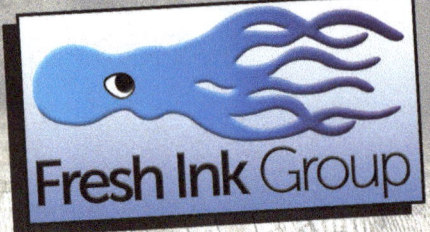

Hardcover, Paperback, Nook, Kindle, GooglePlay, iTunes, Kobo, and more!

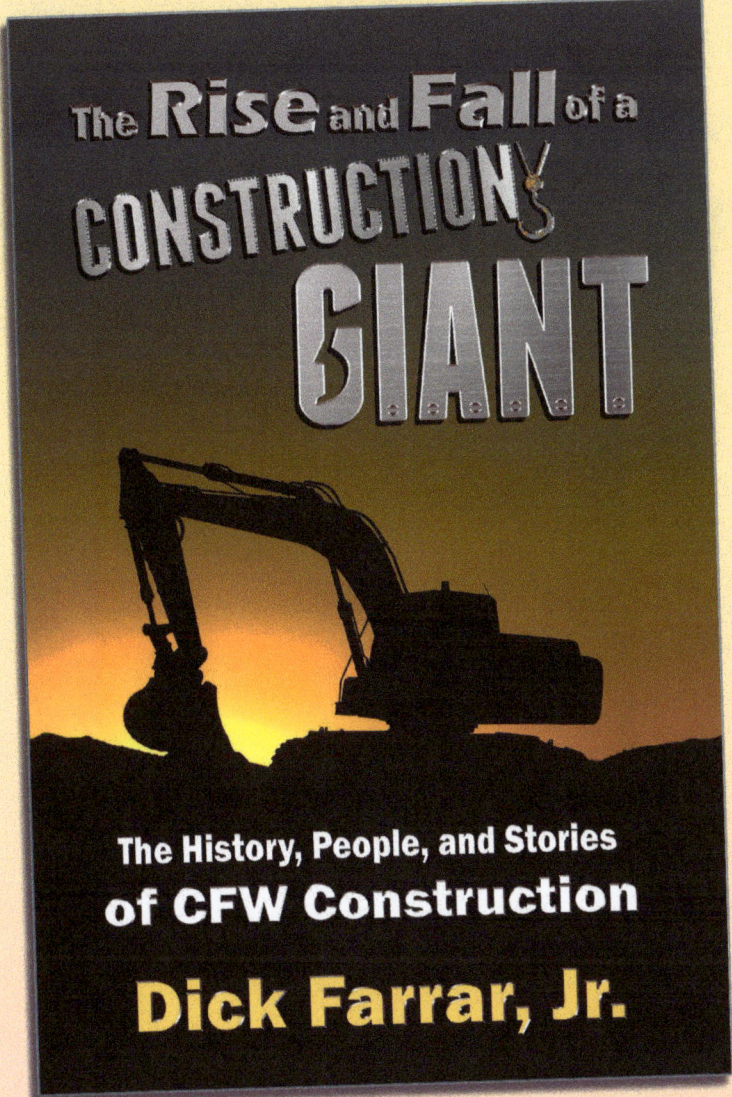

Determined to bring utilities and small-building construction to rural areas, William R. Carter joined with Dick Farrar and John Williams to form the CFW Construction Company in Fayetteville, Tennessee, 1952. Named for the partners, CFW expanded into building plants, roads, tunnels, bridges, and more. Within forty years the company grew to five offices, 14 subsidiaries, a thousand pieces of equipment, and a proud workforce of more than 1,500 across a dozen states. Then came the scandals. By the end of the 20th century, CFW was gone, and the lives of everybody had changed. Dick Farrar's son was there for the best and the worst. Now he's written the definitive history, not just about a company, but a region and its people. With nearly a hundred restored photos, most in color, Farrar, Jr., tells the true story, naming names and documenting the details. The Rise and Fall of a Construction Giant is a keepsake, a historical record, the chronicle of an era, a compelling story told by the man at its center in the end.

Hardcover
Softcover
All Ebook Formats

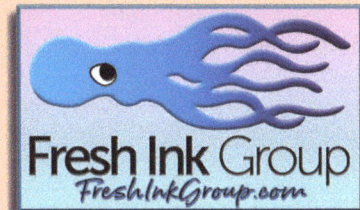